SEVEN TROOP

www.rbooks.co.uk

SEVEN TROOP

Andy McNab

BANTAM PRESS

LONDON • TORONTO • SYDNEY • AUCKLAND • JOHANNESBURG

TRANSWORLD PUBLISHERS
61–63 Uxbridge Road, London W5 5SA
A Random House Group Company
www.rbooks.co.uk

First published in Great Britain
in 2008 by Bantam Press
an imprint of Transworld Publishers

This book is a work of non-fiction based on the life, experiences and recollections of Andy
McNab. In some cases names have been changed to protect the privacy of others. The author
has stated to the publishers that, except in such respects, the contents of this book are true.

A CIP catalogue record for this book
is available from the British Library.

ISBN 9780593059500 (cased)
9780593059517 (tpb)

Addresses for Random House Group Ltd companies outside the UK
can be found at: www.randomhouse.co.uk
The Random House Group Ltd Reg. No. 954009

The Random House Group Limited supports The Forest Stewardship
Council (FSC), the leading international forest-certification organization. All our
titles that are printed on Greenpeace-approved FSC-certified paper carry the FSC logo.
Our paper procurement policy can be found at www.rbooks.co.uk/environment

Typeset in 11/14pt Palatino by
Falcon Oast Graphic Art Ltd.
Printed in the UK by CPI Mackays, Chatham, ME5 8TD

2 4 6 8 10 9 7 5 3

Mixed Sources
Product group from well-managed
forests and other controlled sources
www.fsc.org Cert no. TT-COC-2139
© 1996 Forest Stewardship Council
FSC

This book is dedicated to:

Mr Grumpy
Hillbilly
Padre Two Zero
Nish

SEVEN TROOP

Sunday, 9 May 1998
0200

The cottage stood in the middle of an acre of flat, open land. It was nearly two o'clock in the morning, but light still blazed from the windows. At the front of the building, small spotlights were trained on a footbridge over a stream. I stared down at the water.

Voices drifted from the path that led to the back of the house. They got louder and the tip of a cigarette glowed red in the dark.

Two shapes emerged from the shadows and headed towards me.

I straightened. 'Halt. Who goes there?'

'One big nose, one ayatollah.'

'Advance and be recognized.'

I'd worked with both these guys many times, often undercover. In the old days we'd worn jeans and bomber jackets, whatever it took to blend in with the locals on the Shantello and Bogside estates. Tonight's disguises were something else again. Frank was got up like a refugee from *The Sweeney*, in a spear-point collared shirt, leather coat with big, fuck-off lapels, and stick-on ginger sideburns to match his hair. Nish, in a bright waistcoat and floppy golf hat, looked like he was auditioning for Showaddywaddy.

The muffled thump of music came from the back of the house. I'd set up a marquee with a big TV so the guests could sit and eat while they watched some of the worst numbers ever composed battling it out at the Eurovision Song Contest in Birmingham.

I'd come as a 1970s porn star, complete with a droopy moustache and a gold medallion – my next-door neighbour's brooch – on a lavatory chain. Almost everyone else had come as a member of Abba.

Frank and Nish came and leant on the rail alongside me.

'Together again.' Frank gave us both a nudge. 'The Three Musketeers.'

I laughed. 'Three Wise Men's more your style these days, ain't it?'

'Nah.' Nish sucked at his Silk Cut. 'Three Wise Monkeys. Or, here you go . . .' He gobbed into the water below. 'Three Coins in the Fountain.'

Frank smiled indulgently. They were trying hard. We all were. It should have been a fun night. Building works, mostly to divert the River Stour from my living room, had delayed the housewarming for a year, but now here we all were.

Or not quite all.

Of the eight former Ice Cream Boys on the invitation list, one hadn't turned up. He was in police custody.

'I keep thinking about him.' Frank pushed one of his cardboard sideburns back onto his jaw. 'What makes a man do such a thing?'

Nish studied the water. 'Maybe he's even madder than I am.'

Shanksy had already left Seven Troop by the time I arrived, but he was a legend in the Regiment. Dr Thomas Shanks was a veteran of the 'Secret War' in Oman in the mid-1970s – where he'd won the Military Medal for rescuing a mate under fire –

and had gone on to become a hospital consultant. Two days ago, he'd pulled an AK47 from the boot of his car outside a pub in Leeds and gunned down the girl he'd said he loved.

Shanks had worked in hospitals in the Midlands and in 1995 had become a locum anaesthetist at Pontefract General Infirmary. Within a fortnight he'd met Vicky, a local girl training as a nurse. They began living together and got engaged. But things had turned sour: two weeks ago she'd called things off and started going out with a former patient.

Last Wednesday she'd found a letter from Shanks at her hospital flat; it contained the engagement ring she'd returned to him and told her he was miserable and depressed. The following day, he'd called her in a pub in nearby Castleford, where she was having a drink with her new boyfriend, his son and his son's girlfriend. Over and over again, Shanks demanded that she tell him she no longer loved him. He called her a selfish cow and a bitch. Vicky eventually put the phone down on him and moved with the rest of her party to a neighbouring bar.

When Shanks tracked her there she agreed to speak to him, but he became abusive and bundled her through the doors and out into the street. A fight broke out. Shanks grappled with the new boyfriend and kicked him as he lay on the ground.

The boyfriend's son held Shanks back while Vicky and the others went back to the first pub. At 9.50 p.m. they noticed him in the car park and Vicky went out to speak to him. Moments later she was seen running back, with Shanks in hot pursuit.

She only got as far as the edge of the car park. The first burst of 7.62mm hit her six times in the chest, elbow, abdomen and buttock, but she somehow found the strength to get to her feet. When she reached the pub doorway a second burst took her down for good.

The place was packed for the landlord's farewell. Everyone was watching videos of previous parties when the firing began. At first they thought someone had laid on some

3

fire-crackers or was bursting balloons as some kind of surprise. Then a few rounds screamed through the room, splintering wood and smashing glasses and mirrors. It only lasted a few seconds, but no one dared move. When they got up, they saw the gunman walk casually to his car and drive off.

Vicky was lying in a pool of blood. She couldn't talk. They tried to stem the flow with bar towels and somebody got a quilt from upstairs to cover her until the ambulance arrived.

She died two hours later, after emergency surgery in the hospital where she'd worked.

Shanks bought half a pint of bitter at another local, phoned his ex-wife in Birmingham to tell her what he'd done and headed there to see his nine-year-old daughter. He wanted to see her before the police caught up with him. Then he changed his mind and made for Scotland. He went to see his brother in Glasgow, maybe to get cash and gear before heading into the hills. He gave himself up the next day, after a nationwide manhunt.

'He probably just couldn't decide on his costume,' Nish said.

Tommy Shanks was a legend, not just for his soldiering skills, but also for being a total anal-retentive. He would spend hours working out what to wear for a night on the town. Most people just threw on a pair of jeans and a polo shirt. Not Tommy. It had to be a proper shirt, pressed so you could cut your fingers on the sleeves.

'Don't take it personally.' Nish slapped me on the back. 'Your party ain't that bad.'

Frank gave him one of those despairing looks parents give their kids. He'd been the first through the skylight when the SAS had broken the Iranian Embassy siege in 1980. He'd always been rock steady. If he was covering your back, you were in good hands. But now he was even more off his trolley than Nish: he'd become a vicar.

One of his favourite sayings was: 'I just show them the door to the kingdom of heaven and they can walk through it if they want to.'

I still hadn't opened it. I was pretty sure God would throw the bolts before I turned the handle.

'Cheer up, Frank.' I tugged at one of his sideburns.

'You'll burn in hell, McNab.' He gave me the same disapproving look he'd given Nish. His brow furrowed. 'Why? Why kill her?'

In all the years I'd known him I'd rarely heard him raise his soft Geordie voice at anything or anyone, and now was no exception.

'What's that shit you always say?' Nish grinned. ' "Better to spend one day as a tiger than a thousand years as a sheep"? Well, fuck it, why not?'

Frank wasn't biting. 'I mean, here's a guy who's a hospital consultant one minute, and he drops a girl in a car park the next. What makes a man throw two lives away, after all he's been through?'

Tommy was one of six brothers and two sisters brought up in working-class Glasgow. His father was an epileptic sawmill labourer, and Tommy was only ten when he came home from school one day and found him dead. Five years later, after his mother began drinking heavily and became aggressive towards the children, he went to live with an uncle.

He left school then and became an engineering apprentice, then joined the army two years later. He was posted to Bahrain as a signaller, from where he applied to join the SAS. Within eighteen months of first joining up, Tommy Shanks became one of the youngest ever to pass Selection.

He served for ten years, then worked for a security company specializing in VIP protection. He was stabbed seven times by a gang and very nearly died.

After he'd recovered he went back to the classroom and gained a place at Birmingham University medical school. He and his wife Julie, a teacher, set up home in the Midlands and had a daughter. He graduated in 1986 as a Bachelor of Medicine and Master of Surgery.

He joined the Royal Army Medical Corps as a reservist captain, but resigned in 1989. When Iraq invaded Kuwait in 1991 he joined the medical team at 32 Field Hospital in Saudi Arabia and was given a cocktail of about twenty undisclosed inoculations to offset the effects of chemical warfare.

When his marriage faltered on his return, he took a job as an anaesthetist at New Cross Hospital in Wolverhampton, where colleagues described him as a typical tough Scot, who didn't suffer fools gladly. He ended up at Pontefract Royal Infirmary, but all wasn't well on the work front. He flew into rages when other medics didn't match his high standards.

'What was he doing with an AK anyway?'

He shrugged. Guys often had the odd weapon stashed away as a souvenir. Our first task if a mate got killed was to clear up before his family was allowed into his house. One had had enough PE4, rifles and ammunition in his loft to start the next world war. The MoD didn't have to worry about budget cuts: they could have popped round to his place.

There were already mutterings in the media about Gulf War syndrome, but however horrendous GWS was for the sufferers, it was a world away from post traumatic stress disorder (PTSD). It was a medical issue rather than a mental-health one.

Three guys who served with Shanks in the Gulf, two of them doctors, had already committed suicide – apparently because of the strain of their military experiences. The sight of casualties carried in with limbs missing, horrifically scarred, most of them young men in their prime, must have taken its toll.

After he returned from the Gulf, Shanks had difficulty concentrating and remembering things, and suffered increasingly severe mood swings, irritability and depression – which were consistent with symptoms experienced by others who returned from the Gulf. I wondered if he'd been suffering from PTSD when he'd shot Vicky Fletcher.

From a professional soldier's point of view, two erratic bursts were a sign of a disturbed man. If he'd been in control, he would just have put two rounds into her head.

'That's us two off the hook, Father Frank. We're Gulf War-free.' Nish took a drag on his cigarette. 'Dunno about McNab, though. Reckon he's a walking time-bomb.'

GWS was about the only thing I knew I wouldn't be suffering from later in life. In the SAS we had some control over our lives. The drugs did turn up, but unlike the rest of the army we weren't ordered to take them. We binned ours, working on the principle that if we were attacked with a blood or nerve agent that could kill in seconds, a daily handful of capsules wasn't going to make much difference.

Frank was still brooding. 'Maybe he's just another lad who lost his head. There are enough of us.'

I put a hand on Nish's shoulder and poked a finger at Frank. 'You're the vicar, mate – you're supposed to have the answers. PTSD? Or maybe he really is just mad, like this fucker.'

Nish burst out laughing. 'I'm not mad – not this week, anyway.' He flicked his cigarette into the stream and immediately lit another. 'I wonder if Shanksy wishes he'd saved a couple of rounds for himself. I would have.'

Frank was in Sunday-sermon mode. 'When taking a life has been sanctioned by the state, that's one thing.' He paused to allow the weight of his statement to sink in. It didn't. 'But taking a life out of anger, well, that's quite another.'

Nish turned and grabbed him in a huge bear hug. He beamed from ear to ear. 'Awww, Frank still thinks we're shining knights, agents of wrath to bring God's punishment on the evil-doer. Not just mad fuckers who get pissed off and kill people . . .'

Frank had had years of us taking the piss out of his beliefs. It was like water off a duck's back. He kept on-message. 'Is any of us less guilty than Tommy? I've seen enough killers to know one when I see one.'

I grinned at the pair of them. 'You're both as deranged as each other. Nish, you have regular conversations with your fridge . . .'

Nish nodded.

'. . . and you, Frank, you've got God telling you what to do, haven't you?'

There was a long pause. 'I thought I did, mate. I thought I did.'

Nish and I exchanged a look, and then he followed Frank back to the party.

I watched them fade into the darkness. One of those loonies kept dreaming about freefalling from the edge of space. The other believed there was an old man with a white beard who lived up there. I couldn't help wondering whether the jungle punch we'd all drunk fourteen years ago had had some mad potion in it, and I was next on the list.

For all that, they were two of the best friends a person could ever hope for. We'd been through a lot together, the three of us and the handful of others from Seven Troop. We had killed and some of us had been killed, and the outcome was a closeness that outsiders might find hard to understand and impossible to share. We scoffed at the notion of brotherhood, but that's what we were: brothers in arms. My ten years in Seven Troop were the most awesome of my life. Since I'd left in 1993 there hadn't been a day when I didn't thank my lucky stars that I'd had the chance to be associated with the most highly skilled and inspirational bunch of guys I've ever come across.

The trust between Frank, Nish, me and the others had been total. It had had to be. Would we have died for each other? Yes. But brotherhood forged under extreme danger comes at a price. Some had already gone mad; others were well on the way.

If only I'd known then that Tommy Shanks murdering his ex-girlfriend and Nish trying to kill his a year earlier wasn't going to be the end of the story. Could I have prevented what happened next? Probably not. But that couldn't stop me lying awake asking myself the same questions over and over.

I remembered a mate from A Squadron coming up against the RAF shrink after my release from Baghdad's Abu Ghraib prison at the end of the '91 Gulf War. Mugger had been in overall charge of the SAS recovery mission: he went into Riyadh to organize a few videos for our entertainment while the B Squadron sergeant-major turned up with a hospital trolley loaded with beer. We were smuggled out of the ward and down to the library, where we set about getting blitzed.

Dr Gordon Turnbull had arrived in Cyprus to oversee the recuperative phase. 'What have you got there?' he asked Mugger, when he spotted his shopping bags.

'Videos for the lads.'

'Mind if I have a look?'

Turnbull nearly had a heart-attack. Mugger had bought us *Terminator*, *Driller Killer* and *Nightmare on Elm Street*. 'You can't do this! Those men are all traumatized!'

'Traumatized?' Mugger laughed. 'They were all fucking barking to start with.'

What had sent Shanks, Nish and others to the dark side?

What was it about the landscape we'd crossed and the things we'd had to do that had brought them to this point? Why had I been spared?

And perhaps the biggest question of all: should I have seen it coming? Were the clues there all along?

I didn't often look back. In our line of work, reflection isn't healthy.

But if I was going to find the answers, maybe it was time to revisit the journeys taken by this united but disparate band of men.

I leant back on the rail. A lot of water had flowed under the bridge since 1984.

1

MALAYSIA
July 1984

Two things have stuck in my mind from my first day with B Squadron. First, what a complete and utter knobber I felt in the jungle in all my shiny, squeaky-clean new kit. And second, how loud my ears still rang with the advice I'd been given in Hereford the week before.

'Never forget, it's harder to keep than it was to get,' the colonel had said to the eight new boys as he tossed each of us a sand-coloured beret like they were frisbees.

In the corridor afterwards the RSM (regimental sergeant-major) had added, 'You might have spent six months doing the toughest selection course known to man, but now it's right back to square one. Because, lads, you know jack shit.' He eyed us carefully as he took a long drag on his roll-up. 'When you get to your squadron, make sure you wind your neck in. Shut up, look, and listen. Pick out a role model. See what he does and why he does it. Now, the four of you joining B Squadron, go and draw your kit – you're going to Malaysia. And one final thing.' He took another drag and looked at each of us in turn. 'Good luck. You'll need it.'

B Squadron was famous for storming the Iranian Embassy in 1980. The live TV footage was the very first time I had seen the Regiment in action. It was that footage, and the fact that the Green Jackets had missed out on the Falklands conflict two years later, that made me want to take Selection. After all, I'd joined the army to fight, and they were always in the thick of it.

The SAS consisted of four Sabre Squadrons: A, B, D and G. They, in turn, were divided into four troops, each with a specialist infiltration skill. Air Troop infiltrated enemy territory by parachute. Mobility Troop got in by any overland means. Boat Troop attacked from the water. Mountain Troop went by foot, scrambling over any big lumps of rock that happened to be in the way. Each troop was numbered so you knew which squadron it came from. In B Squadron, Boat Troop was 6, Air Troop was 7, Mobility 8, and Mountain 9.

None of us knew which troop we were headed for. We were just told we'd be allocated once we got in-country.

Two guys came to collect us from a muddy, rutted road-head close to the northern border with Thailand after our day's drive from Kuala Lumpur. One was a Maori, the other a gingernut, with hair thick enough to be made into a rug. 'I'm Al,' he said. 'Ready?'

We shouldered our Bergens and followed them into the twilight world of the primary rainforest. Huge hardwood tree-trunks fanned out into buttresses on the ground. Way up at sky level, the canopy was bushy and tight; hardly any light reached the leaf litter under our boots.

Gingernut didn't look the happiest man on the planet, which I thought was strange: he should have liked being out of the sun. His pale skin seemed even paler under the canopy. He was about six foot tall, and lean, almost bony. He had the look and bearing of an officer, and he even sounded like one, on the rare occasions he opened his mouth. He talked as if the words were being dragged out of him with pincers. I had the feeling I'd seen him somewhere before, but I couldn't place him.

'We have a twenty-minute tab. Been here a while. Jungle training, mostly. And as a deterrent against insurgents.'

The Maori said even less than Al, if that was possible. Lots of New Zealanders and Australians joined the Regiment, but this guy wore different jungle camouflage from Al and the rest of us. The Kiwis had an infantry battalion based in Singapore. Maybe he was with them, or New Zealand SAS. No matter – if they weren't telling, I wasn't asking.

The advantage of thick canopy is that at least the under-growth is sparse and easy to move through. But when the canopy thins and light gets through, you'd be lucky to cover a kilometre in four hours. You're never alone in the jungle. We shared it with red ants, leeches, scorpions, massive ticks that buried themselves in your skin, and every make and model of snake was queuing up to take a bite out of you. And then, of course, there was scrub typhus, jaundice, dysentery, rain-forest ulcers, prickly heat, foot rot and ring worm. But this is still the best environment to fight in. It provides cover and water, and you never get cold or hungry.

Al smacked his neck and a mosquito died. 'Poxy malaria merchant.'

It was stiflingly hot and humid. My jungle greens were already drenched with sweat. What had I expected? It's called rainforest because of the rain. The moisture can't escape the dense canopy, so it's wet, hot and very sticky, twenty-four/seven.

Everything we had, we carried with us. We all had two sets of kit – dry kit to sleep in, and wet kit. First thing we did every morning was put our wet kit back on.

I didn't have great memories of the jungle phase of Selection. Everything was about keeping that dry kit dry. If it got wet, you'd never get it dry. Mine was double-wrapped in plastic Bergen liners, and then in another for luck.

We followed a narrow, muddy foot-track to a commune of A-frame pole-beds. You could tell the guys had been there a while. Some A-frames had sprung extensions; others had duckboards made of branches to keep them above the mud. Figure-11 targets, the standard army target of a man charging, stuck to a hardboard backing, had been cut and nailed to logs to make tables and chairs, and there were angled sit-up boards for a makeshift gym. Here and there, two or more A-frames had been joined together with poncho shelter sheets.

A radio hissed continuously. Food bubbled in mess tins or large cooking-pot-shaped grenade tins resting on one or more little hexamine stoves.

There was a strong smell of cigarette smoke. Nobody wore rank. Everybody had beards and long greasy hair. They lay around outside A-frames reading books, or squatted over hexis brewing up. It was like I'd walked onto the set of *Platoon*.

'This is Squadron HQ. Just sit and wait out.'

Al and the Kiwi disappeared between the A-frames.

Everyone, including me, had two morphine auto jets hanging from their neck by para-cord, along with a watch and sometimes a little button compass. If anyone left their basha (shelter) area they had their webbing and weapon with them all the time – and their gollock. You went nowhere without one tied around your waist. It wasn't part of your belt kit, it was part of your body. It was your most essential item under the canopy – it cut down and dug out food, it built you traps and shelter, and gave you a means of protecting yourself.

The air filled with buzzing as we sat in sweltering 90 per cent humidity. The entire insect population had heard there was fresh blood in town. Tastiest of the bunch, apparently, was the Green Jacket. I rubbed more mozzie rep (repellent) on my face and hands, but it made no difference. The little fuckers still hovered and swooped and were biting me to bits.

2

A guy stood up from his hexi stove with a cigarette burning so low between his lips it was in danger of setting fire to his beard. 'All right, lads – want a brew?'

He passed round one of the black plastic pint-and-a-half mugs that normally went over the water bottle on our belt kit. It steamed with hot, sweet ration-pack tea. We took a swig each and stood there, the sweat gluing our clothes to our backs.

There was a whirlwind between the ponchos over to our left and an educated voice delivering a series of instructions with the staccato rapidity of a GPMG (general purpose machine gun). 'I want this, this, this and this . . .' He approached our little group and clapped his hands. 'I'm Graham.' Everybody seemed to be on first-name terms round here. 'I need one of you for each troop.' He looked us up and down. 'You look like a diver – Six Troop.'

A Royal Engineer, a keen climber, volunteered for Mountain Troop.

'Right, that's Nine Troop sorted, then.'

I breathed a sigh of relief. Anything but Mountain Troop. Graham pointed to the guy next to me. 'Eight Troop. Mobility.'

Then he nodded in my direction. 'Got your shades?'

I smiled back and nodded, not knowing what the fuck he was on about.

'Good. Seven Troop.'

Back in whirlwind mode, he disappeared beneath the shelter sheets once more.

'That's Boss L,' the guy who'd offered us the brew said. 'The OC.'

The Squadron Officer Commanding was always a major. Troop commanders were captains. He was from a Highland regiment and a champion skier. Born for the jungle, obviously.

It wasn't long before our new companions came to claim us. 'What troop you going to?' the first one asked.

'Air Troop.'

'The Ice Cream Boys!'

Sunglasses? Ice cream? I still didn't have a clue what they were on about, and before I could ask, a giant of a man bore down on me, a good six foot three tall and four foot wide. His hands were so big his M16 looked like a toy.

'Who's for Air Troop?'

I stood up. 'That's me.'

'I'm Tiny.' A half-smile crept out from under his beard. 'Get your Bergen.'

Bizarrely for such a big guy, he bounced on the balls of his feet. He had long curly hair but was balding on top. He looked like some kind of spring-loaded hippie monk.

I followed him to the troop location, trying to get my new boots even muddier.

'What's your name?'

Thunder boomed way above the canopy.

'Andy. Andy McNab.'

'What battalion you from?'

'Two.'

'I'm Two Para too. D'you know—?'

'No, mate, Two RGJ – I'm a Green Jacket.'

He stopped in his tracks. The skies opened for the second

time that day and the canopy above us rattled under the down-pour. The din added to the noise of the rain smashing onto my head.

'So what the fuck are you doing in Seven Troop?'

'I don't know. The boss just told me to come here.'

He moved off again along the track. It was bucketing down. 'For fuck's sake, we haven't had anyone in the troop for eighteen months and now they're sending a fucking crap hat.'

I followed behind sheepishly, thinking, Yep, nice one, good start.

We eventually got to the troop area, a small spur of high ground covered with A-frames. In the middle there was a large fire. Six or seven guys sat having a brew under some shelter sheets, which sounded like drum skins under the pounding rain. One of them was Al.

Tiny did the introductions. 'His name's Andy McNab and he's a Green Jacket.'

'What the fuck's a crap hat doing here?' A Viking blond got to his feet. 'I'm Chris.' He stuck out his hand. 'Para Reg.' He grinned. He was about five foot five, hairy, and spoke with a soft northern accent.

The others stayed exactly where they were as he pointed each of them out. No one was coming into the rain to say hello now they knew I wasn't of the airborne brotherhood.

'Nish ... Frank ... Al ... Phil ... Paul ... and Saddlebags ...' It was like being introduced by one of the Tetley Tea Folk.

I nodded as they nodded, and one or two said, 'All right?'

Chris pointed to the right of the fire. 'Get yourself over there and bung a pole-bed up before last light.'

I went to the edge of the clearing, dropped my Bergen into the mud and pulled out my gollock.

3

The theory is that you start with four lengths of wood about two metres long. Tie each pair together at one end, open them out to form the shape of an A then stand them about two metres apart. Get two more stakes about three metres long and no more than two or three inches in diameter, just strong enough to support your weight, slip them through the side sleeves of the hammock, fit the ends over the apexes of the two As, and push them as far down as you can until the hammock is taut. Finally, you tie the webbing straps on each corner, which would normally be attached to a tree, around the poles so they don't ride up. All being well, you've created a bed that's a couple of feet off the floor.

Once that's done, you secure a shelter sheet over the top by bungeeing it to the nearest trees. Now you're protected from the rain; all that's left is your mozzie net. Sleeping without one isn't macho, it's madness. Getting bitten means any exposed skin swells to three times its normal size, and that means you're less able to operate. If you take the time to sort yourself out, you're a much more useful commodity the next day.

That was the theory, anyway. I'd only ever made one A-frame, and that was during Selection a couple of months ago. Now everybody under the shelter sheets was watching me make a total bollocks of the second.

Selection seemed a lifetime ago as I tried to chop branches to the required lengths. Every time I pulled up a pole to make the A it would fall down, but finally I had two half-decent frames. I then had to get the shelter sheet up to keep my hammock dry while I fed through the two poles. The crowd was loving it.

Chris came over and waffled something about a 'kerfuddle' later on with cocktails. He turned and fucked off as quickly as he'd arrived.

Kerfuddle? Cocktails?

Not wanting to intrude, I gave a few exaggerated yawns and prepared to get my head down. I got my wet kit off, rolled it up, and put it at the top of the A-frame. Then I pulled on my dry kit, got under the mozzie net and just lay there.

For the last six months I had sweated, screamed, clawed and crawled towards this moment. 'Selection isn't an exercise,' the training team had told the two hundred hopefuls who'd turned up. 'It's torture. It saves our time and the taxpayer's money to weed out those who can't hack it. We don't fail you on Selection: you fail yourself.'

Selection had been simple and brutal. It took no prisoners. Of the original two hundred on day one eight months ago, only eight had passed. And to rub salt into the wound, I'd given up my rank as sergeant and now had to start again as a trooper.

What was more, I had to become more than a freefaller before I could receive Special Forces' pay. I had to get at least one patrol skill: signals, demolitions, languages, medic. That meant a pay cut for up to a year; I'd thought it would be worth every penny. I'd wanted to join the elite. But these guys were more Special Needs than Special Forces. All they seemed to do was doss and drink tea.

Out of the darkness came a long, drawn-out sound like a foghorn. '*Hooooonk . . .*'

*

The last time I'd felt so disappointed was when I was sent to a juvenile detention centre, and then I'd been disappointed with myself for being such an idiot. The thieving had got stupid. As a gang we couldn't walk past a second-hand furniture shop with a pavement display without nicking stuff to sell at the next place round the corner. We'd saunter past old ladies sitting on park benches in posh places like Dulwich, areas that we reckoned deserved to be robbed, grab their handbags and do a runner.

If we saw a hire car or one with a foreign plate, we always knew there'd be stuff in the boot. I stole from relations' pockets. I even sank as low as tipping over Portaloos in a makeshift Peckham car park so I could snatch the soaked, shocked and frightened occupants' belongings.

I hated everyone and everything, mostly because I didn't have what they had. I'd spent the first fifteen years of my life in South London. Despite what *Only Fools and Horses* would have you believe, Peckham was never full of Del Boy cheeky chappies, having a laugh on the market stall, then off to drink brightly coloured cocktails in the local. It was full of un-employment, drugs, guns and mindless vandalism.

I felt angry with people who had shiny new cars or spotless motorbikes. So much so that I used to kick dents in them just because I could. I vandalized people's shops, messed up their gear, simply because they had stuff and I didn't.

I went to nine different schools between the ages of five and fifteen, so I had a lot of teachers to be angry with as well. I was angry that they kept putting me in remedial classes, but I didn't do anything to get out of them. If anything, I enjoyed being at the bottom of the class. It gave me yet another reason to be angry. I liked the feeling that everyone was against me. I was part of a select club. It justified my resentment: I was entitled to do things that others couldn't or shouldn't do.

It wasn't long before I was in a world of shit, and at that

point I decided I was going to change. But what was I going to do? I wasn't qualified for a decent job; I wasn't qualified for any job. So, why not join the army? Why not do three years, see what it was like? Anything to get me out of this cell . . .

I joined up at sixteen with the reading ability of an eleven-year-old, which was maybe why they wouldn't let me be a helicopter pilot like the guy in the recruiting film. But being in the infantry had its advantages. I was actually in a place where they wanted me to be angry. And they were paying me for it.

I killed my first man at the age of nineteen and was promoted way above my ability to become the infantry's youngest full corporal. I was awarded the Military Medal for a fire fight I was lucky to survive. I was promoted to sergeant when I was just twenty-three and found myself commanding riflemen much older.

That had been a year ago, and now I was in Seven Troop. But I wasn't as sure that this was the place to be as I had been just twenty-four hours ago. As if to underline the point, somebody let rip a huge fart to answer the honk, and the whole group laughed like drains.

4

It was still so dark when I woke that I couldn't see my hand in front of my face, but the luminous dials of my watch told me it was five forty. First light would be at about six. Shit, I was late for stand-to. This wasn't good.

It's a British Army standard operating procedure (SOP) to 'stand to' before first and last light – the prime times for attack. It applies even on exercise. Apart from anything else, it's a way of gripping guys to a routine. If you let squaddies doss and vegetate, they will. Discipline crumbles, weapons don't get cleaned and then they don't work so people die. It might sound a bit drastic, but these systems have evolved over years of soldiers' fighting, and dying, in the field.

In primary jungle, all movement stops at night. The canopy completely covers the sky; there is no ambient light. A patrol stands to at last light, once they have looped their track and laid an ambush on the route they've just taken. Once they've established they aren't being followed, they move off to a harbour position. Once it's dark and no one will be able to move towards them, they put up their hammocks and shelter sheets in the dark, feeling their way between two trees, never cutting or cracking any branches, always trying to minimize the amount of sign they'll leave behind.

Then, before stand-to at first light, the patrol will pack up and sit on their Bergens, ready for an attack. Once it's light enough to move, the patrol commander will do just that. So I'd fucked up big-time.

There was silence all around me, not a peep from anyone else. They must have got themselves up and were sitting on their Bergens, waiting with weapons in the shoulder. I threw on my wet kit like a man possessed. The cold, clammy material was coated with grit and leaf litter that rubbed against my skin. I pulled on my belt kit as quietly as I could, which wasn't quiet enough. I could only hope no one noticed the Laurel and Hardy routine going on around the new boy's pole-bed.

I finally settled down and waited with the rest of the invisible troop as insects buzzed around me, taking lumps out of my neck and hands. I covered myself with mozzie re and watched as pale light penetrated the canopy and yet more wildlife stirred into life. Last night's rain was still working its way down onto the leaf litter. Soon the order would come to stand down, and I was expecting one of two things to happen. Either Chris would bollock me for not getting a grip of myself for stand-to or, worse, no one would say anything. That would mean they definitely thought I was a crap hat.

Forty-five minutes past first light, and still I waited for the stand-down. It never came. Instead, in the gloom, I saw the glow of hexi stoves, and birdsong was replaced by the sizzle of luncheon meat frying in mess tins.

I turned back into the troop area to see Chris squatting by the remains of the fire, sparking up some wet wood, nice and smoky to keep the mozzies off.

Al sat astride a massive blue plastic sack of rice, stirring a grenade tin of porridge on his hexi. It dawned on me that I was the only one who'd stood to.

I quickly got my kit off and hoped they hadn't spotted the nugget sitting on his Bergen in the foliage. I was out of luck.

'A word, mate.'

Al had somehow materialized next to me.

'We don't bother out here. Not your fault. I suppose nobody told you.' He grinned and waved his hand over the troop area. 'Who'd want to attack a refugee camp anyway?'

He turned to go. 'You know, it's good having a new boy about. Until yesterday that was me. Takes the pressure off, know what I mean?'

I got a brew on and Chris held up a log as his porridge bubbled away between his feet. 'You know the price of these things in Hereford?' He didn't wait for an answer. 'Forty-five quid a load. Fucking disgrace. You can get them for forty-three down in Pontralis.'

I knew where he was talking about. It was a village with a timber yard, about ten miles out of Hereford. If he'd been one of my mates back in the Green Jackets I might have made a crack about tight-fisted Yorkshiremen, but I wasn't part of this group yet – I wasn't even sure I wanted to be. I sat and listened as he made a brew. Like the RSM said: mouth shut, eyes and ears open. As for the bit about role models, they seemed a bit thin on the ground.

In any case, Nish did the joke for me from behind his mozzie net. There was a touch of West Country burr in his voice. 'Pontralis? You'd spend more than the two quid on petrol getting there. What is it with you northerners? You're supposed to be our leader, for fuck's sake. Corporal fucking Tight-as-a-duck's-arse. Give us some of your porridge.'

Another loud 'Hoooonk!' rang out from the canopy. Nish couldn't help himself: he replied with a fart just as loud, then got up and changed into his wet kit. He was six foot and a couple, and lean, but his body was muscular. With his dark brown hair, big nose and light blue eyes, he reminded me of a timber wolf. Assuming there was a timber wolf that picked its nose and farted all day.

Chris passed me his mug while I waited for my brew to boil.

He had a moan about the phantom honker. 'Fucking Snapper, he needs help.'

Al shook his head and kept stirring.

Nish giggled, then got back to begging for food.

I took a sip from Chris's mug. At least that bit felt familiar. Wherever you are in the battalions, you always share your brew.

I nodded as if I knew who he was talking about. I got that Chris was the troop boss, but only a corporal. Maybe Seven Troop didn't have a sergeant or troop commander. I didn't care.

5

The rest of the troop were sorting themselves out, just as we were.

Tiny and Saddlebags's pole-beds were near each other, and they seemed to have a mate living between them. Both were on their knees by a small hole in the mud, pushing down small lumps of luncheon meat.

'Come on, Stan, breakfast.'

Tiny's voice was completely at odds with his physical presence, which said loud and clear to me that he ate babies three times a day. He spoke so softly he could call you an arse-hole and you wouldn't be sure if he meant it or not. He was good at everything he did but, annoyingly, made it look easy.

Saddlebags was a southerner with a mop of thick dark brown hair, the sort that went wild if it wasn't cut every half-hour. He reminded me a lot of Jon Pertwee in his *Doctor Who* days. His claim to fame was that he'd been almost a child when he'd passed Selection. He was only nineteen when he got in; he shared the record with a guy called Shanksy.

After a couple of days of not shaving, the best he could manage was a light coating of bum-fluff; he looked like a university fresher. But he had done it all: the Falklands, the embassy, lots of stuff in Africa. He'd been sent on so many jobs because he was a dab hand at languages.

The troop waffled away among themselves but I didn't have a clue what anyone was talking about. Different terminology; different personalities. These guys knew each other well. They talked about their wives and kids, their house-building and cars, all the everyday stuff that people do, whether you work in a chicken factory or you're sat in the jungle.

I finally got up to go for a piss.

'You'll be in my patrol today, Andy, all right?'

'OK, Chris, good.'

I turned to Tiny. 'What should I be doing now?'

'Just getting ready to go, I suppose.'

'What time?'

'We'll get out when we get out. Stan's got to be fed first.'

When I got back from my session in the troop pit, Nish was back on his pole-bed. He didn't bother getting up, just turned over towards the smoke and reached out both arms like Oliver Twist. 'I'll cook tomorrow, Al, promise.' He let go a fart as loud as the one that had rattled the canopy the previous night. It immediately started to rain. Nish patted his arse. 'I could rent this boy out one day as a rain-maker.'

Eventually, after about an hour of Nish honking about having to go out in it, we grabbed our belt kit, Bergens and M16s and headed into the jungle.

I clung to Chris.

'Four-man contact drills, OK?'

Great! Jungle lanes: tactical movement and actions on encountering the enemy. I knew what I was doing now. At last I could show them I wasn't a crap hat.

Patrols from other troops were already training. The forest echoed with the rattle of automatic gunfire and the whine of rounds bouncing off trees. The idea of jungle-contact drills is to put down the maximum amount of fire and get the hell out, so you can box around the problem and carry on with your job.

Tiny and Nish were in Chris's patrol as well. Frank was the other patrol commander.

I looked around me. It was like a switch had been thrown. All of a sudden these guys were alert, professional, business-like. They moved with purpose. It seemed I might have some role models after all.

'Speed, aggression, surprise.' Chris gave a sniff. 'SAS – get it?' He slid off into the jungle.

I was number two: butt in the shoulder, sights up, safety on single shot.

The jungle canalizes movement. The dense vegetation, dead-fall, deep gullies, steep hills, ravines, and wide, fast rivers make cross-country movement difficult unless you use high ground and tracks. But that's where every Tom, Dick and enemy moves, and where ambushes are laid – so it's not where the SAS goes. That day we navigated across country, using a technique called cross-graining. Up and down, up and down, not keeping to the high ground.

We didn't so much move through the jungle as melt into it. We didn't use gollocks to cut our way; we bent the branches aside and eased ourselves over obstacles as we came to them. Always, butt in the shoulder, sights up, safety off.

Rivulets of sweat carried the mozzie rep into my eyes and stung them severely. This issue stuff was almost 90 per cent Deet – strong enough to melt plastic.

We'd been patrolling for about half an hour when up popped a Figure-11 target, then another, five metres ahead.

'Contact front! Contact front!'

I moved to Chris's right and opened up. I expected him to turn back on his point, so he didn't cross into our arcs of fire, and move past me, while Nish and Tiny, still behind me, peeled off to one side and got some fire down so I could also move back. That way there was always fire heading towards the enemy while we broke contact. Shoot and scoot, that was the name of the game I'd been trained in. But it wasn't happening.

As I turned to move back, everybody else started coming forward, firing as they went. Chris stood his ground, still giving it a full thirty-round mag on auto. The weapon's gun-oil coating burnt off and formed a grey cloud around him. When he ran out of ammunition, he dropped to his knees and slammed in another mag.

Tiny and Nish ran past him, stopped and brassed up the targets.

Then it was Chris's turn again. He moved ahead of the other two and looked back for me, staring at me like I was a total dickhead.

Nish and Tiny joined in. 'What the fuck you doing?'

The pall of smoke and smell of cordite from the contact hung heavily beneath the canopy. I narrowed my eyes and shrugged sheepishly. 'We weren't taught like that on Selection.'

Nish got a fag on the go and gave me a sympathetic grin. 'You can forget all that shit. The fun starts here.'

6

Every squadron had its own way of doing things, and so did every troop within it.

For the rest of the day it was me, Chris, Nish and Tiny patrolling by our own rules. Fuck the shoot-and-scoot I'd been taught, there was none of that falling back and boxing round shit. With Air Troop it was just go forward. Chris had me running to and fro on the range until I was decimating targets with the best of them.

By the time we'd finished that night and rocked up at the troop location, soaking wet and plastered with mud, my gear looked the same as everyone else's. All I needed now was the beard.

Later that night, we sat round the fire. The smoke stung our eyes, but who cared as long as it kept the mozzies off? I sampled my very first jungle cocktail. It was a big-time B Squadron thing, made from all the boiled sweets out of the rations, with a lot more sugar poured in for luck. Well, I thought it was sugar, but in fact it was rum. The Regiment was still eligible for a gunfire ration and wasn't about to look a gift horse in the mouth.

Al held court on his new private armchair. Ages back he'd put in a request for a large bag of rice, and instead of a two- or three-pounder, a fifty-pound sack had turned up. The only problem was, every time we scooped some out, his arse got lower. 'There'll have to be rationing,' he said, without smiling. Not for him the troop banter. He preferred to sit back and listen.

The mail had come through with the same drop. Al sat on his rice chair to open his letters. He looked inside the first and gave a grin, the first I'd seen from him. 'I think this must be a hint.' He held up three sheets of paper, a stamped, addressed envelope and a pencil. It was from his parents. I'd overheard Al talking to Frank about them. They were obviously a close family.

Nish lay back in his pit again and pulled out a book. Everybody else was cooking and sorting themselves out around the fire. Chris had gone with Tiny down to the HQ area for squadron 'prayers', Boss L's daily orders for the squadron. Chris was the only one of us who had to attend, but you never went anywhere alone in the jungle at night. We weren't tactical, so you could use a torch, but you still went with another lad and never without your weapon, belt kit and gollock.

I cooked up my dehydrated lamb stew and some ration-pack porridge, while Nish read *The Holy Blood and the Holy Grail* by candlelight, and treated us to his full repertoire of nose-picking, farts and burps.

'Oi, Frank.'

Frank glanced up. The look on his face said he knew what was coming. 'Come on, lads, not again . . .'

Frank had fine ginger hair, not dark and thick like Al's, and the fair complexion that tends to go with it. He was slim and a little taller than me, and had eyes of the palest cornflower blue. He sounded like he came from slap-bang in the centre of Geordieland, but he never raised his voice. He seemed more forthright than blunt, unlike Chris.

'How do you get around all this thou-shalt-not-kill business? How does that work?'

31

Frank shook his head and laughed. I kept my head down. This sounded like piss-taking, but it was family shit.

Nish took a big puff and really went for it. 'Come on, Frank, how do you get out of it? Soldiers kill. It's what we do. How do you square the circle, mate?'

Al shook his head. I still couldn't place him. I definitely knew him from somewhere. Nish grinned at me. 'Frank's a new boy too. Fresh to the God Squad – born again.'

Yesterday I was a crap hat, now I was sort of all right. Someone even passed me a brew. But I still didn't know what the fuck was going on.

Frank nodded at me and I nodded back.

Chris delved into his Bergen and produced a Bible. 'Yep, it says it here, Frank, "Thou shalt not kill." Come on, we've got to think about this – what are you going to do?'

Nish started humming a hymn. 'Know what, Frank? You haven't quite perfected the turn-the-other-cheek thing, have you? I read that you lot have killed about six billion in the name of religion.'

This was getting more surreal by the minute: eight rough, tough Special Forces soldiers comparing passages from the Bible in the middle of the jungle?

'Tell you what, your boss's boy didn't walk on water, either. My dad was in the Middle East during the war and he visited the Sea of Galilee. He got all the int. Not many people could swim in Roman times, especially in the desert. No wonder the crowd on the shore was gobsmacked. The gospel writers were as bad as the tabloids today, mate – swimming across to his mate's fishing boat somehow became walking on water. Simple as that.'

Frank smiled quietly to himself. He wasn't biting.

Al sat on his throne and scribbled the letter to his parents.

Everything went quiet until Nish sat bolt upright and swatted at something on his neck. 'Jesus Christ!'

Frank flinched. 'Nish, have you ever stopped to think what you're saying?'

Nish rolled over. The tip of his cigarette glowed in the gloom.

Everybody laughed – except Al and me. And it was then, as I watched him scowl into the fire, that I remembered where I'd come across him. Alastair Slater was the training corporal I'd seen about a year before I went on Selection: he'd been giving recruits a hard time in the BBC series *Para*. He'd gone to public school, and although you wouldn't know it, he was a Scot. The army had wanted him to be an officer, but he'd chosen to be a tom (private soldier).

I remembered one thing in particular that he'd drilled into the recruits. 'Getting noticed,' he'd growled, 'is absolutely the last thing you want to do.'

7

The next day started the same way, only without any nuggets standing to. The troop dossed around again, brewing up and frying luncheon meat. Tiny and Saddlebags were enticing Stan, whoever he was, with dried lamb, while Nish came good with his promise on the porridge.

Food plays such an important part in anybody's life in the military – not so much for the calories as for the fact that it's one of only three sources of entertainment in the field. The other two are taking the piss and honking – or ticking, moaning, whatever you wanted to call it.

In the infantry, we'd spent more time than Gordon Ramsay talking about what we were going to cook and how, and all the different mustards or spices we'd be using. Everybody here seemed to have brought their own Tabasco, Worcester and other more exotic sauces to jazz things up.

Sitting in state by the smoky fire, Al Slater looked every inch the tribal king. Occasionally he leant down to scoop another handful of rice out of his throne for those who'd decided to go the risotto route with their Spam. 'I wish to look after my people.'

I sat in the middle of the kerfuddle, sipping a brew, but still only looking and listening, speaking only when spoken to. I was beginning to measure the various friendships.

Al Slater and Frank Collins were close.

Al was a freefall nut, just like Frank. The pair of them jumped at Peterborough Parachuting Centre every weekend they could. Al got on really well with Frank's family, and so did his parents. They all got together whenever they came south.

I never met another soldier's parents my entire time in the army, and I never introduced anyone to mine. Mind you, I'd never met my biological parents either – though I knew that whoever my mother was, she must have wanted the best for me. She left me on the steps of Guy's Hospital in a Harrods carrier bag.

I was fostered from the age of five by a South London couple. They brought up three boys – I was the middle one – and had to take every low-paid job going to make ends meet. My dad drove a minicab; my mum juggled office cleaning and factory work. Like most kids I knew, I wore welfare clothes and ate free school dinners. I slept on a camp bed in the bathroom for a year because there was nowhere else. It never got steamed up; there was no hot water. A bit later on, my parents must have decided I was OK because I got promoted to the front room, and they adopted me.

I wasn't abused, I wasn't beaten, I wasn't mistreated, but I still couldn't wait to leave home. I felt a little jealous of Al. I bet his parents turned up at open evenings and knew his teacher's name.

Frank's wife didn't like Regiment guys as a rule, but Al was the exception. She was house-hunting for him, and had even promised to find him a wife while we were away. From what little I'd seen, I wasn't too sure that Al was the marrying type just yet. He was more Action Man than Barbie and Ken. I decided every square inch of his room back in Hereford would be crammed with diving, climbing and parachuting gear. No space to store an engagement ring.

I liked Al. I didn't think he was Mr Grumpy at all. I reckoned he didn't say much because he spent a lot of time thinking. Whenever he did open his mouth, what came out was sensible and to the point. I liked that. But I also liked his nickname. Great Piss-take.

Chris was strong mates with Frank, despite the divide over Frank's new-found religion. Tiny was pretty much mates with everyone, perhaps because he didn't give a fuck about anything: he just got on with the job and gave everyone a hard time. As for Saddlebags, he was much like Tiny, but talked quite a lot to Stan, who never seemed to join in the conversation.

I thought some more about Frank and the banter the night before. How did it work, being a Christian soldier? When I was a sixteen-year-old recruit, the only time we had off was Sunday afternoon – but every other Sunday we were marched down to the garrison church for an hour of hymns and a padre moaning about this and that. It meant we only had the evening free, when we weren't bulling our boots and doing all the rest of the stuff for Monday-morning inspection. So I'd never had much time for religion. Quite frankly, I hated it.

The metallic clang of a gollock rang out behind me. Chris looked over my shoulder. 'What the fuck you doing now?'

I swung round to see Nish leaning forward with his gollock in one hand and the other down his trousers, scratching his bollocks. He was inspecting the cuts he'd made in a massive buttress tree.

'Thought we'd have a Seven Troop sun-trap, somewhere we can wear our shades. The Ice Cream Boys have a reputation to maintain.'

'For fuck's sake.' Tiny stood up from his brew and headed for the tree surgeon. 'It's going to land on top of us if you keep fucking about.'

Nish grinned. 'Nah, nah, nah. If I do the cuts right it'll fall down towards the river, no problems.'

'Sure?'

'Trust me.'

Al picked up his belt kit and weapon. 'Don't believe a word of it.' He headed down towards the river, passing Nish on the way. 'Going to get some mud off me. I'm not waiting to be crushed by that thing.'

'You'd better watch yourself when you get back, mate. Careful the sun don't catch those freckles.'

We went back to sharing brews around the fire as Nish resumed operations for the next twenty minutes. Behind us, the massive buttress tree began to creak.

The creaks turned to groans and the next thing we knew, Nish was running towards us, laughing his head off. 'Might have fucked up! Save Stan!'

We grabbed our belt kit and weapons and ran for it. Nish stopped by Stan's hole and checked he wasn't outside having his breakfast.

There was an almighty scream of splintering wood and the tree smacked down just inches from the pole-beds.

'There you go.' Nish grinned. 'A very professional job.'

A shaft of sunlight streamed through the canopy and I could feel the warmth on my face.

Nish lit up as he surveyed his work. 'See, Frank? God. You got a direct line.'

Chris wasn't impressed with the near disaster. He told us to kit up and move out.

Almost immediately, we heard a couple of five-round bursts down by the river and went to see what was going on. Al appeared with a big multicoloured snake slung over his arm. Hissing Sid had crept up on him while he was washing and paid the price.

Frank clapped a hand on my shoulder. 'You're with me today. More contact drills. Let's see if you're as bad as Chris makes out.'

8

We were practising two-man contact drills, the lead scout and number one in the patrol coming under attack. I was ahead of Frank, moving tactically: butt in the shoulder, safety catch off and, after my day with Chris, finger on the trigger, on full automatic.

I came to the crest of a hill and gave the hand signal at waist level to stop. Frank waited while I crawled forward to see what lay in the dead ground beyond.

We were already soaked to the skin from the morning rain and the jungle was sticky and steaming. I had sweat running into my eyes again, and it stung like fuck.

I stared at the jungle and listened. Everything more than ten metres ahead merged into a big haze of green. I literally couldn't see the wood for the trees.

As I snaked through the mud and leaf litter, a Figure-11 target popped up about five metres in front of me. I opened fire and hosed down the area with a full thirty-round mag.

Frank came up on my right and moved two paces ahead. He put down some quick bursts while I dropped to my knees and changed mags. I got up, advanced another four or five paces, loosed off more rounds. The target was so close I could see the wood splinters flying.

'Stop!'

The shout came from the guy who'd been following us. His job was to point out any targets we missed, and to check those we'd fired at to make sure they'd been hit.

Frank and I reloaded, swapped positions and patrolled on. This continued for a couple of hours, until we reached a river. That marked end-ex (end of the exercise) for us. We were to wait there for the rest of the troop to come through.

'Get a brew on, Andy – I'm taking a rinse.'

I watched Frank walk down the bank and wade in fully clothed, complete with belt kit and even the green canvas satchel holding a Claymore anti-personnel mine and firing cable that always seemed to be slung over his shoulder.

The hot barrel sizzled as it hit the water. The American-built Colt M16 was a brilliant weapon, almost totally soldier-proof. You never have to worry about any weapon getting wet – that's just film stuff. The firing doesn't stop when you have a bit of rain.

When he was in up to his chest, he ducked down below the surface, and when he came back up, all the mud and leaf litter he'd accumulated on the range had disappeared.

I pulled a hexi burner from my belt kit and lit a block. I poured water from my bottle into my alloy mug, rested it over the flame, and sat down against a tree. The black plastic mugs that go with the water bottles are usually binned from belt kits because you can't cook or brew up with them.

Frank came back up the bank and joined me. Strangely, because there wasn't any wind, he leant forward and packed some mud around the burner. Force of habit, I guessed. Or some weird Christian ritual.

I left him to it and went into the river for a rinse. By the time I got back, Frank was oiling the working parts of his weapon.

It started to rain. When it rained in the jungle it came down vertically, whether or not there was wind. The water hit the canopy forty or fifty metres above us, then worked its way through the leaves and came down in torrents.

The rain made the hexi spit. Frank hunched over the burner. 'Tell you what, get a sheet up to keep this dry.'

The rainforest echoed with bursts of automatic gunfire as the guys carried on with their contact drills. I got my shelter sheet out of my belt kit, together with four elastic bungees I'd bought in Halfords. I hooked one to each corner and stretched them out to the nearest trees, adjusting the angle so the water ran off. We both slid under it, and Frank lay down with his head on his belt kit while the new boy got on with the brew.

The water pounded on the poncho. We had at least twenty-four hours' rations in our belt kit, and enough teabags, sugar and powdered milk to see us through the decade. I also carried extra sugar. I never used it except when I was in the field.

I emptied a milk sachet into the water once it was warm so it didn't go lumpy.

Frank was silent, and I felt a bit awkward. I thought maybe it was my job to make conversation. But not about work; he'd be debriefing me later on how well or badly I'd done.

'Frank, that God thing last night – does that happen all the time?'

'They're just worried about me. They don't understand.'

Frank didn't carry on waffling like I'd hoped he would. I over-concentrated on the brew. 'You been a Christian long, then?'

I'd fucked up. I'd opened a door I'd meant to keep closed.

Frank sat up straight and his eyes widened. He spoke louder than he usually did to make himself heard above the rain.

9

'It was on a Deltex. Just this March. The seventeenth. That's the day I really knew I'd found God.'

'Deltex? I don't know what that means, mate – I'm learning a new language here.'

'It's an exercise in Germany – the Russians have invaded, we go in to blow up key points, like power stations and bridges, anything to break the supply lines. You'll be doing enough of that later on, don't worry. But that was when it happened, the last Deltex.'

The water was boiling. I dropped in a teabag. 'So, did, er, God talk to you then, or what?'

He smiled. 'Sort of. He spoke to me through Larry, one of the Delta lads.'

At last, something I knew. Delta Force was the US equivalent of the Regiment. The unit was started by Colonel Charles Beckwith in 1977. Following the disastrous operation in 1980 to free the US hostages in Iran, Delta had been totally remodelled along SAS lines, with a lot of input from Hereford.

They were stationed at Fort Bragg in North Carolina.

Deltex, Frank said, was designed to further an atmosphere of co-operation between the two units, but all it did for him was evoke huge amounts of envy. 'I was bowled over by the sheer

41

size of the place: you could have fitted the entire town of Hereford twice over into what they called a "fort".'

Apparently, the quantity and quality of equipment on show was beyond belief. 'Delta had indoor 7.62 and 5.56mm shooting ranges; at Stirling Lines we only had the 9mm equivalent. We also had only one gym, while they had dozens of them, including Jacuzzis, saunas and a massive climbing wall for their mountain troop.' No wonder they'd renamed the place Fort Brass. They had more helicopters in one unit than we had in the whole of the British Army; come to that, there were more personnel in just that one base than in all of the British armed services put together.

'I was on a patrol with Larry. I'd already spent six months with Delta on exchange in the US and met him then.'

The US Army teemed with Christians of all persuasions. I'd spent a couple of months with the 101st Airborne in Fort Campbell, Kentucky, when I was a Green Jacket, getting my Air Assault wings. Even in the cookhouse, soldiers would pray at the table before eating, and down at the range you were just as likely to see a guy reading the Bible as firing a weapon. It was only natural that Delta would be full of them too.

I stirred the teabag. Anything to avoid eye-to-eye.

'Larry had never been one of the lads. He was too blond, too upright, Mr Clean. He probably did have a sense of humour, but it wasn't our sense of humour. People thought he was a bit weird.'

I nodded and fished out the teabag with a twig. I hoped that was the end of it.

'Larry always carried his Bible and he was always reading it. Even in the States I used to tease him, just like the lads tease me, but he always answered my questions seriously. He'd reach for his Bible and say, "Let's see what the Lord has to say on that subject."'

I was starting to get worried he was going to shift into full conversion mode, but there wasn't much I could do. I was the new boy: he had me over a barrel.

'Larry would always come up with an answer to my questions, but do you know what? I didn't really understand. I found it incomprehensible.' He chuckled to himself. 'But I found myself compelled to keep asking. I wanted to know the answers.

'So, one night, on the Deltex, we were out in a German forestry block doing a bridge recce to stop the Russian supply line. I asked him three questions. The first was, everybody knows about evolution, so how can people like Larry claim that God created the world? Then, if God loves us so much, how can he allow so much suffering? And finally, the one the lads keep on at me about: how can someone be a soldier and a Christian? Nish is right, you know – religion has killed billions. But do you know what Larry said to me?'

I made sure that the edge of the mug wasn't too hot, and shook my head. I had a couple of sips before handing it over.

Frank gripped it. 'He said, "If you want to know more about God, just ask him."'

He brought the mug up in a toast, and nodded.

I was starting to flap big-time. Were we going to end up on our knees?

'That night I just lay there in my sleeping bag and said quietly, "God, if you really exist, if you really are out there and listening to me, just give me a sign, some kind of sign."'

I had to look away. All I could think of was that bit in *Monty Python and the Holy Grail*: 'Give me a sign, give me a sign.'

'Also I said, "Look, God, if you don't send me a sign tonight, then it means, once and for all, that Larry's talking shite."' He took another swig and passed it back to me.

'I just lay there waiting. There were no angels, no glows in the sky, no doves with olive branches. Nothing. I slept, but I kept waking up in the night, opening my eyes, checking to see if God was there doing His thing.' He grinned. 'I would have hated to miss Him.'

He paused. It was obviously time for me to say something.

'So you didn't see anything, then?'

'Nothing at all. But I wasn't disappointed. Well, I was a little. But who doesn't secretly want to see an angel?' His hand was out for the brew. 'But then, just before first light, I had to send the sitrep that we'd recce'd the target. When I'd done that, I kept my earpiece in and started listening to the World Service.

'I caught the end of the news, and then the next programme was announced. It was about a guy who'd been in Bomber Command in the Second World War. He was being challenged on how he could reconcile what he'd done during the war, and his role as a scientist, with his religious convictions. He was going to be asked three questions . . .'

Frank held up a finger. 'One, how could God have created the world in a few days, when as a scientist he must agree that it evolved over aeons?'

Two fingers. 'Two, how could he believe in God's love when he had seen so much suffering? And three –' now he had three fingers up, as if I couldn't hear him '– how could he be an airman in Bomber Command and a Christian? Christians don't kill people, do they?'

Frank beamed at me. I wondered how I could steer the conversation round to house renovation or the price of logs in Pontralis.

'You know, Andy, I just lay there in my maggot, electrified. My three questions! This man was going to answer them! Was this the sign I'd asked for?'

I took the brew off him and got the last bit. Maybe there was a God: there was still a bit of undissolved sugar in the dregs.

Frank was waiting for me to ask the obvious question, but I was a bit preoccupied all of a sudden. I was starting to feel a bit uncomfortable between the legs. I scratched myself through my wet camouflage bottoms. You're always getting bitten by something in the jungle, but this felt different.

I tried to give him my full attention. 'So did he answer them?'

'Yes! First, he said there was no contradiction between the Bible and any scientific evidence for evolution. The Bible explains why the world was made, and science is just beginning to suggest *how* it was made. All of our scientific understanding is frequently wrong or incomplete, and all these so-called certainties that we've been brought up with have been disproved by subsequent discoveries. All we can really be sure about is the extent of our own ignorance. That's all it is, Andy. Does that make sense?'

I didn't want to say yes. I felt like I was in a resistance-to-interrogation session: if I gave a direct answer, I might find myself signed up for daily Bible readings or some shit like that. I sort of nodded.

'At the beginning of the Bible, God makes the world in six days. It doesn't say anywhere that a day is twenty-four hours, does it? A day might be an aeon, just as evolutionary theory suggests. So for God a day might have been, like, a million years. Who knows?'

'What about the suffering, Frank? Why does He give that the nod?'

Fuck me, I had a bit of suffering going on myself. The itch between my legs was becoming a lot more than just an itch. It felt like something was actually getting its teeth into me down there. I was on fire.

10

Frank frowned as I rummaged inside my trousers. 'It's all God's plan. Suffering has its benefits. It's only by knowing pain that we can experience real joy. Pain is a necessary part of our existence.'

I nodded again but my mind was on my own pain, not the world's. I wore Lycra cycling shorts under my camouflage bottoms in the jungle to stop my bollocks chafing, and that was where my thoughts were focused. I was hunched over in the poncho, bouncing my feet up and down, having a good scratch. 'I'll have to think about that one, mate.'

'A man drops his hammer on someone and hurts his toe. Suppose God intervenes to save the toe. That man will never be responsible with his tools. He'll keep on dropping hammers all over the place and hurting people's feet. When I realized this, it was a revelation.'

'OK. But what about the big one: being a Christian and a soldier?'

He smiled. 'Easy. Soldiers play an important role in the New Testament. They're God's agents to ensure submission to authority and the common good. Soldiers are appointed to carry out God's punishment on evil-doers. I really believe it, Andy. I believe that the Regiment exists to fight evil. That was exactly what this man was saying. The words made soldiering noble, an important mission.'

I undid my trousers. I was going to have to have a dig around to find out what was going on. Meanwhile, Frank could think what he liked but I certainly didn't see joining the Regiment as a noble cause. I wasn't here to wreak God's punishment on evil-doers. This was all a bit heavy for me – I was only on day three.

'It's like the embassy, Andy.'

'You were there?'

'I was twenty-three, the youngest soldier on the job. The terrorists were killing people and had to be stopped. Killing is sometimes the best way to save life.' Frank's face glowed. 'I was overwhelmed. I went over to Larry and shook him awake. I said, "Larry, pray with me." And he did. He prayed, I repeated the lines after him. I apologized to God for the way I'd lived my life up till then. I told God I understood it had all been wrong. I'd been selfish and hurt people and I'd turned God away. I asked for His forgiveness. I wanted Him to help me live by His laws, and all the things I thought were important weren't any longer. God was important.'

He picked up a handful of litter. 'Look at this forest – every leaf, every twig. It's a work of art, Andy. I see craftsmanship in everything I hadn't even noticed before. Everything is jumping up at me, wanting to be noticed. Everything looks different now I'm a Christian. I believe I've been selected in some way.'

I believed I had been, too. As Frank picked up his Claymore bag, I pulled down my trousers and felt something drop down my right leg. I wanted to have a good scratch and make sure everything was all right down there.

'So now I carry my Bible with me everywhere. Just like Larry.' Frank pulled one out, wrapped in a plastic bag.

I began to hear other voices. I'd never felt so relieved.

Nish and Chris had finished their ranges over the other side of the river and were wading across. They must have spotted the shelter sheet or smelt the tea.

Nish saw Frank and waved. 'Oi, Vicar, get the Holy Water boiling.'

Frank looked up at me and shook his head. 'They're just wayward children. Despite all the swaggering, they're clinging to the Regiment instead of forming a lasting relationship with God. They're lost, Andy. I was, too, until March the seventeenth. Now I understand my life is part of a bigger plan.'

Thank fuck the Bible disappeared back into the bag.

'Well, what do you do now, mate? Do you have to go to church?' I had my trousers down to my boots. 'What sort of church? Catholic, or what? Do you have to see a vicar and sign up? What's the score?'

As I peeled off the Lycra I felt a warm, wet sensation all round my bollocks. I looked down. The whole of my groin was covered with blood.

'Whoa! Fuck!'

It was only capillary bleeding, but my skin was so wet from all the rain and sweat it looked like it was everywhere. I almost went into shock. I was flapping big-style.

Nish and Chris ran up. 'Look at that ugly thing.'

They weren't looking where I thought they were. Down by my boots was the world's fattest, happiest leech, as big as my thumb. It had got inside my clothing, attached itself to my cock and drunk so much it had fallen off. When leeches bite they usually put in an anticoagulant and anaesthetic twistball so you keep bleeding and don't feel a thing. This one obviously hadn't had much practice.

'Fuck, have a look!' I pushed my cock towards Frank. The other two lads were rolling up.

'Shame on you, Vicar.' Nish grinned from ear to ear. 'We turn our backs for ten minutes and you're having your evil way with the new choir boy.'

The leech was very proud of himself, and rightly so. I kept

him to one side for ten minutes or so while I tried to decide what to do with him. Eventually I gave him a burst of mozzie rep, which really pissed him off.

By then the other two lads had their brew kit out and Nish was lying down having a fag. 'Well, Father Frank, what's going to happen now? Is this dearly departed leech going to heaven, and is this sick murderer going to hell?'

11

The next four or five days were spent in much the same way as the first few: two-man contact drills, four-man contact drills, always with live ammunition, white phosphorus grenades and high explosive (HE). Live firing had one great spin-off. The more HE and rounds thrown about, the more collateral damage there was for our cooking pots. Al's snake had been first in. It was gritty and tasted bitter, but half a bottle of Tabasco and some garlic soon sorted that out. Stan, who I finally discovered was a giant scorpion, didn't like it, though.

We practised being attacked from the front, behind, left, right, then with a man wounded, so we'd have to move him out of the contact area, and when we were halfway through crossing a river, with two of the patrol already on one bank, two on the other – how did we deal with that under fire? On and on, drill after drill, day after day. I loved it.

Then we moved on to ambushes: as we patrolled, we'd carry out the anti-ambush drills I'd learnt on Selection. We'd loop our track so we'd come off at an angle and back on to lay an ambush for anyone following. I learnt to lay Claymores at each end of the killing area as cut-offs, with others facing into the killing area to make it more 'kinetic' – a great military understatement.

Again, it was always with live ammo. What's the point in training with blank ammunition? It means you're training for training. Live ammunition focuses the mind wonderfully. Or, as Nish said, leaves a fucking big hole in it.

It was true. If you fuck up with live ammo, there's no going back. All you can do is keep the body alive until a helicopter arrives.

The benefits outweigh the downsides. You gain more confidence in yourself and in your weapon and, most important of all, in the people around you. That's why the Regiment is the best there is at what it does. There have been plenty of casualties, even on Selection. But if the squadrons were wrapped up in cotton wool or had to listen to the health-and-safety brigade, there would be even more deaths – not in training but on operations. Then there would be even more hand-wringing.

People tend to forget that the SAS are paid to fight, kill and perhaps be killed themselves. To make sure that the last doesn't happen too often, training has to be realistic and therefore dangerous. I felt very comfortable with it. I was a volunteer; no one had forced me to catch the sand-coloured beret.

Life here was very clear. 'This is what we do, this is the way we do it. If you don't like it, get out. There are thousands wanting to take your place.'

Every night, we'd brew up and waffle in the dark and the rain. By now I had some hair growing on my face, my kit was in shit state like everyone else's, I stank, I had zits like the others, and was starting to get into the routine of the kerfuddle and communal cooking. I'd brought a frying-pan that fitted nicely in the back of my Bergen, and everything I cooked I shared.

I was joining in bits of conversations as I began to feel more comfortable around the guys. I liked them all. Nobody was being horrible to the new boy, trying to make him fall flat on his face. That stuff didn't happen in the Regiment. Everyone was a professional soldier getting on with his job. And, besides, I was on probation for a year; plenty of time to do my own falling.

The only thing I didn't join in with was the piss-taking. I was so happy being in the squadron there was no way I was going to jeopardize my chances by getting on the wrong side of anyone.

Frank was the friendliest to me and I always seemed to land up sitting next to him round the fire as he got a hard time from one or other of the troop. Maybe he saw me as moral support, or a good target for conversion.

One particular night everybody was doing his own thing, brewing up and eating. Frank slapped me on the back as he added the rum to the punch. 'I can see the Regiment's occupying the number-one spot in your life, isn't it? You're ambitious, you want to go on and get all your skills. It's everything to you, isn't it?'

'Course. Not much else matters.' I looked at him, surprised. I couldn't understand why he was even saying it. I thought everybody here would think the same way. Surely the only reason you joined the Regiment was to become the best soldier you possibly could be.

Chris had just come back from prayers with Saddlebags. He fed the fire with wet wood. Nish lay on his pole-bed, moaning that the fresh clouds of smoke were interfering with his own.

'OK, listen in. Boss L is pissed off with the honks. He knows it's Snapper starting them off. It has to stop right now.'

On cue, a 'Hoooonk' rang out in the darkness.

Everyone laughed, including Chris.

Nish took a deep breath but Chris was waiting for it. 'Don't even think about it. We'll all be in the shit.'

'Wasn't going to, mate. Just about to say Snapper must be deaf as well as mad.'

The general waffle now was about Frank leaving for a few

weeks to do some hearts-and-minds stuff alongside medics from other troops.

Tiny was on the other side of the fire, once more reading *The Holy Blood and the Holy Grail*. Al sat next to him, on his rice sack, poring over a Bible like a detective at a crime scene. They were in their own little world, occasionally swapping notes and conferring.

All of a sudden there was a frenzy of noise, voices and torch-light heading our way.

A slow northern accent rang out from behind the torch. 'Mason hunt! Snapper and the anti-lodge approaching. Where's the new boy?'

12

Nish rolled out of his pole-bed as five guys came into the fire-light.

'Here he is – Andy.'

Snapper went down on his haunches the other side of the smoke. He was very tall, with a flat face and a nose broken so badly it headed east when he was facing north. His accent was dramatic Lancashire, and he stretched the last word of each sentence until it broke. 'Andy, you a fookin' masooooon?'

'What?'

'Lodge, Andy. You a fookin' apron-wearer?'

The other four were waffling with Nish about the new sun-trap and passing round a mug of punch.

'No, mate.'

He stared at me. I wasn't sure if this was a joke or not. An apron-wearer? What the fuck was he on about?

He stood and took the alloy mug that Saddlebags offered. Nish introduced me to the other four, who weren't as mad-looking.

Des Doom had thick dark curly hair and a face that said, 'Come and try it, if you think you're hard enough.' He was wearing a green vest that exposed arms and a chest that were meaty rather than muscle-toned. Every square inch of exposed skin was covered with Para Regiment tattoos and what looked like a Chinese takeaway menu without the English translation. He grinned as I took in the art gallery. 'If you don't want to talk to me, read me.'

Harry was a Royal Marine and it stood out a mile. His looks could have sold toothpaste and there wasn't a zit in sight. Thankfully, he wasn't the full Adonis: he had more blond hair on his face than he had left on his head.

Hillbilly looked like Chuck Connors's shorter and less successful brother. His nose was more squashed than Chuck's and his chin was a bit more bent out of shape. Miraculously for someone who was obviously no stranger to a fracas, all his teeth looked intact.

Schwepsy also had blond hair, but his was thick and wild. His face was acne-scarred, but unlined. He clearly wasn't a man prone to worry.

Snapper's manic eyes, still staring at me over the mug, told me all I needed to know about him. He finished the brew. 'OK, no masons here. One more new boy to check.' He took a deep breath as they moved back into the darkness. '*Hoooonk!*'

Chris sniffed and shook his head as the rest pissed themselves with laughter. I felt I could join in on this one.

The general waffle for the rest of the night was about the anti-masons. Snapper was obsessed: he was sure that freemasons were infiltrating the Regiment and it was his mission to expose and kick them out. He'd even set up a covert observation post (OP) opposite the Lodge in Hereford and filmed whoever turned up.

Nish grinned. 'Just because you're paranoid doesn't mean no one's out to get you!'

Des Doom, Hillbilly and Harry had all passed Selection with Nish in 1980.

Hillbilly claimed to have a background in the Merchant Navy. In fact, he'd been a croupier aboard a cruise ship. The navy wouldn't let him apply for the SAS so he'd had to leave and become a civilian. He'd been on the dole in Hereford while training for Selection.

Schwepsy had been an instructor at Depot Para in a past life, and looked perfect for the role. There was a frustrated RSM inside him.

Snapper? Well, the conversation went on and on about him. He was a regimental institution. Mirbat, Kubat – all the Aden battles – and back again. He'd also been in the Falklands and on the embassy job. He'd had 'B Squadron Smoke Embassy' emblazoned on his T-shirt.

Snapper had been sent to Hong Kong once to train the Gurkhas in unarmed combat. He'd had a punch-up in a pub and become the last British soldier to be publicly flogged. He said he didn't think it'd hurt much – but then the biggest Chinese he'd ever seen in his life came out with the longest cane in history. He got six strokes, and for months he claimed to be the only sergeant with twelve stripes: 'Three on each arm and six on my arrrrse!'

Snapper knew he was sane and had a bit of paper to prove it. Al voiced what the new boy could only think: 'That means he really is mad, doesn't it?'

The thought of having a bit of paper to show you're OK in the head sounded great to me. I wanted one.

Things started to die down around the fire as we had a mug of punch and sorted our shit out, but the tranquillity didn't last long. Behind his mozzie net, Nish used a box of ration-pack matches to get another No. 6 on the go. He propped himself on one elbow and shouted into an imaginary mike, 'Welcome to the show, ladies and gentlemen, boys and girls. My name is Nish Bruce, and I'm your Red Devils commentator for this afternoon's display. About three minutes from now, the aircraft will appear overhead. I'll just see where they are now . . .' He rolled over and stuck his head out from his mozzie net, peering up at the canopy. 'Today we have eight jumpers in the aircraft, including His Holiness Frank, Certifiable Snapper –

What happens when a paranoid has low self-esteem? He thinks that nobody important is out to get him, ba-boom – and the newest member of the team, young Trooper Andy from Sarrrf London, and this is his first display . . .'

Al had had enough and threw a log at him. Nish fell out of his pole-bed trying to avoid getting hit.

Frank leant over to me. 'Nish knows about freefall. He was in the Red Devils. Got about three thousand jumps in his log book.'

Tiny muttered, 'Here we go, two crap hats talking about the airborne.' He didn't even look up.

Frank wasn't Para Reg, but a scaley (signaller) attached to Hereford before he did Selection, because that was the only way they could apply.

Nish brushed himself down and came over to join us. 'Oi, Father Frank, tell him who's the daddy . . . Who got wet in the Falklands, eh?'

13

The interrogation phase of Nish's Selection had ended on a Saturday night in May 1982. 'By first thing Sunday morning, me and the other four dickheads you just met were badged and screaming round the Lines (the camp in Hereford) getting issued with kit and zeroing weapons.'

An Exocet missile fired by a Super Étendard had taken out HMS *Sheffield*, with the loss of twenty crew. Downing Street were shitting themselves: if the same thing happened to an aircraft-carrier, it could mean the end of the war before the islands had been reclaimed.

The head shed (command) started to look at ways of destroying Étendards and Exocets on the ground. While Nish had been pissing around on Combat Survival, Frank and the rest of this lot had been training for an assault on Argentina.

One option was for a pair of C-130s (Hercules transport aircraft) to fly from Ascension Island into Argentina and deliver them directly on target. The two airfields were Rio Grande and Rio Gallegos, either side of the Strait of Magellan, at the very tip of South America. B Squadron practised flying under radar at Heathrow and doing mock assaults on airfields all over the UK.

B Squadron patrols were already on mainland Argentina,

setting up OPs. They started sending information back to Hereford and a plan of attack was formulated. The aircraft would be circling out at sea. When they got the all-clear from the OPs, they would fly in below the radar and land in the airfield. As soon as the ramp dropped, out would stream the motorbikes and cut-down Land Rovers. They carried machine-guns and M202s, American-made, multi-barrelled white phosphorus grenade-launchers. Air Troop would bomb-burst into small groups to take out the control tower, blow the fuel tanks and attack the accommodation blocks to kill the pilots.

But time was tight. A military base two miles away housed a couple of thousand Argentine marines. Escape options were limited. The nearest British Task Force ship would be five hundred miles away, and helicopters had the fuel capacity to reach the mainland but not get home again so there would be no pick-up after the job. That only left the border, forty miles away, in vehicles or tabbing. They'd have to get there and give themselves up to the Chileans.

But that wasn't the only plan the head shed was considering. The troop left Brize Norton. Nish got chosen for the advance party because of his freefall experience, even though he was so new he didn't have any patrol skills. Seven Troop would jump into the attack and be first on the ground, taking out the pilots and control tower as the rest of the squadron flew in, landed and destroyed the aircraft.

The winds in the area averaged about forty m.p.h. at that time of year so there were six guys in each patrol instead of the normal four – they didn't expect everyone to get down in one piece.

They reached Ascension Island. They wanted to close down the airfield so they could practise the drop. A C-130 was going to fly in low, climb again to 600 feet, its maximum height for the radar, and they'd jump off the tailgate.

Nish didn't know it yet, but nobody in any Air Troop had ever jumped from so low. Even he wondered if he'd stay stable enough on exit to pull the handle immediately, but he kept his mouth shut. He thought the head sheds must know what they were talking about.

He had kept his doubts to himself right up until the point where Ken, the troop sergeant, whom I was yet to meet, asked if they should do the dummy run with or without the chainsaws needed to cut through chain-link fences.

Frank said the OC (officer commanding a squadron) had already been binned because he'd said it was a suicide mission.

Tiny gave a jerk of his wrist. 'That's because he was a crap hat.'

Nish smiled. 'Yeah. Anyway, what's the point of practising something you can only fuck up once?' He gassed a bunch of mozzies with a lungful of smoke. 'We got the warning order: leave in twelve hours. I was jumping with just a chainsaw, no other kit. The rest of my gear was in one of the Land Rovers.

'Then we were told there was a delay. Then that it had been put on hold. Then it was on again, but changed. Fuck me, it went on like that all week. Apparently Thatcher wasn't happy about the predicted sixty per cent casualty rate. The crabs (RAF) weren't too thrilled either about having to dump the aircraft and have the crew tab to Chile with us.'

Frank shook his head sadly. 'We were called together by the new OC. We thought it was to announce another delay, but a Sea King had crashed while cross-decking between ships at night. About twenty from D and G Squadrons and their signallers were dead. All of us had friends in that helicopter.'

Then, on 8 June, two transport ships, *Sir Galahad* and *Sir Tristram*, were hit by Argentine jets in Bluff Cove. Dozens of soldiers were killed or burnt, most of them Welsh Guards. All of a sudden, the mainland op was back on.

'We were due to take off at 0700.' Nish was now blowing smoke rings. 'I was in the baggage party, humping gear into the cargo hold. A Land Rover screamed up and we heard the news: the op had been cancelled. One of the newspapers had gone and published a story about us practising for a mainland operation! Within hours, the Argies had moved their aircraft away from the airfields and scattered them in ones and twos.'

B Squadron were deployed instead to join D Squadron on an assault on Port Stanley airport.

'We were going to fly down there in two C-130s so the Argies couldn't get all the Special Forces with one hit.' Frank smacked his neck and killed a mozzie. 'We were going to do a wet landing and be picked up by ships in the area. Next morning, our two C-130s took off. The flight was thirteen hours – a long time when you're sweating in a dry suit.'

Finally, the plane lost altitude, and they could see ships below.

I couldn't see the other plane with Nish aboard but I knew it was ahead of us. We circled. We circled some more. Suddenly we were gaining height and flying back in the direction we'd come from.

The jumpmaster appeared, waving his hands. 'It's off, no jump.' Back at Ascension Island after twenty-six hours' flying, they were told they had six hours before re-boarding and flying back.

'That was when we learnt why we'd been sent back . . .'

14

Frank handed over with a flourish. Nish gave a huge grin and smoke poured from his mouth. 'Fucking right. We reached the convoy and prepared for a static-line jump from a thousand feet, directly off the ramp.'

Their dry suits would give them about five minutes in the water before they froze, so it was all down to the navy. There were twenty-one guys, but only seven could jump on each pass because there weren't enough inflatables to pick them up. Nish was in the second stick.

'Red light, green light . . . I sat under my canopy, watching the last guy in the first stick just missing the stern of a ship. Ten feet from the water, I hit the release box and dropped away from the rig. Fuck me, the water was cold. Huge swells.' Nish's hand moved up and down. 'The coxswains were surfing down the waves to get to us. They pulled me on board and the Herc made a final pass and dropped all the kit. Bang . . .' Nish punched one hand into the other. 'The whole fucking lot burst open and sank. Bergens, weapons, personal stuff, everything.'

The drop was halted. The aircraft turned back to Ascension.

Nish giggled. 'When they did the final tally-up, the blokes were claiming enough lost kit to sink a couple of battleships. I lost a couple of Rolexes and a mink coat in my Bergen.'

He took a big suck from a brand new No. 6. 'We were on the deck, waiting to be heli'd in, when they announced white flags had been seen over Port Stanley. Story of my life.' Nish held his thumb and forefinger half an inch apart. 'So near, and yet so fucking far . . .'

Frank got up to bin it for the night. Nish picked up a log and lobbed it like a warning shot across a ship's bow.

Tiny wagged his finger. 'C'mon, Frank, what's the most Christian way for a soldier to kill a man?'

Frank was uncomfortable, but happy to defend his views. 'There is no Christian way to kill . . .'

'OK, then, as a Christian soldier, would you kill any differently?'

'No. You've still got to nullify the threat. In Romans thirteen it says something like, "He does not bear the sword for nothing for he is God's servant, an agent of wrath to bring God's punishment on the evil-doer."'

'What the fuck does that mean?'

'Killing is sometimes the best way to save life.'

'You going to heaven after all this, Frank?'

'I believe in the afterlife. Death is the next great adventure.'

'You think Jesus would have passed Selection?'

'He lasted forty days and nights in the desert, didn't he? Christ was hard.'

'You still coming over the water, then, or you off to Bible college?' Tiny was getting bored with the non-biting Frank. He leant back and stretched. He was going to get his head down too.

Frank got up, scratched around. He'd heard it all before. Chris looked up and smiled. 'No, come on, Frank, what are you going to do?'

'I'll do my job, like everybody else.'

I looked around me, bewildered. 'Are we going over the water?'

He nodded.

'When?'

Chris laughed. 'We get a long weekend off and then we start training. Soon as we get back, it's out of this lot and into jeans and trainers.'

That night, I lay in my A-frame as the rain pounded the shelter sheet and thought about Frank. He was a complicated piece of work. It was as if being Frank Collins wasn't enough.

He'd gone into the army to escape the fighting, alcoholism and misery at home and joined 264 Signal (SAS) squadron, then passed Selection as one of the youngest ever. During the embassy siege he had taken a pillow up onto the roof during the many stand-tos for an assault. He reasoned he might as well get some sleep while he waited. When the assault finally happened, Frank was number one into the building.

The Royal Signals had a strange system when one of their own passed Selection: they wanted him back after three years. But Frank had changed that system for ever. When it was his time to return he'd simply refused and said he'd rather quit. It was a risky bluff, but it worked. Maybe, though, just like his conviction about God, he would have carried it through.

15

It was a shock, but a good shock. I was excited about going back to Northern Ireland. I'd been there on plenty of tours with the Green Jackets, doing all the normal army town patrols in places like Crossmaglen and Belfast, but ultimately we were just mobile Figure-11 targets.

It was nearly seven years since I'd started my first tour, at Christmas 1977. So many seventeen-year-old soldiers had been killed in the early years of the Ulster emergency that you now had to be eighteen before you could serve there. So, when the battalion had left on 6 December, I couldn't join them: I had to wait until my birthday at the end of the month.

I was in Crossmaglen, a cattle-market town known to us as XMG, right on the border, in bandit country. This meant the players could prepare on the other side, in Dundalk, then pop over and give us the good news, or just rig up their mortars in the south and get a few rounds down on us.

We didn't use vehicles because so many had been blown up by improvised explosive devices (IEDs). Everything came in by helicopter, but even they weren't immune. Our CO (officer commanding a regiment), Corton-Lloyd, was killed when one was brought down as he left the location. By the time peace was finally declared in the Good Friday Agreement in

1998, more than 2,300 civilians had been killed in Northern Ireland. So, too, were more than 950 members of the security forces – a greater number than so far in Iraq and Afghanistan combined.

It was in XMG that I first met a guy from the Regiment. At least, I thought he was. I didn't see him for the first two months I was there, but I knew his name was Rob, and was told he wore a dirty white submariner's polo-neck jumper, minging jeans and wellies, and lived near the operations room. I'd go past his door sometimes, hear the hiss of radios and catch a glimpse of maps of South Armagh. His place was a dump: there were Bergens, belt kit, old crisps packets everywhere. But no Rob.

Then he turned up in the washrooms one day and didn't look at all as I'd expected. He could have been anyone in a crowd. He was wearing just a pair of pants, T-shirt and flip-flops. His washing and shaving kit consisted of a toothbrush and a bit of soap in a plastic cup from a vending machine. We, at the bottom of the food chain, had been told not to talk to him.

'All right, mate?' He was from up north somewhere.

I'd smiled back through a face full of shaving cream. Not that I needed to shave that much at eighteen. 'All right.'

That was as far as my introduction to the Regiment went from Rob. I was to see him quite a lot in H (Hereford) in the future, but never got round to asking if he remembered the zit-covered dickhead in the washroom.

That tour had been the first time I'd had to shoot at real live people, and the first time a friend had been killed in front of me. Nicky Smith was a year older than me when he got blown in half by a booby trap on the outskirts of town. His head was cut off diagonally at the neck, and his lower legs were missing. The bit in the middle was intact – badly messed up, but intact. I felt his blood splatter on my face, could smell the flesh that now hung from a fence, and it took hours to find his left foot.

It was an abrupt end to soldiering just being a good laugh. I still had Nicky's map: I'd picked it up from the bloodstained street to remind me this was serious business.

It was a different story when the Special Air Service showed up. These were the guys who carried the war to the Provisional IRA (PIRA), the Irish National Liberation Army (INLA) and the rest. What they did was proactive and aggressive. And now, wearing jeans and trainers rather than helmet and body armour, I was going to be joining them.

Frank left for the Cameron Highlands the next day to do his hearts-and-minds thing. I was happy he could dodge the flak for a while. Everyone gave him a hard time, but I knew now it was only out of concern – for his wellbeing, and their own. We depended on each other for our lives, and if Frank's finger hesitated on the trigger because of stuff a guy had allegedly been spouting a couple of thousand years ago, well, it was just plain scary. At the same time, I was sorry he wasn't there. It's fun to take the piss out of someone, and if the other lads didn't have him as the butt of their jokes, they might turn their attention to somebody else.

I wondered what the next few months held in store. I was still on probation. I was still on an infantry sergeant's pay, but it was less than a qualified trooper earned in the SAS.

To qualify for Special Forces' pay I still had to get a patrol skill. Everyone has to have signals – if the shit hits the fan you've got to be able to shout, 'Help!'

I would also need my entry skill. Mobility Troop need to know how to drive a whole range of vehicles; divers need to be able to dive; Mountain Troop need to get themselves up and down hills; in Air Troop, we needed to know how to freefall. No patrol skill, no extra pay, but it was Catch 22: we wouldn't be paid unless we'd got the qualifications to do the job – but we couldn't get the qualifications because we were too busy doing it.

Seven Troop was off to Northern Ireland; the other three troops would comprise the counter-terrorism team.

Chris gave me another bit of good news. We were going to Oman as soon as we got back from over the water, and would be on a 'fast glide'. I eventually found out that meant military freefall training, and we'd be doing it for weeks on end. And I discovered, at last, the reason we needed sunglasses: it's no good having an expensive aircraft sitting doing nothing because the weather's closed in, so it's cheaper and more effective to go somewhere with a guarantee of sunny skies. And where there's sun, there has to be ice cream.

I needed my entry skill before the Oman trip so that when the other blokes in the troop mentioned riggers, risers, brake-lines, baselines or flare I'd understand what the fuck they were talking about.

The public image of the SAS is synonymous with Land Rovers screaming around the desert, men in black abseiling down embassy walls, or freefallers leaping into the night. But freefall, like the other entry skills, is just a means of getting from A to B.

To count myself proficient I would have to be able to jump as part of a patrol and keep with the others in the air at night on oxygen, with full equipment loads weighing in excess of 120 pounds. Basically, I would have to get up there and jump my arse off until the entry phase of the operation became second nature. If the entry phase went wrong, there would be a domino effect of cock-ups.

For all that, it was addictive, from what I'd heard round the fire. There were world-class freefall jumpers in the Regiment, people who had represented the UK in international competitions. Nish, for all his farts and eccentricity, was one of them.

16

Al was worried about Frank. Not so much about him getting God, but what he was proposing to do now that he had. His rice sack was empty so he had to sit on a log like the rest of us. 'Do you think he'll get out?'

The general consensus was that he wouldn't. It was a phase; he'd soon see the error of his ways.

'Moving on . . .' Chris had a more pressing point. He'd had a letter. Frank and Chris were corporals, the senior ranks here, but the troop sergeant was Ken. He was away on a German course in Beaconsfield, west of London. I had no idea why, but that didn't matter. The main thing was that now Frank had gone the piss-taking had shifted, not to me but to Ken, even though he wasn't there – and, as I would discover, that was the only time to take the piss out of him.

Chris read out a snippet about German being a very interesting language. The grammar, apparently, was very similar to English. Both had identical pluperfects, or something.

Nish couldn't stop laughing. 'What the fuck is he on about? He eaten a dictionary?'

Tiny had only two words to say: 'Crap hat.' He looked across the fire at me. 'Even you can call him one. He's Int Corps.'

That made my day.

*

The next month under the canopy was taken up with a tracking course. That was why the Kiwi regiment were there. Those lads really knew their stuff. In fact, their course is famous, the best in the world. The Regiment send people there all the time. Not only are they really good at it, but also they've got all the different terrains in New Zealand to practise in: rainforest, mountains, snow, ice.

After we'd come out of the jungle there was a two-day clear-up of all the weapons and equipment. Nobody shaved. They were saving it for our week off in Singapore.

17

Hereford

I felt good after the Malaysian trip. I'd blended in. I'd also been lucky, although I didn't realize it until I got back to the UK. The jungle trip turned out to have been one of the few times the entire squadron was together in one location. One or all of the four troops were often away training, then there were team jobs: six, ten, twenty guys, however many were required, might be away on operations. Others might be at specialist training establishments, learning everything from demolition to trauma care. The squadron is like a clearing house; it's not like a rifle company, where everybody's together all the time.

My freefall course was starting in three weeks. It would entail two weeks back at No. 1 Parachute Training School at RAF Brize Norton in Oxfordshire, the same place I'd learnt to static-line jump at the end of Selection, then two weeks in Pau, in the foothills of the Pyrenees, and finally two more weeks in Brize Norton. But first I had to go and get all my black kit for the counter-terrorism (CT) team build-up, and get some basic training with the Counter-revolutionary Warfare Wing (CRW). I was going to be part of the team I'd watched storm the embassy. I just hoped I didn't fuck up.

CRW had been born out of the Munich Olympics massacre. On 5 September 1972, eight Palestinian terrorists had burst into a room housing eleven Israeli athletes. They'd shot two dead and taken the others hostage, demanding the release of PLO prisoners held in Israel and members of the German Red Army Faction held in West Germany. They also wanted a plane to fly them to Cairo.

The West German government, who had no specially trained counter-terrorist forces, gave in to the terrorists' demands after a day of negotiation. They were flown to a military airbase in two helicopters, and army snipers opened fire as they prepared to board the aircraft. Visibility was bad, and the snipers were too far away. The terrorists had time to blow up both helicopters, killing all nine hostages and a policeman.

To avoid a similar disaster in the UK, the British government turned to the SAS. The CRW had been created, among other things, to be responsible for training every member of the Regiment in counter-terrorism techniques.

An entire squadron was 'on the team' in the UK for six to nine months, on permanent standby. The squadrons rotated, and it was B Squadron's turn. While Seven Troop was over the water, the other three troops would comprise the team. I'd been sent straight for CT training so that while I was mincing around for a month at Brize Norton on my freefall course, I'd also be on standby. It was a national and international responsibility, and they needed every spare bit of manpower they could get their hands on.

It sounded to me like the best of all worlds. I got to do team training, collect my entry skill, and finally to go on operations with my own troop.

18

We were split into two sub-teams, Red and Blue, which meant that two incidents could be covered at once if it was a really bad day. One team was on thirty-minute standby, the other, three hours. There was a signals set-up from Frank's unit, and each had an assault group and a sniper group.

The assaulters were the guys in black who jumped out of helicopters and went in through embassy windows. Depending on the target, they tended to work in four-man teams. One of the assaulters was also the method-of-entry (MOE) man, responsible for taking down any door the team were trying to get through with explosives, or by simply turning the handle. Then there was the MOE heavy brigade. They were the guys who cut through walls using shaped charges, and made sure that everything from window grilles to steel-plated doors didn't get in our way.

Until everything went bang and an attack went in, the most important component of the team were the snipers. They were always in their fire positions so we had eyes on target supplying real-time information. They reported any movement they could see, the exact construction of the window frames, whether there were any covert approaches to the target, so that the lads could have a close recce. The snipers knew exactly the kind of information required because they, too, were trained as assaulters.

The squadron HQ comprised the OC – a major – and the SSM (squadron sergeant major) – a warrant officer – who were responsible for both teams. B Squadron had just got a new OC. Boss L was off to bigger and better things.

Stirling Lines, our camp, was named after the founder of the SAS. It was usually just referred to as the Lines, and had been rebuilt about five years ago. The old camp, Bradbury Lines, consisted of wooden spider huts from the 1950s, long barrack rooms in a star shape joined at the centre by the toilets and washrooms. Now the camp looked more like a university campus, with red-brick buildings, white-framed double-glazing, and no parade ground. It was so un-army. I loved it.

I lined up at the quartermaster's and was issued with my ready bag – a black canvas affair big enough to hold a family car, containing everything an assaulter could ever need. The idea was that you could throw it straight into a vehicle or a heli in a call-out. Ready bags always had to be ready.

First into it was a set of black overalls and Nomex tops and bottoms to go underneath, like pyjamas. Nomex was the fire-proof kit racing drivers wore. I was also given an NBC (nuclear, biological and chemical) suit, which would go between the two if we were using dodgy gas that was designed to attack the skin as well as the respiratory system. Next came a respirator and six spare canisters. The Kevlar body armour had two ceramic plates, front and rear, to protect the major organs in the chest area. A thick suede waistcoat to go over the top was festooned with small webbing loops and pockets. And last, but not least, there was a pair of green leather aviators' gloves. They protected your hands, but were thin enough to let you feel the trigger. Everyone loved them.

I was handed a 9mm Browning semi-automatic pistol, and the legendary Heckler & Koch MP5, with an under-slung torch. The torch was zeroed to the weapon. If you were firing from up to about eight metres, the rounds would hit where the beam did. It was great for target acquisition in the dark, but the beam was also powerful enough to penetrate smoke.

I was given half a dozen thirty-round magazines for the MP5 and three for the 9mm, and thick leather mag holders to strap to my legs: 7.62 mags on the left, 9mm on the right. They didn't go on your legs so that you could walk around like Wyatt Earp: it was because your belt was under your body armour, so nothing was accessible until it came off.

The webbing hooks in the waistcoat were for grenades, flash bangs and/or gas canisters. Flash bangs – not stun grenades, as the media like to call them – came in different formats. Bang, flash or scream: all of them fucked people up in their own special way. Some just gave off crushing bangs that made your body shudder – as well as the enemy's. Some gave bangs and a brilliant flash that caused temporary blindness. Some emitted high-pitched deafening screams. About the size of an aerosol can with a handle down the side, they had a rubber skin that contained three levels of small alloy canisters. When the pin was pulled and the flash bang was thrown, the small charge inside kicked off and sprayed the room with whatever special brand of fuck-off stuff was inside.

On the left-hand side of the vest there was a pouch with a bit of strapping to hold the next bit of issue, a fireman's axe – very handy if the MOE guy fucked up. High on the left shoulder a survival knife was positioned so you could grab it easily with your right hand, even with a weapon butt in the shoulder. It was not so much for fighting with, more for cutting away the abseil rope if you got caught up. It was added to the kit after the embassy siege when a couple of lads got tangled and couldn't cut themselves free. They were badly burnt by fires set off by flash bangs, which billowed from the windows below.

As soon as we had our ready bags we went to CRW and started training. CRW also evaluated new equipment and techniques for the CT team. They sourced different training areas and buildings. If they could get their hands on a 747 jet they would, and we'd fly off and meet it wherever it was. They organized trips to the London Underground, ports and airports, and assessed major venues where heads of state were likely to gather. They were big believers in the Seven Ps: Prior Planning and Preparation Prevents Piss Poor Performance. A large two-storey building with a flat roof that was used as a stronghold stood within the training area. It got stormed about six times a week.

The Regiment used Agusta 109 helicopters. Some were captured in the Falklands; others were bought once the head shed saw how good they were. They were perfect for moving fast in built-up areas and delivering assault groups to the top of buildings or wherever they needed to be. They were also in wide use by civilians, so offered concealment.

The idea that particular night was to practise a new technique for inserting an assault team onto the top of a building fast and in darkness. I'd only abseiled a couple of times before on adventure training, and never from a helicopter. Back in the Lines, the lads had shown us how to rig up the seat harness, which was part of our ready bags, and the metal figure-of-eight the rope went through so you could control your descent. And that was it. Again, it was all about barrel time: just get on with it.

The normal abseiling technique from an Agusta was to stand on the skid, leaning out on a rope secured to a D-ring on the floor. It was tried and tested, but the disadvantage for the pilot was having guys hanging out as the helicopter swooped into position. The new method we were going to try was to stay in the aircraft so the pilot could fly faster and manoeuvre round targets without worrying about guys falling off the sides.

We all knelt inside, rigged up and ready to go, with only three metres of slack rope, secured to a D-ring, coiled in our hands. When the command came to jump, we did exactly that. There was three metres of freefall before the rope bit on the figure of eight, and then we abseiled normally. The only thing to make absolutely sure of, the instructors said, was that you really had a grip of the rope in your right hand. That was the free one, the one that was going to do the braking.

It all worked fine, until one of us had a drama and lost his grip. He hit the roof like a runaway sack of shit, and his ankle cracked so loudly I could hear it from ten metres away.

As he lay there waiting to be cas-evac'd off, the heli's rotors blasting us with downwash, Snapper walked over, lit two fags and passed one down. 'You'll have to work on that last bit, laaaad.' He winked. 'Only four point five for styyyyyle.'

19

We were taken to what used to be called the Killing House. I'd heard hundreds of rounds being fired in it while I was on Selection, and now I was actually going in to have a cabby (a go) myself.

'We have to call it the CQB building noooow.' Snapper wasn't impressed. 'Things are starting to get all politically correct. I blame Maggieeee!'

Whatever it was called, the single-storey building in the corner of the Lines was designed for us to train in hostage rescue with live ammunition, and make entry at any level – anything from a four-man assault group to a complete team.

The smell of lead and cordite clung to the walls. After a while you could taste it at the back of your throat. There were extractor fans, but they couldn't keep up with the number of rounds fired – more than the rest of the army put together.

Snapper had just been posted to CRW, but still thought he was with the squadron. He hung around, and generally joined in with the guys, honking about everything and anything, like any soldier in any army on the planet.

Even with all the lights on, the rooms in the CQB (close-quarter battle) house were still gloomy. Some rooms had bullet-proof glass with little portholes so people could look in from outside or video us.

Live ammunition could be used because the walls were covered with overlapping sheets of conveyor-belt rubber. Behind them there was a gap of about three inches, then thick steel plate. The rounds would go through the rubber, hit the steel, and if they ricocheted it would only be back against the rubber. It was a brilliant system. You could ram an MP5 right against the rubber, blat away on auto, and not a single round came back.

We were separated into four-man groups. I was with Hillbilly, one of the lads I'd met when Snapper was doing his anti-mason hunt. He was in Boat Troop.

He gave me a nod. 'How you getting on? Seen anything of Nish?'

'Nah, they've been in the training area since we got here.'

Snapper appeared. 'You, you and you – let's go.'

Hillbilly, another lad and I fell in behind him.

Snapper looked and sounded as mad as usual. 'OK, laaaads, let's smoke 'em and doke 'em!'

I'd thought he was going to do his CRW training thing, not be the team commander.

I was number three on the door. I looked at Hillbilly. 'What do you want me to do?'

No one had given me any instruction about four-man room combat.

'Just get through the fucking door. Go where we're not. If Snapper and me are to the right, you go left. Just get in where you can. If you see an X-ray, drop him. Simple as that. Just get on with it, mate. No time for mincing.'

I loaded the MP5 with thirty rounds, pulled the cocking handle to make the weapon ready and put the safety catch on. I let the weapon drop in front of me to hang from its chest sling and pulled out the 9mm, cocked it, applied the safety, and pushed it back into the thigh holster.

We were on the left of the door. Snapper was number one

and on the hinges. Hillbilly was so close behind he could have got him pregnant. I was the same distance behind him. It had to be this way so we'd get through the door almost as one.

Over the next decade I'd get used to the deafening thuds from other rooms and the smell of lead and cordite.

The number four, the MOE guy, was on the handle side of the door.

Snapper must have heard Hillbilly. He grabbed hold of my arm and dragged me close enough to shout into my ear through the respirator and above the din: 'It's all about barrel time, Andy lad. Time on the weapon, that's what it's about. Don't you fucking worry about all the walk-through talk-throughs. I'll soon tell you if you fuck up.' He let go and I got back on the door, but then he came back and dragged me towards him again. 'Or Mr Nine Millimetre will. Awww.'

Snapper got back on the door with the butt of his MP5 in the shoulder, weapon up, facing where the gap would appear as soon as the door opened.

Hillbilly had his weapon in the shoulder but was pointing it down at the floor. I saw his thumb click his safety down onto single shot. All the way down would have been automatic. It's all about taking rapid, controlled shots to conserve ammunition.

Snapper had just remembered he was now on CRW. 'We want the fuckers to drop like liquiiiid – no chance of zapping back at us. Double taps to the nuuuut.'

I knew all this anyway. The CQB phase was part of Selection, but not room combat. I knew that in real time the place could be full of X-rays (terrorists) and Yankees (hostages). If you started blatting automatic fire all around, you were going to land up killing the very people you were there to save. You only made head shots. Terrorists were allowed to wear body armour as well, and they could be totally out of it on drugs or adrenalin. I'd heard about Jocks in the First World War charging on, skirts flying and bayonets fixed, sometimes taking six or seven rounds before they understood they were dead.

20

I checked my safety catch, muzzle pointing down. My left shoulder pressed against Hillbilly's back. We waited in silence, but it was a noisy silence. As well as the din of gunfire and shouts I could hear my respirator's rubber diaphragm clicking each time I breathed in, and the breathing itself was amplified; I sounded like a pervert on the phone. That wasn't the only problem with respirators. There was also a strong smell of rubber, and pungent, peppery traces of old CS gas. On top of that, my lenses were steaming up. I was beginning to feel like I was under water.

Snapper shouted, 'Stand by, stand by – goooo!' It was muffled by his respirator, but I got the drift.

Number four pushed open the door and Snapper and Hillbilly disappeared. They'd go as far forward as they could before firing, to leave room for others to come in and join the attack.

As I followed them a split second later, butt in the shoulder, both eyes open, torchlight burning into the gloom, I heard a series of quick double taps to my right.

I couldn't believe my eyes. There were real people in here. Some team members were sitting at tables. One was standing to my half-left, another was sitting on a settee.

I moved to Hillbilly's left. He was firing at a Hun-head between two lads at a table.

I spotted a Hun-head in the far corner, stopped, illuminated the target, gave it a double tap and moved forward. There was hardly any recoil from the weapon.

I double-tapped again, shuffled forward, double-tapped. And again. Finally, I was close enough to see the rounds making holes. That was it. He was dead, and there were no more targets, just guys sitting or standing around me.

We had all stopped firing within seconds of making entry. Snapper screamed through his respirator: 'Clear.'

We covered the number four as he swept from the right, pistol drawn, MP5 dangling over his front, checking behind the settees and in the wardrobes for any hidden X-rays.

A double tap from him into the wardrobe, then another, said there were.

The threat was only considered eliminated when a body went down and wasn't moving any more because it was dead. That was why a target sometimes got zapped by sixteen rounds. You had to fire until you *knew* the guy was dead. It was dark in the wardrobe and the number four couldn't see the strike marks as he fired the first double tap. So he fired again until he did.

After the embassy, I remembered listening to armchair experts complain about the number of rounds the dead X-rays had in them. 'Why didn't they just shoot him in the leg?' they were saying, or 'Why not kill them with just two rounds? This is overkill.' The people who made those comments were lucky enough never to have had a gun pointed at them.

Snapper pulled off his respirator. 'Too fookin' sloooow!'

I took off mine too. I must have had a big line round my face from the seal, just like the other three.

All the hostages, lads from Mountain Troop, gave Snapper a slagging. They said he'd gone off to the right as he came in, when the main threat, the nearest target to him, was to his left.

Snapper wasn't having any of it, and gave a perfect demon-
stration of why he'd earned his name. An argument kicked off
in less than a second.

I unloaded my weapons and Hillbilly did the same. He
pushed my arm to hustle me out, and went into Snapper mode.
'Let's leave him to iiiit.'

My hair and the back of my neck were wet with sweat. Cold
air attacked it as we left the CQB house and wandered towards
the 'Norwegians'. Huge Thermos flasks the size of wheelie-
bins, they were picked up each morning from the cookhouse,
along with the team's packed lunches. The meal never varied:
a couple of beef rolls, a packet of crisps, a Yorkie bar and a
battered apple. Everyone honked about them, but ate them
within a couple of hours. Both of us got a paper cup of sweaty
old brew.

A Worcester to Hereford train rumbled past about thirty
metres away. Commuters must have had a great view every
morning. The old camp was situated right next to the track and
on the edge of town.

I still didn't know Hillbilly that well but at least he was
making an effort with the new boy. 'When are you going on the
freefall course?'

'About two weeks, then straight over the water with the
troop. Were you and Nish the same battalion?'

'Nah, I met him on Selection.'

Hillbilly was from Portsmouth. He didn't have the accent,
but he'd mentioned the place a couple of times. His ex-wife
and daughter still lived there.

He was fanatical about fitness – but it had nothing to do with
keeping on top of the job. 'Training, plus lots of, equals women
pulled,' was his motto. Hillbilly lived life at maximum revs.
Saturday night was new-shirt night. The local clothes stores
made a fortune out of him. It was as if he'd taken on sole
responsibility for keeping the women of Hereford happy. He
was no Robert Redford with his punched-in face, but he had

charm, lots of it, and few could resist. As he always said, once he was dressed up in a new shirt with neatly groomed hair, 'They stop, they stare, they care.'

21

I still didn't understand about Snapper. Was he part of the team, or CRW, or what?

'CRW.' Hillbilly unwrapped the cling-film from the last of his beef rolls. 'But he still turns up with the troop in the morning. We have to fuck him off.' He chuckled. 'Fucker's mad as a box of snakes.'

Snapper's latest derailment had come when he'd started a fight at Boss L's wedding reception. He ended up cutting down the hanging baskets with a ceremonial sword.

'What's all this stuff about him having a certificate to prove he's sane?'

'Just before Malaysia he got sent to Woolwich – Ward Eleven.'

All soldiers knew what that was: the psychiatric wing of the military hospital.

'They put him through the tests and he came up clean. He must have worked them out before they worked him out—'

The rest of his sentence was drowned out as Snapper appeared and grabbed a paper cup. He was in a good mood. 'They were wrooooong. They admit it. Snapper knows beeeest.'

He stirred enough sugar into the brew to make the spoon stand up on its own.

Hillbilly almost choked on the last of his roll. 'Snapper, tell Andy about you going to see your gun – you know, the Mirbat gun.'

'They couldn't hold Snapperrrr! Slipped away to the artillery museum cos I fancied seeing it. Then when I got back there was pandemoniummmm.' Snapper loved his stories. 'They said, "Where you been?" I said, "To see the twenty-five-pounder. I was one of the Mirbat survivors."'

He waited to make sure I knew what he was on about. Of course I did: it was embedded in regimental history. A picture of one of the casualties, Labalaba, hung in the cookhouse. We saw it almost every day.

In many ways, Oman was the Regiment's spiritual home, the place where battles like Mirbat had happened and Snapper had gone loopy. Operation Storm had been a covert war, fought to stem the flood of Communism after the falls of Aden and Vietnam. The campaign was strategically vital. The West had been terrified of Soviet expansionism ever since Stalin had taken over the whole of Eastern Europe as far as Berlin. Now the Red threat was gathering momentum in Arabia, and the People's Front for the Liberation of the Occupied Arabian Gulf – or, as the Regiment guys knew them, the Adoo – were gaining ground in Yemen and moving into the rest of the peninsula. A line had had to be drawn in the sand.

The site chosen was Dhofar, a province in the south of Oman, immediately next to the border to Aden. The operation would be tough. The place was remote, which was an advantage because it was a covert war, but at the same time little was known about it. Dhofar was isolated from the north by a 400-mile-wide desert, which rose up at its southern tip into a huge plateau, the Jebel Massif, a natural fortress 3,000 feet high, nine miles wide and stretching 150 miles from the east down to and across the border with Aden, renamed by the new management as the People's Republic of Southern Yemen.

Since early 1970, small SAS groups supported by *firqats* – bands of local tribesmen loyal to the Sultan of Muscat and Oman – and Baluch Askars, tough little mountain guys from Baluchistan, had established toeholds on the coastal plain immediately facing the Jebel. The war had to be fought quietly or it would affect the price of oil as producers and consumers worldwide got jittery. Operation Storm was a classic guerrilla war that was kept covert, contained and controlled so the region didn't become unstable – and it was won.

At 6 a.m. on 19 July 1972, the Adoo were still fighting hard and sent 250 well-armed men against the isolated British Army Training Team (BATT) house near the coastal resort of Mirbat. Snapper was manning the .50 calibre Browning machine-gun on the roof.

Against overwhelming odds, he and the eight other SAS soldiers stationed there resisted fiercely, holding the Adoo back for several hours until reinforcements could arrive.

The twenty-five-pounder, now known as the 'Mirbat gun', which was used by Sergeant Talaiasi Labalaba (a Fijian SAS soldier) during the siege was now housed in the Firepower Museum at the old Royal Artillery garrison in Woolwich. 'Laba' Labalaba was killed in action, continuing to fire the twenty-five-pounder although he was seriously wounded. Snapper had been alongside him, in one of the most famous ever small-unit actions by the SAS, and one of the Regiment's proudest moments.

Snapper chuckled. 'They gave me a brew and tucked me into bed saying, "There, there, of course you were. Now have a nice rest and everything will be all right . . ."

'Fookin' not a clue! They must have thought I was mad, but they still gave me a piece of paper showing everyone I'm nooot!'

The grin dropped. Snapper seemed to have got bored. 'We're going to bin it. We've had enough for now. See you later.'

He wasn't talking social. We were going down to the

training area for yet more freefall abseiling, but at night. With luck I'd get to see the troop, because that was where they were doing all their training.

22

Des Doom and Schwepsy came over with their brews and cornered Hillbilly. They both had the line around their faces from their respirator seals, and Schwepsy's dirty-blond hair was damp with sweat and sticking up as if he'd had an electric shock.

Schwepsy always strode rather than walked, like an RSM on the look-out for recruits to bounce around and shout at. His back was straight as a ramrod and his shoulders were so square they looked like the hanger was still in his jacket. With his Aryan hair combed back, he came straight off a recruitment poster for the Panzer Korps.

He peeled off his pilot's gloves and I noticed, yet again, that he didn't wear a watch. Even without one, he still checked his wrist every few seconds to make sure he was five minutes early for any parade – or anything, really. If he'd been a car, he would have been a solid, reliable, value-for-money Volvo. Only this Volvo would deliver a barrack-square bollocking if your hair was too long or your beret wasn't straight, you 'orrible little man.

Des Doom got his face into Hillbilly's like he was about to conduct an interrogation. Des only had two speeds, aggressive and more aggressive. Life, to him, was one long bayonet charge. He was the only guy I knew who could make asking a server in McDonald's for ketchup sound like a demand to step outside. If the poor guy didn't hand it over quickly enough he wasn't an idiot, he just suffered from NBPE (not being punched enough). For all that, somebody loved Des Doom. He'd been married to Mrs Doom for a long time, and they had kids. In the field, nothing ever fazed Des; no matter the task, he just got on with it – aggressively, of course. If Des had been a car – well, he wouldn't. He'd have been one of Schwepsy's panzers.

'You're coming with us for a brew.'

Hillbilly was hesitant. 'Too much to do at home. Gotta sort some kit out.'

Lads streamed out of the Killing House now it had been binned for the day.

Harry was heading our way. He was in Mountain Troop, and just as Nish was a champion freefaller, Harry had become a big-time mountaineer. He was always running round Norway in his weeks off, climbing, skiing, *langlaufing*, all the snow business. He wasn't married, but lived with a woman down town; unlike his best mate, Des, he was very quiet and stable, a guy who just got on with the job and wished his fine blond hair wasn't thinning so quickly. Des and Schwepsy decided that because I was in Seven Troop it was OK to take the piss out of Harry because he was a marine. Harry always had other ideas. 'Try it . . .'

Harry would have been an E-Type Jag: understated but with plenty under the balding bonnet. Hillbilly? They hadn't yet built a car with him in mind.

Des turned the lasers on me. 'What you doing now?'

'Nothing. Just killing time until later.'

'Fall in.'

We got the black gear off and back into the ready bags as Hillbilly slunk away.

Des checked his watch and glanced at Schwepsy. 'Give him

a head start. It kicks off at four, right? We'll make the last fifteen minutes.'

We dumped the bags in the hangar and the four of us piled into my minging white Renault 5. I'd lost the ignition key long ago, so started the thing with the wires that hung under the steering column. The right-hand wing was held on by two bungees. But the wheels went round.

We weren't going for a brew, it turned out, but to catch Hillbilly at an aerobics class in a local gym. We were like a bunch of school kids, excited at the chance of embarrassing a mate.

The aerobics class was one of Hillbilly's many and varied plans to get laid. He thought if he joined the class he'd get to talk to young fit females, and then to ask them out for a drink. What he hadn't planned on was that some of the women would be going out with or married to Regiment guys. The secret got back via Mrs Doom.

The gym was in two parts: the weights in one warehouse and, across the courtyard, the aerobics studio.

The music pounded out as we crawled under the windows.

Hillbilly was in the thick of it: the only male in a class of thirty, all dancing away as the instructor kept up the pace.

'One, two, three, four – yeah! That's good, keep going! Feel the pump!'

Hillbilly was even wearing the right gear, though his vest was too tight and his Spandex shorts were a couple of sizes too small – perhaps not entirely unintentionally.

Schwepsy savoured every moment. 'Feel the pump? He's there to feel their arses.'

Hillbilly knew all the moves. He smiled at the class as they bounced around the floor in a sea of leg-warmers and, in his case, blue socks to match his vest and wristbands.

Des wasn't pleased. 'He's going at this half-cock.' He rested his tattooed forearms on the window-sill. 'Where's his headband?'

Harry swayed to the beat. 'Fuck it, we'll say he wore it any-way. Lovely little mover, isn't he?'

We ducked back from the window as the class ended. Thirty women and Hillbilly gave themselves a clap before streaming out and crossing the courtyard to the changing rooms.

Hillbilly was in big chat-up mode; he still hadn't clocked us. 'Yeah, I really feel I've had a work-out. She plays such good music, doesn't—' At that moment he spotted the four mug grins hanging on his every word. 'Shit ... Lads, let me explain . . .'

One of the women he'd been targeting called out, 'Can you make Gingerbread this weekend?'

'Er, don't know. But I'll try.'

Des got his face into Hillbilly's. 'Feel the pump, eh?'

Hillbilly was red as a beetroot, and it wasn't from the work-out. 'I'm bang to rights, aren't I?'

Harry wasn't letting him off that lightly. 'Gingerbread? What's that? You're not going to give us an even worse name than you already have . . .'

Hillbilly almost collapsed in embarrassment. Gingerbread was a single-parent group that came together to talk about emotional issues and give each other practical help and arrange day trips, that sort of thing. His plan was to become their only single father when he had his daughter with him for the weekend. 'You know, give the girls a shoulder to cry on.' He beamed. 'Let them see my vulnerable, caring side. It's worked a treat so far.'

23

A couple of hours before last light we heaved our ready bags into the team's Transit vans and Range Rovers. It had been raining, turning the day damp and miserable.

There were four of us per Range Rover. The wagons were fully laden and heavy. Mine rolled left to right as the driver practised his fast-driving drills. He looked at his watch and grinned. 'Ten minutes, doing well.' There was always a race to get to the training area in a quarter of an hour.

The lead vehicle came on the net as it rounded a corner. 'Road clear.'

The carload of civilians we overtook going into the blind bend stared at us as if we were madmen. And so we were, I supposed, apart from Snapper – he had that bit of paper to show he wasn't.

Snapper wasn't with us. He'd finally realized he was meant to be on the other side of the fence, and had gone ahead to plan the abseiling party.

I'd got to know the training area pretty well during Selection. We were heading for the drive-in range, an open square of earthworks about fifteen metres high, like a three-sided berm. Targets could be engaged left, right and forward.

Three or four wagons were parked off to one side. Those

range cars were used for live contact drills and they took a severe beating. Bodies milled around them. It just had to be Seven Troop.

There were a lot more bodies around the vehicles than there had been in the jungle. It wasn't just Seven Troop going over the water. Lads from other troops were going as well to make up the numbers. At least twelve guys were needed on the ground.

Everyone was in jeans and jackets. Their hair was even longer than it had been in Malaysia, and a couple even had beards. Most drank brew from white paper cups while making ready MP5s and reloading magazines.

They turned to see who was coming. As we got nearer I picked out Frank, Nish and Al near a green Astra.

The Range Rovers stopped and we clambered out. There were general slaggings and honks, then smiles when we produced the packed lunches we'd collected from the cookhouse. One of the wagons dragged out a Norwegian and a stack of paper cups.

As I walked over to Frank, I could see that the Vauxhall's windscreen was held in place by bungees. There was a neat stack of brand new windscreens on the grass, next to a pyramid of shot-up ones.

Frank was in a good mood. Al gave something approaching a smile as he shoved a Browning into the pancake holster behind his right hip. I smiled back, but mostly because of his pullover. It was one of those multicoloured Scandinavian fishermen's things that Abba might have worn when they were doing a winter video.

An arse was sticking out of the driver's door. Al grabbed its belt and pulled. 'Ken – this is Andy.'

Mr Grumpy said, 'Ken, he thinks you're a crap hat.'

The giant stood up and turned. I immediately saw why no one took the piss out of Ken. With his wavy brown hair and a few days' stubble on top of a slightly acne-scarred face, he looked more like a lifer than a soldier. The top set of falsies he was readjusting didn't soften the effect. The originals could have been punched out in a prison riot. There wasn't a hint of a smile as he looked down at me. His mouth opened, but only so he could insert a cigarette before he lit up. 'Listen in, I might be crap-hat green slime, but I'm the boss, geddit?'

At last there was a smile and a laugh as he lit up, took a quick drag and took it out again. He stretched out a hand. 'All right, mate?' His accent was Sarf London, like mine, but I already knew that that was where the similarity ended.

Ken was a big-time Bruce Lee merchant, who'd represented the UK in martial-arts competitions all around the world. I'd been warned he'd fight you for a bite of a Mars bar.

I'd done a bit of Mr Lee stuff myself, but only to get girls. At the age of fourteen I was hormonal. I might have slept in a bathroom, but without hot water in the house that didn't count for much. I started to have a shower every night down at Goose Green swimming baths, just in case I had the chance to stand next to a girl.

I wore fresh market socks and was kissably clean, but I was also overweight. I always had been. And the girls didn't seem to go a bundle on fat boys smelling of Brut in fluorescent orange socks. I needed something more.

The craze swept the country. People would roll out of the pubs and into the late-night movie, then come out thinking they were the Karate Kid. Outside the cinemas, curry houses and Chinese takeaways of Peckham on a Friday night, the pavements were heaving with guys head-butting lampposts and each other. I joined a club like everyone else, got into running and the weight fell off. The way of the dragon worked for me. But, of course, I didn't tell Ken any of this. He'd have wanted a fight to see how bad I was.

I also knew that because Ken had come from the green slime (Intelligence Corps), he had done quite a few jobs on the dark side, jobs that never got talked about. Maybe that was why he'd been sent away to learn German.

Ken leant back into the Astra and retrieved his MP5 from the rear foot well. 'All right, then, this crap hat had better get out the way. Time to showcase your talents, Andy boy. Get your weapon and go rear right.'

'What?'

'Get in the fucking wagon – four-man contact drills.' He turned to Frank. 'For fuck's sake, brief him up.'

24

Frank followed me back to the Range Rover and I grabbed my gear. I loaded my MP5 and shoved the pistol into my jeans before jumping in behind the driver's seat. Al came in next to me. None of us used seat-belts, and we were all sitting on wet seats and broken glass.

'Met Ken, then?'

Nish jumped into the front left and Frank reversed past the Range Rovers. 'All right, mate. You on your freefall soon?'

Frank had his left arm over Nish's seat. He leant back and waffled away to Al about a girl his wife had lined up for him. She was also helping decorate Al's new house.

Nish wasn't impressed. 'Al, you don't need the Collins escort service. Bin the jumper, get a decent shirt and go down town with Hillbilly.'

Frank stopped the car about a hundred metres from the range.

Nish turned to Al. A light switch had been thrown in his head.

'I know why they're trying to get you a woman.' He pointed at Frank.

'It's him. He wants to do his pastor stuff on you. Be the man who marries you!'

The rest of the squadron had set off for the top of the berm and stood or crouched over the wet soil with their brews. Ken was jumping up and down at the entrance to the range, shouting for us to get on with it. Frank hit the gas. 'Here we go.'

Nish stared through the bungeed window as Frank put his foot down. 'Give us a nice skid, Frank. Put on a show, eh?'

As we screamed into the range a fireball kicked off in front of us, followed a split second later by a loud boom.

Nish got his weapon into the shoulder. Frank hit the brakes and the rear end slewed round on the wet shale. He battled to keep the car pointing forward as we skidded towards the fireball.

I could see Figure-11s in front of us on the forward berm. Nish kicked off his MP5 in short bursts through the windscreen. The pressure waves banged against my ears and spent cases bounced off the ceiling and onto my shoulders and head.

Al's door was open before we came to a stop, and he was gone. So was I, running four or five metres to the side to dodge the rounds the car would take in an ambush.

Nish finished off his mag through the shattered glass and jumped. Frank bailed out as well. Fire and manoeuvre: someone's always got to be firing while others are moving. That way, you're killing enemy or, at the very least, keeping their heads down so you can advance.

I cleared the line of fire and moved forward, past the front of the car, stopped, and kept double-tapping the nearest targets. The fire was still burning around it.

Frank sprinted past me, stopped and fired. He did short bursts, three or four rounds.

There was movement to my left, the other side of the car, and a lot more firing. It never stopped as we all kept moving to target.

I squeezed the trigger and nothing happened.

'Stoppage!'

Frank wasn't stopping to cover me. He kept moving forward.

I had to draw down on the pistol. I kept firing, holding the MP5 in my left hand but still putting down good double taps, both eyes open, glued to the target.

It took just a few seconds but we were right on top of the targets now. We kept double-tapping into every one. Different landscape, same principle: fire and manoeuvre, keep going forward, keep hitting the enemy.

'Stop! Stop! Stop!'

I applied safety and spun round to see Ken striding towards us. He had a cigarette in his hand. The rest of the squadron had had their show and started to move – or get pushed – down the berm. Snapper shouted them on. 'Let's get to worrrrk! The helis are comiiiing!' He added his own debrief on the attack: 'Shiiiite. Only four point five for styyyyle.'

Ken turned to me. 'See you after the freefall, yeah?'

'OK.'

Tiny and yet another big tall guy sorted a Mazda saloon. He gave me a nod. 'You've met Ken, then, eh?' He snorted with laughter.

The tall one broke away from what they were doing and came up to me. He put out a shovel-sized hand and smiled. 'Cyril.' He had a slight lisp and looked like the oldest man in Hereford, let alone Seven Troop.

'Hello, mate – I'm Andy.'

'I know.' He smiled again. 'See you over the water, yeah?'

I walked back to the wagon. Snapper was still hollering and shouting. 'Get a fucking move on – we're burning dayliiiight . . .'

25

Brize Norton was even more fun the second time round. There were just four Special Boat Service (SBS) guys and me on the course. Technically, we were already part of the brotherhood, and the instructors treated us almost like mates. I nearly felt sorry for all the baby paratroopers getting marched around on the static-line course. Nearly.

Most of the instructors were members of the Falcons, the RAF display team. They apologized straight away that the stuff they were going to teach us was outdated. 'We have to go by the manual, even though it was obsolete before it was printed.' On top of that they didn't jump the same rigs as us, but we had to start somewhere. For all I cared, we could have used the ones Noah had on the Ark.

I liked having long hair in preparation for Northern Ireland. I liked wearing my sand-coloured beret. I felt how an actor or singer must feel when they hit the big-time, though of course I didn't show it. I still had a lot of learning to do. The RSM's words rang in my head: 'Wind your neck in, look and listen.'

The boy soldier who'd started out in September 1976 with no intention of being in the army long had certainly fucked up on that plan. The first three months in the Infantry Junior Leaders Battalion (IJLB) at Shorncliffe, Kent, had been nothing but marching, bullshit and being shouted at, but I'd had constant hot water, my own bed and locker, and we even did our bit to keep the defence budget down. At IJLB you could only use three sheets of toilet paper: one up, one down, one shine.

More than the material comforts, I liked being part of something, the way the training sergeants shouted words like 'we' and 'us'. I couldn't understand why some lads didn't stay the course. Maybe they had something better to go back to.

Even the teachers who had to take lads like me, who were well below their reading and writing age, made me feel special. My very first day in the education block changed my life. The captain, an old sweat who had come up through the ranks and now wanted to pass something on to the new generation, came into the classroom of twenty zit-faced, uniformed sixteen-year-olds and pointed out of the window.

'Out there, the other side of the wire, they think you're all as thick as shit.' He stopped and looked at us as if we were going to disagree. I certainly wasn't. I was in the infantry because no one else in the army would have me.

'Well, they're wrong. The only reason you cannot read or write is because you do not read or write.'

He wandered between the desks, checking all the raw, pock-marked faces. In the army you shaved even if you didn't have to.

'But as from today, young soldiers, that stops.'

Not only did the army educate me, they even paid me to be angry and fight. I became the junior army welterweight champion – something I certainly wasn't going to tell Ken about. It all began because of the company 'boxing' competition. It wasn't boxing as Muhammad Ali would have known it. The army called it 'milling'. You had two minutes to beat the shit out of the other lad. If you won too easily, you went in and fought again; if you lost too easily, you went in and fought again; and if you didn't hold your ground, you went in and fought again. After six or seven bouts IJLB had found its boxing team.

It suited me down to the ground. They wanted me to fight and kill people, and gave me a great life and an education in return. I loved it. At last I had found something I was good at. I even won the Light Division Sword for the most promising boy soldier. For me, each day was better than the last.

The freefall lessons at Brize Norton were one-to-one, and my personal instructor was called Rob. The first thing he asked me was what troop I was going to.

'Seven.'

His face creased up. 'You know Nish?' I asked.

They certainly did. The military freefall circuit was small. With Nish being a Red Fred and them being Falcons, they'd done a lot of jumps together, civilian and fun events, as well as military.

The first few lessons were a bit awkward for all of us. I felt strange learning for the sake of learning, and they felt strange teaching the stuff. I'd really thought the bullshit-baffles-brains bit was behind me. The basic problem was that freefall was driven by the sport rather than by the military. The sports clubs were where all the rigs and techniques were being perfected. They were adapted for military use, but it took a very long time. Usually it was the other way round. Military technology drove civilian technology, certainly in time of conflict.

Over the next two days it got better, even though I was just learning how to put on the basic rig. Our first jump was to be a very straightforward freefall from 12,000 feet, taking about fifty seconds, under a round canopy called a PB6, very similar to the static-line parachute. Then we'd progress to the TAP, an antiquated bit of kit that still wasn't a square chute like the sports ones the instructors were using. It looked more like a quarter of an orange. All you could do was turn left or right.

26

On day three, the ten of us took our places in the back of a C-130. I wasn't scared; I just didn't want to look a dickhead. I was going to jump, no problems with that, but I didn't want to cock it up.

Everybody was going through the drills, even the professional jumpers who'd been doing it for years. Mentally and physically, they're dry drilling all the time, simulating pulling their emergency cutaway of the main rig and deploying the reserve. It doesn't mean they're scared, just that they're thinking about the future.

We all sat in the plane with our arms in the air, as if in freefall, miming as we chanted in our heads, 'Thousand and one, thousand and two, check the canopy . . .' And if it hadn't opened, we mimed looking for the cutaway pad on the right of the rig, pulling that, then pulling the red reserve handle on the left.

I checked both my wrists. In training we carried two altimeters, great big things that looked like they'd been salvaged from a Lancaster bomber.

By the time we'd got to about 6,000 feet it was already getting really cold. I started to feel light-headed as we climbed to 12,000 and the air got thinner still. This was the maximum height we would jump from without oxygen. At just 10,000 feet – less than the height of Mont Blanc – the amount of oxygen present and the pressure at which it enters the body is not enough to keep you operating at maximum efficiency. As you go higher hypoxia – lack of oxygen – kicks in, followed by unconsciousness and death.

Nobody was talking. We'd have had to yell to make ourselves heard. The noise inside the aircraft was deafening. We weren't sitting in first class, waiting for the drinks trolley to arrive.

When the time came, the tailgate slid downwards. Sunlight streamed in, along with the rush of the slipstream. I thought of Frank. He'd have loved this. He'd have seen it as a message from God.

Way below us, Oxfordshire was bathed in sunlight. As the pilot manoeuvred left and right, I could see tree-lined roads and buildings.

Rob pointed me onto the tailgate. When I got there, I turned around and he pushed me backwards until the balls of my feet were right on the edge of the plate and my heels were en route to Oxfordshire. He gripped the front of my rig and fixed me with a stare as the slipstream battered my jumpsuit. We had to have eye-to-eye as the aircraft lined up and he steadied me. His eyes swivelled left and right for the jump light.

'RED ON!' he screamed, into my face.

I nodded.

'READY!' The green light must have come on.

'SET!' He pulled me so I rocked forward.

'GO!'

I leant away from him and launched myself backwards off the tailgate, feet first. I adopted the standard 'frog' position – knees bent at ninety degrees and arms outstretched, level with my shoulders. I fell straight down, eyes fixed on the aircraft above me as normal wind forces took over from the slipstream.

Rob's face was just a foot from mine. One second between

jumpers equated to well over a sixty-foot gap. He must almost have jumped on top of me, but I hadn't been watching. I was too busy trying not to fuck up.

I didn't tumble. I kept looking ahead. The aircraft was way above us and getting smaller by the second. I concentrated on keeping in line with Rob. He was about ten feet away now, level with me and staring hard.

I was still more or less stable-on-heading and I wasn't tumbling. I allowed myself a moment to enjoy the pure adrenalin rush of falling at terminal velocity. It was like standing up through the sunroof of a car doing 120 m.p.h. The wind pressure was doing its best to rip off my jumpsuit. I grinned and my cheeks blew out. My whole face rippled. I started to wobble and flailed my arms to compensate. I nearly inverted.

Keep looking at Rob!

His face resembled a pug's, complete with flapping jowls. I guessed mine wasn't much different.

I was now supposed to pick a point on the ground and check I wasn't moving left or right of it. I might be stable-on-heading, I might be pointing the right way, but I might also be drifting right or left. I wanted to fall straight down, not sliding backwards or forwards, left or right. Everything below me was tiny. I focused on a bend in the A40 dual carriageway. I was going down straight – I thought . . .

I checked my altimeters non-stop. As soon as I reached 4,000 feet I went in for the pull. Physically looking down at the red steel ring on the right of the rig, I brought my left hand up above my head and gripped the handle with my right. I wobbled and started to turn, but it was nearly pull time and I wasn't sure how to rectify it now I was out of the frog.

I stuck both elbows out to keep symmetry. If I'd only stuck one out, the air would grab it and I'd start spinning.

I wasn't perfectly stable, but I was all right. Rob was there somewhere, just feet away, but I couldn't see him. My eyes were filled with the alti readout on my left wrist.

At 3,500 feet, I pulled the handle. The pin that secured the canopy came away. I checked I had the ring in my hand. Not that I needed to: the pack on my back was rattling from side to side as the spring pushed the drogue (small chute) clear to catch air and pull out the main canopy. Then the para-cord lines bounced off my back and, *BANG*, the canopy grabbed air. I was Bugs Bunny sprinting round a corner straight into a whack from a frying-pan.

27

I wasn't as worried as I should have been about where everybody else was in the sky. I was busy enough sorting myself out.

I heard another canopy crack open, so someone must have been close. I looked up to make sure I had a canopy rather than a big bag of washing about eighteen feet above me. The ends of the canopy still hadn't fully inflated. I grabbed hold of the brake lines, ripped them from the Velcro on the risers just above each shoulder and pumped them hard.

I looked up, going through the drills. Everything was where it should be as the parachute fully inflated. But, fuck, my bollocks hurt! The leg straps had worked their way into my groin and it felt like someone was giving the bad boys a violent squeeze.

I checked around my airspace, ready to take evasive action. There was no one else around, no other parachutes turning left when they should have been turning right, screaming in towards me. That was it. All I had to do now was enjoy the ride.

I could see the instructors under their square canopies, swooping like buzzards round their pupils as we fell towards the earth beneath our steam-driven PB6s, with no control beyond left or right turns.

Vehicles made their way along the A40 like toys. Sheep the size of cotton-wool buds were sprinkled across the fields. The guys manning the drop zone (DZ) kicked off blue smoke. We needed to turn into the wind when we landed.

There was nothing else to do, suspended in the silent sky, but before I knew it, I was getting ground rush. As you get level with the horizon, you realize how fast the hard stuff is coming up to meet you. You're dropping at 20 m.p.h., the same as jumping off a ten-foot wall. I tucked myself into the parachute-landing-fall (PLF) position, knees bent, feet together, ready to accept the landing.

I hit the ground and rolled. Sort of. There wasn't any time to savour the moment. I had to field-pack the canopy into the big green nylon bag I had stuffed down the front of my overalls, drop it off with the RAF riggers, jump in a wagon and scream back to Brize Norton for another drop. We were doing three a day and getting debriefed in between.

The first few jumps felt clumsy and unnatural; then I started to get the hang of things. We were jumping 'clean fatigue': no Bergen, no weapon, no equipment, no oxygen gear. Before we graduated to Pau we had to be able to control ourselves in the sky: left turn, right turn, back and forward flips, track, spin, and recover from any kind of unstable exit.

Freefall is a combination of acrobatics and aerodynamics, and it can't be mastered in a classroom. Like learning to ride a bike, you just have to get out there and do it. You can be taught the physics of balance, but after that, as Snapper would have said, it's all about barrel tiiiime. And until the grown-ups took the stabilizers off, we wouldn't be going to Pau.

A lot of the manoeuvres were like trampoline work. For back flips, you tucked your knees into your chin, pushed your arms down in the air and threw your head back. The world was blue sky, then green, then blue again before we flared out back into the frog.

To achieve horizontal movement – tracking – you held your

arms near your sides like a swept-wing jet, and made tiny correcting movements. You could generate enormous speed this way, and end up travelling much faster than someone falling vertically at terminal velocity.

Even after a week of it I felt the same exhilaration each time I left the aircraft. It wasn't just the freefall itself. It was passing the point of no return. Mobility Troop could pull over and stop to sort out a problem. Mountain Troop could find another route over their lump of rock, or come back down. Boat Troop could get out of the water or even float on it. But Air Troop? There was no going back once you'd exited the aircraft. Unless you were Frank, of course, and had the angels on your side.

28

Monday morning, week two, we were in the crew room, just coming to the end of our daily brief. It was going to be very much the same sort of stuff to start with, lots of 360s and somersaults, staying with the instructor, making sure you completed the manoeuvre and stopped directly in front of him.

A bellow echoed down the corridor outside. 'All right, mate?'

Even if I hadn't recognized the voice, I'd have recognized the fart that followed.

A burst of laughter was followed by a soft Geordie accent telling Nish to get his arse to shut up and go and fetch some brews.

We walked out to the rigging shelves to collect our gear. Frank, Al and Nish were in a huddle with the instructors. They obviously knew each other well.

Al looked over at me and shook his head. 'Fuck me, a crap hat in the brotherhood. What next?'

Everyone laughed, even the SBS lads.

There were three sports rigs on the shelves, much smaller than ours, and three plastic Pro-Tec helmets, the kind canoeists wear. Ours were much heavier Para Reg pudding basins.

Nish picked one up and grinned. 'Don't need much.'

He tapped his skull with his knuckles. 'Tough as a coconut.'

It was Al's turn to smile. 'Thick as, more like.'

Nish dived into one of the neat white RAF lunchboxes and took out an orange. He threw it to Frank before coming over and studying my rig as if he was the resident expert on *Antiques Roadshow*. 'We came in on one of the 109s – he's waiting to pick up the CO, so we thought we'd cadge a lift and get a couple in.' He grabbed one of the sports rigs. 'Besides, old Father Frank wants to have a one-to-one with his boss . . .'

I watched the three of them rig up over their baggies – civilian jumpsuits, multicoloured and a lot looser, designed to grab air – in the back of the C-130. They had handles on the bottoms of the legs and on the forearms so they could grab each other more securely during relative work – something I wouldn't be learning till the last third of the course. Then they got their Pro-Tecs on and ran through the drills, exactly as the instructors had said the pros did. It was almost like watching a *t'ai chi* session: they slowly raised their hands and mimed the pull, looking up, then down at their rig, tugging the imaginary handle that would cut away the snared canopy. Then they went into freefall again, and pulled their reserve.

When we were over the DZ, Rob signalled me forward onto the ramp as usual. As I turned to him, I saw that the other three weren't facing back into the aircraft like I did, but forward, and bunched up really close to each other, immediately behind Rob, for a mass dive exit. They were coming with me.

Frank bit into the orange to clamp it in his mouth.

I thought, OK, not a clue what the fuck's going on.

Rob gave me the ready, set, go. I jumped and looked up to get eye-to-eye before I got stable-on-heading to start my exercise.

Nish, Frank and Al were directly behind him. They flew down to me, all smiles, apart from Frank. He still had a face full of orange.

They linked arms just off to my right. I still had to get my exercise done within the fifty seconds of freefall. I did my left-hand 360, making sure I stopped facing Rob. Rob nodded. I did a right-hand 360, and just overshot him. I managed to correct it and got a nod.

Nish pushed out his legs to catch air and the three of them slid towards me. Their heads were so close together they were almost touching.

Frank opened his mouth and let the orange go. It bounced about between their heads for three or four seconds before it was caught in the air and pushed out of the vortex.

My arm shook. Rob had grabbed hold of me and was gesturing. I still had exercises to do before 5,000 feet.

I did a forward roll, then a backward roll and banged out of it to stable-on-heading. Nish gave me a big thumbs-up, back-flipped out and tracked away with a wave. Frank turned, drew his arms back like a delta wing, and screamed across the sky. Al did a forward flip that took him into a rapid descent.

I checked my altimeter. It was just coming up to 4,000 feet. Looking down at the handle, I grabbed it and waited for 3,500 before pulling down and away.

It turned out that not everyone was looking forward to going to Pau as much as I was. One of the SBS lads, the biggest, tallest, strongest on the course, one of those annoying guys who just naturally shit muscle, started to look a bit worried about it and kept asking the instructors what other units would be there.

'A couple of companies from 2 REP,' was the answer. The Deuxième Régiment Étranger de Parachutistes (2 REP) or 2nd Foreign Parachute Regiment, was part of the world-famous French Foreign Legion. They served as its elite rapid-reaction force. There was never any shortage of volunteers for 2 REP, but selection was tough and restricted.

The SBS lad went very quiet. I guessed it was because he was a hard nut; maybe he didn't want to come up against the Foreign Legion and find himself lacking.

When we got there, he hid half the time and never went to the cookhouse. He lived on chocolate bars and scraps his mates brought back. It was his loss: 2 REP were great lads; they wanted to know all about us, and we wanted to know about them. They had shaven heads, but looked rather Gucci with their *porte-monnaies* and smart clothes. Many of them were Austrians, maybe grandkids of the hundreds of Nazis who joined the Legion in 1945 and went off to fight in Vietnam. They were hard, but we got on all right with them. Most were well educated; they spoke good English and French, as well as their own native language.

Our lad still wouldn't show his face. I thought he was a bit strange, but fuck him. Chances were I wouldn't see him again. It was only on the final night when we went down town to a fish place that he finally confessed. He'd gone AWOL from the Marines before he went to France. When he did the big romantic thing and joined the Legion, he eventually landed up in 2 REP. He only did three of the five years to which he'd committed himself. 'I just got bored.' He pushed a big lump of fish round his plate, the first real food he'd seen in two weeks. 'So I did a runner from them as well, went back to the Marines, faced the court-martial, did my prison time, went back to my commando and eventually got into SBS. When I was offered the freefall course I couldn't turn it down because every man and his dog wants to get onto military freefall. Going back to France was bad enough, but then I found out 2 REP were going to be here . . . And then it got even worse. I spotted one of my mates who'd joined up at the same time. It's something like a ten-year sentence when they catch a runner – hence all the Mars bars . . .'

29

November 1984
Belfast

Gloria Hunniford's white perm helmet was perched in front of me on the British Airways shuttle from Heathrow, but that wasn't my biggest buzz. With three days' growth around my chin, long hair, and cheap trainers I'd bought with my clothing allowance, this was the first time I'd ever been to Northern Ireland on a civilian flight. I was normally crammed into the back of a C-130 with a couple of rifle companies on the way to a tour, or in the early years, aboard a Royal Corps of Transport ferry from Liverpool docks. They were the worst. The boats were flat-bottomed for beach landings, which turned the Irish Sea into a rollercoaster – and the ride usually lasted something like fourteen hours. They were literally steam-driven.

Now here I was, sitting with a plastic cup of very black, well-stewed coffee, a dodgy, plastic-wrapped cheese sandwich and a one-finger Twix bar, listening to Gloria waffle away with her mate. Both were wearing some strange perfume, but it was heaps better than the diesel fumes on a ferry or the BO from sardine-packed soldiers in the back of a C-130.

I unwrapped my Twix and used it to stir the tiny carton of

milk into the coffee. I read a bit of my newspaper. They were asking readers to write in and rank the most momentous events of the year. There were plenty to choose from. The Aids virus had been identified. The Indian prime minister, Indira Gandhi, had been assassinated. Ten million people were starving in Ethiopia. The Soviet bloc had boycotted the Los Angeles Olympic Games. Michael Jackson had sold billions of copies of *Thriller*, and the whole world seemed to be moon-walking to work.

Closer to home, and certainly closer to what I was about to be involved in, John Stalker, deputy chief constable of the Greater Manchester Police, had arrived in Belfast in May to begin an investigation into the alleged shoot-to-kill policy of security forces in the region. In September, security forces in the Republic of Ireland had intercepted a trawler, the *Marita Ann*, off the coast of County Kerry and uncovered seven tonnes of arms and explosives believed to be en route to PIRA. And, just a couple of days ago, PIRA had carried out a bomb attack on the Grand Hotel, Brighton, in England, which was being used as the base for the Conservative Party's annual conference. Four people were killed in the attack and another person died later from injuries received. PIRA issued a statement directed at Margaret Thatcher: 'Today we were unlucky; but remember, we only have to be lucky once – you will have to be lucky always.'

Frank had been lucky just two weeks ago. The madman had walked straight towards a possible PIRA firing point to check if anyone was in position. He had taken a patrol to an isolated house belonging to a part-time member of the security forces. The Tasking and Coordinating Group (TCG) had found out that he was being targeted and would probably be shot as he left the house.

The plan was to set up an ambush outside the house and wait for PIRA to turn up. The problem was that there was only one bit of cover in which to set it up. What if PIRA had got

ANDY McNAB

there first and was already in the bushes waiting for the target to leave the house at first light?

Frank's solution was to walk across the 300 metres of open ground between the house and the cover and see if anyone either ran for it or shot him.

They would have been flapping as Frank came towards them. What the fuck was he doing? How many more of them were there? Was it a trap? If they killed him, were they signing their own death warrants?

Frank kept walking, expecting at any moment to get a burst in the face. He finally got to the bushes and parted them. No one was there.

Now the boot was on the other foot. The patrol took up position in the cover. They waited four days, but PIRA never came. Maybe they'd heard there was this guy in the area whose next trick would be to turn them all into pillars of salt.

The seat-belt sign came on, and Gloria autographed one last in-flight magazine for a fellow passenger. I looked out of the window, down at the five-mile sniper range that most people called Belfast. With my new entry skill, I felt a completely paid-up member of Seven Troop and now I was going on ops.

There hadn't been too much of a brief before I'd left. I'd collected my ticket from the squadron clerk, and he'd said someone would pick me up at the other end. And that was that, because that was all he knew.

Al was waiting for me, dressed in a pair of jeans and a bomber jacket. At least he'd ditched the jumper. 'Hello, mate, how you doing?' He sounded as though he had a cold you couldn't climb over, and there was no colour in his face.

We went through our warm and wonderful greeting ritual for the benefit of any prying eyes looking for military targets to shoot at as they left the airport, and walked off towards the car park. We got into a Mazda saloon. Al handed me a Browning and an extra mag. 'It's loaded and made ready – safety catch is on.'

I shoved it under my right thigh. He got his out of his holster and stuck it under his leg and away we went.

Al was straight into his briefing. 'We're going to the troop location. You'll be sharing a room.'

I flapped straight away. He saw it and smiled. 'No, it's OK – nothing involving Bibles or farts. You're in with Paul.'

'How's it going on the jobs?'

He gave a wry smile. 'Just done one in South Armagh – there's a little tension in the air.'

'How's that?'

'You'll find out.'

We drove along narrow lanes. Eight-foot-high hedgerows hemmed us in on each side. I decided Al wasn't Mr Grumpy at all. He just found it hard to talk to people and seemed quite happy with his own thoughts.

I wasn't. It felt strange just sitting there, saying nothing. 'How's the new house? Frank's wife finished decorating?'

I reckoned it wasn't as big as the house by the sea he'd grown up in. He'd spent his childhood fishing and crabbing, having adventures in rock pools. Now he'd progressed to freefall, diving and driving about with a 9mm under his thigh.

'Looks good. She organized the paint, carpets, you know the sort of thing. I think she and Frank want me to babysit the kids as payment.' He smiled. 'I don't mind.'

'What'll she do when she finds you a wife? Build a nursery?'

The smile turned into a surprising, open-hearted laugh.

'Maybe when I get back. Maybe . . . I'd like to, but, well, you know . . .'

Al was a soldier. He didn't do emotions much, except to his family. But I knew what he was trying to say: when the time was right, he'd commit himself to someone outside the Regiment. But not just yet.

We drove into the confines of a well-protected army camp, then into a camp within a camp.

'Welcome to our world.'

30

The Regiment stockade was like a big, windowless B&Q warehouse, with doors big enough to drive trucks through and high enough to house a six-storey building. Floodlights bathed the whole interior, which was filled with blue or white Portakabins, some low level, some stacked up three or four high, like on a construction site. There were areas for vehicle maintenance, stores and equipment.

Al pointed through the windscreen. 'The armoury. Sauna. That's the gym. And those are the squash courts. They're for fights. If you want one, just get in there, get on with it, and tell no one.'

'Ken not approve?'

Al shook his head. 'He always wants to join in.'

Frank wasn't the only one in the Regiment famous for his religious beliefs. Ken believed in reincarnation: he'd been here once before as a Viking marauder and, like any self-respecting Norseman, he loved to fight. It had even got him temporarily chucked out of the Regiment.

Ken would invite guys to play squash, then say, 'Let's do some sparring.' That always got out of control, of course, so no one in the troop was that keen to take up the invitation. The only person who regularly obliged was one of the cooks. He wasn't going to be pushed about by anyone and they were cage fighting at least once a week. It had to be stopped. A bruised face was too easy to pick out in a crowd, and the cook couldn't focus properly to fry the eggs. He'd crack them open but miss the pan.

Al pointed out the cookhouse and the ops room, all the bits and pieces I'd need to know immediately. 'You'll work it all out. You're here long enough.'

A pack of six or seven supersize dogs mooched around.

'Who do they belong to?'

'Not sure.'

'Who feeds them?'

'They just get fed . . . lots.'

With a squeal of tyres, Al parked beside a one-storey breeze-block building. I followed him into a dark central corridor. The faded white-brick walls were bare and peeling. There were doors off to left and right, maybe six sets. Game-show-type TV voices jangled behind a couple of them.

We stopped by the second on the left. 'That's it. See you later.'

I entered a room fit for a Spartan. There were two heavy old metal beds, the sort that were being phased out of the army. They had been designed to be used for a thousand years, but had one fatal flaw. The bed ends slipped very easily into the metal tubes that formed the legs – and came out just as fast. And five inches of solid steel tubing with a wider bit at the end made the perfect weapon. The army was still trying to erase the phrase 'So I had to bed-end him' from its vocabulary.

A TV sat at the foot of the two beds. Two lockers, belt kit, a Bergen and all kinds of other gear had been shoved in one of the corners.

Paul was stretched out on a Desperate Dan duvet. 'All roight, boy?'

He had kept himself to himself in the jungle. The thing I remembered most about him was when we reached the road-head and were waiting for transport. He'd looked up when he heard a plane going over and said, 'You know what? The distance we've walked today, someone up there just travelled with one sip of his gin and tonic.'

Paul was shorter than me, but much stockier. He'd played rugby for the army and had a mouthful of false teeth to show for it. There were a lot of false teeth running round in this squadron. He'd been on the embassy job and in the Falklands. He'd also been on some team job in South East Asia just before Malaysia, and another in Sudan. Originally he'd been in the Ordnance Corps, from what was called Heavy Drop, the airborne contingent, based in Aldershot. He was married and had a couple of kids, and must have been born and raised near Hereford, going by the accent. I liked him a lot.

I dropped my bag. 'Where do you get a brew, mate?' I was gagging for one after the shit airline coffee.

He pointed down the corridor. 'Can't miss it – the Burco.'

'You want one?'

He eyed me with something approaching disgust. 'No! I got Channel 4 – *Countdown*'s coming up, then it's soup time. I don't want no tea, boy.'

I wandered back into the corridor. The first room on the right was now open. I poked my head round it to see Tiny crashed out on one of the beds. His hair was longer, exaggerating the bald patch and making him look even more like a mad monk.

A guitar nestled among a pile of magazines and old newspapers strewn across the other bed. The floor was littered with plates encrusted with dried Marmite and dog ends. Something was blaring from the TV but I couldn't tell what it was – the screen seemed to have been liberally coated with bogeys.

'All right, Crap Hat – nice of you to drop in. Freefall OK?'

I guessed this was Tiny's way of being nice, approachable, even. I told him the SBS and 2 Rep story and he nearly fell off

Seven Troop, Oman, 1985. Nish is far right.

Left The author as a Royal Green Jackets squaddy, Crossmaglen, 1977.

Below Green Jackets in Arctic camouflage, 1978, getting ready for a border patrol in South Armagh in snowy conditions.

Above My brick, South Armagh, 1979. Lance Corporal McNab is far right.

Right Nish abseiling into the jungle, Malaysia, 1984.

Below Nish landing. Hillbilly is on the rope.

Right A-frames.

Below Frank Collins on his pole bed.

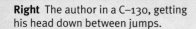

Left Saddlebags (*centre*) rigging up to jump with a GPMG.

Right The author in a C–130, getting his head down between jumps.

Below Three-man exit off the tailgate of a C–130, New Zealand, 1998.

Right Saddlebags exiting.

Below Posing at 12,000 feet. The author is on the right.

Below right The author coming in on full brakes, New Zealand.

Left Seven Troop mortar team, Oman. Nish is far left. Paul looks through the sights, the author holds a round.

Below Mortar rounds in their containers. Nish is seated.

Above From our mortar pit, watching Six Troop prepare to cheat. Paul has the binos.

Right A round has just left the tube. Paul leans back; author is nearest the camera.

Left Chris in shorts; Tiny with the binos. Author seated, cabbying on the GPMG in sustained fire role.

Below Mincing around in the desert. Saddlebags on the left; Cyril on the right.

Above Seven Troop getting their shorts out in the heat.

Right The ice-cream run, Oman. Note the shemag over the cool-box.

Seven Troop have an Ambre Solaire moment. Author second from the left.

his bed. 'Yeah, but that's not all. He told me what happened when he tried to sign on.'

The SBS boy had made it all the way down to the Marseille recruiting office, but it was so late in the day the place was shut. The bloke was penniless, and he had fuck-all kit, so he went to the park over the road and hid in the bushes, just zipped up his jacket and tried to stay warm. Then it started pouring with rain. He was drenched for about three hours and spent the rest of the night shivering big-time.

'At first light he came out of the bushes to get himself sorted for when the office opened, and noticed that the only wet area in the entire park was the patch of shrubbery where he'd been hiding. That was when he realized he'd been curled up right next to the sprinklers . . .'

A voice boomed behind me. 'You're here, then, are you?' There was a series of trumpet-like farts. 'They said some wanker from the Green Jackets was on his way. About fucking time.'

31

I turned. 'All right, Nish, how's it going?'

He was wearing a pair of jeans, flip-flops and an old T-shirt that matched the plates. His hair stuck up on end and a cigarette was wedged in the corner of his mouth. 'Want a brew?'

'Just where I was going.'

He poked his head in through the door. 'Tiny?'

'No! *Countdown!* But you can bring one.'

Nish turned for the corridor.

'And take some of these fucking plates back!'

There was a war going on in that room. But who would be the first to surrender? The more Tiny complained, the more Nish enjoyed it. I bet the bogeys didn't belong to Tiny.

Nish chuckled to himself as we headed for the other end of the corridor, turned left, and came out by the toilet block, yet another Portakabin.

We got to the brew area. A Burco boiler that looked like it was kept going twenty-four hours a day took pride of place. Next to it was a big box of Naafi biscuits, jars of coffee and sugar and mountains of teabags and white paper cups. Nish carried his own blue and white striped pint mug.

'You any good at conundrums?'

'What?'

'*Countdown*. Don't tell me you don't like *Countdown* . . .'

'OK, I suppose . . .'

'It's prayers at half six every night, scoff'll be on before that, about half five. Ken and the lads are on a job, but he'll sort you out later tonight.'

I could hear the chimes for *Countdown*. Nish rushed off with his mug and a paper cup. 'Duty calls. See you later, mate.'

I made myself a brew and wandered back to my room. I didn't unpack, just lay on the mattress getting the swing of things with Paul. We watched Carol Vorderman add a consonant here and there.

When we got to the maths question, Nish had obviously got it right. A loud *yee-ha* echoed down the corridor before he gave Tiny a hard time for being so thick. Carol and the crew finished and waved goodbye to the troop.

Paul jumped up and rubbed his hands together. 'Soup time, boy – you coming?'

It was only four thirty. Nish had said scoff was at five thirty, but I followed him anyway to the cookhouse, another one-storey brick building, just the other side of the washrooms. The two lads behind the stainless-steel counter could have been manning any canteen in the world. A large steel vat of something steaming stood in front of them, and stacks of white bowls. We helped ourselves to minestrone lumps. Tiny grabbed half a loaf of bread. 'It's healthy, soaks up the juice.'

Four or five cars pulled into the warehouse, normal saloons like the one Al had picked me up in. Each was two up in the front.

The troop got out, in jeans, trainers and bomber or leather jackets. A couple of guys still had beards. They looked like factory workers at the end of a shift, until they started to unload their G3s, the 7.62mm German Heckler & Koch assault rifle, and MP5s. The staccato rattle of working parts being pushed backwards and forwards echoed off the Portakabins.

Nish glanced out of the window. Al came in and slapped him on the arm. He seemed even paler than he had at the airport. 'Looks like those two haven't made up yet, eh?'

I didn't know what he was talking about.

'Frank and Ken.'

I followed Nish's gaze. It was true: they weren't exactly heading for a group hug as they climbed out of their separate cars. Ken went over to Frank. Frank gazed up at him, not flinching or backing away. It looked like he was being invited for a game of squash.

Tiny was obviously thinking more or less the same. 'Why don't they just sort this shit out?'

I didn't say anything. Whatever they were on about, it wasn't any of my business. Maybe it was some God-squad stuff – Frank not wanting to shoot people on Sundays or something. What did I know? All of a sudden I didn't feel as much a part of the troop as I had when I was admiring Gloria's hairdo.

32

The soup was over and the rest of the team had dispersed. There were lots of others running around too. Seven Troop was small, so lads from other troops were making up the numbers. On my way back to my room I passed Saddlebags taking his pancake holster off his belt.

I gave him a nod.

'How's it going?'

I got one back, but he didn't hang around to answer. He disappeared into the room he must have shared with Al. There was a Mr Grumpy sticker on the door.

I tipped out my bag and made up my bed. I found a well-worn blue duvet cover that must have been left by somebody years before and passed down the line. It was only a little bit musty. I was stuffing the duvet into it when Frank appeared. 'Hiya. I'm next door, opposite Nish and Tiny.'

'You been out long?'

'Nah, just been playing around. Nothing much at all. Had soup yet?'

'Yeah. And *Countdown.*'

'You know about prayers at half six?'

'Yeah.'

As I carried on with the bedding, Ken came down the

corridor. He gave me a wave.

'Andy. All right, mate?'

'Ken.'

'I'll see you after prayers, and get you rigged out with all the party gear.'

He carried on walking. At least he was smiling, which was more than Frank was.

'You heard about what happened?'

I shook my head. 'Just there was a bit of drama.' Of course I wanted to know, but I wasn't going to ask.

He didn't let me down.

'Two of us dropped Ken and a couple of the guys off from a van to do a job on the border. We didn't even know what the target was. All we knew was the drop-off point, the pick-up and the emergency RV.

'We drove out of the area and parked, waiting for the call to pick them up. It was up a little track, set back from the road. I'd got the Thermos open when a car crept along the road, on sidelights. It stopped further up and came back, all very slow. It was two up.

'They came to a complete stop near our track, looked up, and then drove on again. They must have seen us.

'We got on the net, reported a possible compromise, and moved out. As soon as we were back on the road we spotted it again. It started to follow us.

'We were right on the border. The car stayed with us and was joined by another, both on sidelights. I got on the net again, expecting to take rounds any second.

'The road got wider, and the lead car suddenly accelerated to come alongside. As I got my safety off, this old Ford came alongside, two up. Both wearing masks. If I'd seen a weapon, I was going to open up. But nothing.

'We were coming up to another junction, and just as we got there, a third car joined in.

'I got on the net, giving a running commentary. It carried on

like that for ten minutes. More cars joined in. It was madness –
soon there were six of them. That was at least twelve players,
probably more.

'We still had to stay on the target area to pick the patrol up
but there was no word yet from them – and, of course, there
wouldn't be until the job was finished. We were driving round
in big circles and they'd even barricaded a road with rubble.

'The patrol called in ready. I told them the situation and said
we'd try to lose the cars behind, but no guarantees. They'd
have to be on their toes.

'Then I suddenly realized something. "There'll be five of us
at the pick-up. Five against twelve – let's go for it."

'I had my G3 in my lap, and I was operating the radio with
one hand and reading the map with a torch in the other. It was
like navigating for a rally driver, only with six cars in pursuit
and I had to be ready to draw down on them.

'We screamed to a halt at the pick-up point, and the guys
jumped in the back. I radioed the pick-up was complete. But
Ken cut me off.'

Frank was very bitter.

' "I'm in charge," he said, "and I'm saying we get straight out
of the area."

'I said, "But we've been chased for half an hour! We've got a
chance here to take out multiple players!" He said to do as he
ordered. What could I do?

'The six cars chased us until we were well clear of the area. I
couldn't believe it. I saved it till we got back here, then laid into
him.

'I'm still angry about it now, Andy. We missed a major
opportunity, and all because he didn't have the full picture,
and didn't take the time to find it out. If you ask me, Ken is—'

'Oh, for fuck's sake, Frank.' Paul was back with a mug in his
hand. 'Just let it go, will you?'

33

There were no shouts or bells to get up to prayers, everyone just assembled. The ops area was eight Portakabins, four on top, four below. I followed a couple of guys up a metal fire escape.

The briefing room was furnished with standard psychedelic army married-quarters furniture, a mixture of plastic chairs and armchairs that looked as though they'd done time in the Killing House. It was in shit state. On the walls were general maps of the Province, street maps, newspaper cuttings and piss-taking pictures of the guys. A selection of daily news-papers covered an old wooden six-foot folding table. A sign warned everyone not to take them from the room. A big black bin liner hung from a nail for the crap.

The room filled up. Some faces I knew; some were lads from the squadron I hadn't met in Malaysia. There were about fifteen of us altogether – not including the big fat Doberman panting in the corner – in tracksuits or jeans and flip-flops. Everyone had a mug of brew apart from the new boy, who had a paper cup.

Ken stood by a white marker board, a notebook in his hand. He looked around as we settled down. 'Where's Al?'

At that moment, Mr Grumpy came through the door. He

looked a little better. Nish threw a crumpled-up sheet of A4. 'There he is. There's the EPC swot.'

The Educational Promotion Certificate was a qualification you needed at different stages of your career. Al must already have done his EPC Standard, or he wouldn't have been a corporal in Para Reg. No matter how good a soldier you were, you wouldn't be promoted to sergeant even if you had a degree unless you'd passed EPC. Once you were aiming for warrant officer you had to pass EPC Advanced. I'd already done my EPC and I was glad it was over with, but EPCA was somewhere out on the horizon. Nish leant forward as Al found a seat. 'I hope you've done my homework for me, or there's no apple.'

Ken had one last look round. 'Right, listen in.' His delivery was short, sharp and aggressive: to the point. He spoke about the job they'd done earlier today. An MI5 operator had met with a PIRA source. Informant, tout, traitor – they had many names. The meet was covered by Ken and the team in case it was a come-on. They happened all the time. PIRA would explode a bomb, the green army would come in and set up their cordons and incident command posts. Once the area was saturated with squaddies, PIRA would detonate another couple of devices.

The prime example had been Warrenpoint.

At least eighteen soldiers were killed in August 1979 in two booby-trap attacks in South Down, close to the border with the Republic. It was the highest death toll suffered by the British Army in a single incident since it had arrived in Northern Ireland in 1969, and only hours after the Duke of Edinburgh's uncle, Lord Louis Mountbatten, had been killed by an IRA bomb in Donegal Bay.

The ambush had been carefully planned. The first device, weighing half a ton, was planted under some hay on a flatbed lorry beside a dual carriageway on the border, seventy kilometres from Belfast. It killed six members of 2 Para in a four-ton lorry at the back of a three-vehicle convoy.

The surviving troops in the other two vehicles were immediately deployed to cordon off the area and call for reinforcements. The Queen's Own Highlanders flew to the scene by helicopter twenty minutes after the first explosion; as it cas-evac'd some of the injured, the second device was detonated, killing twelve more soldiers – two Highlanders and ten Paras – who had been taking cover in a nearby gatehouse.

The job today had been to prevent anything similar happening, like the SIS's man getting head-jobbed and the Figure-11s coming to find out what was happening.

Ken ran through all the other admin points that had to be dealt with when troops are living together. Block jobs, like cleaning the cookhouse and communal areas, and the general stuff, like weapons checks. All weapons had to be accounted for every single day.

There was a definite undercurrent to the proceedings. Frank was being *über*-calm. He just sat and nodded and agreed when necessary, not really joining in. It was like part of him wasn't there. If he hadn't told me about his problem with Ken, I'd have assumed God was running through his own admin points and Frank was listening to Him instead.

'Finally, Andy's here – obviously.'

I got some waves and smiles.

'Any questions?'

There weren't.

'One last thing – the dogs. Stop feeding them. Including my fucker.' He pointed at the Doberman, which, legs flailing, tried to stand to accept the applause.

Tiny, Nish and Saddlebags almost split their sides.

Ken jabbed a finger at Tiny. 'No – more – sausages.'

The laughter died and Chris stood up with his notebook. 'Block jobs, then the bar.'

I stayed in my chair and Nish got stuck into the *Daily Telegraph* crossword.

34

Once Ken had sorted out his papers, he took me down to the Portakabin under the briefing room and issued me with my weapons – a pistol, an MP5, an M16, a G3, plus all the magazines, ammunition and night sights.

'Frank and Chris are the patrol commanders, but you just go with whoever needs you. Everyone's mixed. When a job comes up, you'll be put on one.'

He moved back towards the metal staircase, heading for the ops room, then turned and fixed me with a stare. 'Look, everything we do here is strategic. That's what we are – strategic troops, sent to task. And that comes from TCG. We work for them.'

TCG (Tasking and Coordinating Group) were Special Branch, MI5, all the spooks and government advisers who got together and planned this dirty war.

'So there are no speculative ops. I don't want you floating. That, mate, will lose us the war, all right? You don't drive around, you don't look for trouble, you go and do the job you're meant to do.'

I thought I'd chance my arm. 'Frank just told me about the South Armagh job.'

Ken took a breath. He clicked his fingers at the world's

fattest dog as he struggled to keep up. 'Frank didn't know what we were planting out there, and he still doesn't – no one does, because nobody needs to know. I told him, I've told everyone else, and now I'm telling you – it's intelligence that'll win this war. Intelligence, not body counts. We could have dropped those fuckers but it would have put us back months. Their time will come, don't worry.'

He clicked his fingers again and headed off, with the dog waddling behind him. 'See you at the bar.'

I found Chris in the toilet block and relieved him of his mop. Ken had made sense to me. Why compromise whatever was happening, whatever they were planting – a listening device, a camera? PIRA would have known there were Special Forces on the ground if they were taken on. Instead, by the sound of it, they knew fuck all. The van could have been pig or cigarette smugglers coming up from the south, shitting themselves try-ing to get away as these cars came up and checked them out. PIRA had to be asking: 'Was that van SF? But they didn't shoot, so it couldn't have been.' If Frank had opened fire, there would have been a body count. But maybe PIRA would have suspended operations in the area or stopped them altogether, and there wouldn't have been any information coming in from whatever devices had been planted. Then we would never get to deal with the rest of them.

It wouldn't be long before I came to find out Ken was right: intelligence did win the war. I was to spend a lot of time over the water getting to grips with active service units (ASUs) – not to kill them, but to get to know them better than they knew themselves.

Frank clearly did think of himself as God's agent, appointed to carry out His punishment on evil-doers, and that the Regiment really did exist to fight evil. But Ken knew the Lord sometimes had to work in mysterious ways.

I threw my paper cup in the bin by the Burco and started mopping.

I had killed one of these so-called evil-doers when I was nineteen, and it hadn't exactly felt as if I was doing God's work. It had felt like I was just trying to stay alive.

It was on my second tour and during my fourth ever contact. Despite my age, I was 'brick' commander. One Saturday evening, I was out with a multiple, two four-man patrols, in South Armagh. The overall commander was Dave, a corporal.

We came to a housing estate on the edge of town. From there it was cuds (open countryside) all the way down to a place called Castleblaney on the other side of the border, just a few minutes away.

I took my three over a river and up onto a patch of waste-ground just short of the estate. Dave took his along the river; we would meet up inside.

At that time on a Saturday night the streets were full of coaches that had arrived to pick up the locals and take them to Castleblaney for the *craic*. They'd go for a night out, then come rolling back at two o'clock in the morning. And rightly so: if I was stuck in Keady on a Saturday night I'd want to put on a new shirt and go over there on the piss, too.

We were patrolling in dead ground. The locals couldn't see us, and we couldn't see them. I was expecting that to change once we got nearer the estate; in the meantime, we'd leave them alone. It was pointless forcing our way through crowds: it just incited them to throw rocks and bottles and our lives got even more complicated. Our intention was to outflank them and have a quick mooch around the estate to see what was going on.

A stationary patrol picked up more information than it did on the move. It was called 'lurking': we'd get to a position and just stop. It might be in somebody's back yard; we'd move into the shadows, wait and listen. It used to be great entertainment for the squaddies: we'd watch everything from domestic rows in kitchens to young couples groping in Mum's front room.

Dave's patrol was to the right of me, about 150 metres away, in dead ground to us. There was no need to talk on the radio. We'd been out there quite a few months and worked well together.

We were still hidden from the estate by a row of three or four shops. I turned right and went along the back of the buildings until I came to the fence line. By now the wasteground was more like disused farmland; there were old wrecked cars on it, tin cans, bags of garbage. I jumped over the fence and came into view of maybe 120 people on the other side of the street.

I heard hollering and screaming, which was unusual. Normally there would just have been a lot of talk and laughter; lads smelling of Brut and hairspray, and girls in sharply ironed blouses.

As I looked at the crowd I realized they were really frightened, grabbing their kids, pulling them out of the way. Some fell as they tried to run. As I panned left towards the shops and crossed the road, I came across three or four saloon cars and a cattle truck. It wasn't an unusual sight in this neck of the woods. But as I passed them, I spotted a group of men with masks and weapons.

I latched onto a boy with his fist in the air, doing a Che Guevara with his Armalite as he chanted to the crowds across the road.

He couldn't have been more than ten metres away. Close enough for me to see his eyes as wide with shock inside his mask as mine must have been.

Fuck!

He fumbled with his Armalite and shouted. The other masks ran from the cattle truck.

His weapon was already cocked and he started blatting away at me. I fired back at him and the other masks, a blur of movement behind him.

Another mask joined in from behind the wagon and I fired at him as well. They were flapping as much as I was, in a frenzy to get into the truck and away.

One of the boys jumped into the back of the wagon and started firing, covering the others as they clambered over the tailgate.

I hit one of them. I saw the two heavy 7.62mm rounds rip into his chest, and a split second later blood exploded from the exit wounds. He screamed like a pig as he was pulled inside the truck.

More screams came from the cab. They were also taking rounds.

By this time Scouse, the number two in my patrol, was giving them the good news from the far side of the fence. The other two were still in the dead ground, totally confused. It had all happened so quickly.

I knelt, still firing, then got the dead man's click.

The working parts still worked, but there wasn't a round in the chamber.

I was flapping. I knew what to do, but the faster I tried to do it, the faster I was fucking up.

I hit the ground, screaming my head off as bursts came our way from the truck: 'Stoppage! *Stoppage!*'

As I reached for another magazine everything seemed to go into slow motion. It wasn't, of course: it was fast and fumbled, but it felt like an out-of-body experience, as if I was watching myself going through the drills.

I clipped on the fresh mag and cocked the weapon. I heard more firing, I heard shouting. But the loudest sound of all was the hollering inside my head: 'I don't like this! But I know I've got to do it!'

The vehicle was on the move, and by this time Scouse was firing into the cab. But that cattle truck was sandbagged up at the back, and they'd welded on steel plates to protect the driver.

I was still the only one on my side of the fence. I ran forward, past the shop fronts. I didn't know if anybody was left outside the wagon, maybe lying between the parked cars. Or had they done a runner into the housing estate? Or the shops? Or to the junction only ten metres away and turned left? Or right, up a disused railway line? I had no idea.

Out of the corner of my eye I saw people cowering on the floor of the nearest shop. One of them jumped to his feet. I turned and gave a couple high through the window so he got the message. The glass caved in and the bloke threw himself back to the floor.

'And stay down!'

I didn't know who was more scared, them or me. It was a stupid, bone reaction to shoot through the glass, but I didn't know what else to do. I was so hyped up, anything that moved was a threat.

I legged it to the junction. Time and time again during the build-up training we'd practised two ways of looking around corners. You can get very low and close up or, better, you can move away from the corner and gradually bring yourself round so you present less of a target. It was all very well in training, because I knew there was nobody on the other side with an Armalite. I took a deep breath, got down on my belly with the weapon ready to swing round, and had a quick squint. There was nobody there.

Back at the scene of the contact, one poor guy was crawling towards the housing estate, cursing and shouting, as his wheelchair lay on its side in the road. Locals spilled from their houses to help him.

Mothers shrieked at children. Doors slammed. A woman in the shop screamed, 'There's nobody in here! There's nobody in here!'

Later, a body turned up in the south with a couple of 7.62mm wounds, and a couple of the masks received treatment in hospital for gunshot wounds. Their plan had been to drive past one of our patrols on the other side of town. The masks in the back would brass up the patrol on either side of the street, then keep driving until they'd crossed the border. My patrol had bumped them as they were doing their PR bit outside the shops and climbing into the cattle truck.

At the time, I had mixed feelings about the contact. On the face of it, the whole thing was great. They had taken casualties, and none of us was hurt. I had the credibility of the first kill of the tour and, thanks to an army incentive scheme, I had two weeks' extra leave. But there was another side to it. I hadn't felt like one of God's enforcers, just scared and fucking lucky it wasn't me who'd taken the rounds.

35

After block jobs I went to my room and carried on unpacking my gear. I could hear Nish's very bad version of 'Smoke On The Water' echoing its way down the corridor. To add insult to injury, he had linked it up to an amp and speaker. Music lovers all along the block yelled for him to shut the fuck up.

My Bergen and military kit had come over by helicopter the week before. I gave it a bit of a sort-out until it was time to head for the bar. As anywhere else in the army, the new boy's first job was to buy everyone a drink.

The bar had a tiled floor and maybe a dozen tables with three or four chairs round each. The counter looked like it had been lifted straight out of a pub, and maybe it had. Enough of them had been bombed, on both sides of the religious divide. It was about three metres long, bristling with optics and so on, and laden with Tennants cans, each sporting a picture of a page-three-style Lager Lovely. The girls took up about half the can, and I was a great fan.

I worked my way round the tables, collecting orders. There must have been about twenty-five guys there, including the signallers and green slime. The bar wasn't manned. There was an honour system. You signed your life away on a sheet and paid at the end of the month. I liked that kind of trust. It was a bit of a first for me.

Nish and Al were sitting with their EPCA folders on the table in front of them, unopened. Nish was bent over the *Telegraph* crossword, a can of Tennants in one hand, a stub of pencil in the other. Al chipped in with the occasional answer.

EPCA wasn't going to be remotely difficult for those two. Nish and Al had a lot more in common than it appeared. They weren't just intelligent, they were well educated. They came from comfortable middle-class families. Nish's father, an engineer, had flown Spitfires in the Second World War and been shot down twice. He became an inventor; Sir Francis Chichester used one of his pumps in *Gipsy Moth* when he sailed single-handed around the world. 'They got on well,' Nish joked. ' "Oh, how do you do, old chap? Awfully nice to meet you." '

The only big difference was that Nish was married with a small son, and Al wasn't yet – although he soon would be if Frank's wife got her way.

Nish called Frank over. 'We've got to clear this up, mate. That job where you walked up on the firing point, what was all that about? You on the fast track to heaven?'

A couple more lads turned and listened in. Tiny tipped peanuts down his neck but didn't move from the bar. I stayed put too.

'I keep telling you, I can't be killed.' It was the first time I'd heard Frank raise his voice. 'I'm guaranteed eternal life, Nish, I really am.'

Nish wasn't impressed. 'For fuck's sake, what next? We going to see you walk on water?'

'It's not about miracles.' Frank took a swig from his can. For a moment it looked as though his hand was the only thing stopping Fiona falling out of the front of her dress. 'If one of us has got to be killed, it should be me. I'm a Christian, I'm guaranteed eternal life. I'm the best one to die. That's why I did it.'

Nish's eyes narrowed. 'So what are you saying? That you've got some kind of holy insurance?'

'What I'm saying is, if any of us has got to die, it should be me. Besides, it's better to spend one day as a tiger than a thousand years as a sheep.'

Tiny rolled his eyes and guided me towards the pool table. 'You any good?'

I shook my head.

'Good.'

Frank was in full flow. 'All right, I should have got the lads to check out the bushes. But there was no way we could do it without risking someone's life. As a Christian, I felt I couldn't do that. Look, I wasn't being brave – it's just that I'm not afraid to die.'

Nish stabbed the air with his pencil stub. 'You saying that I am?'

'No, Nish, no. But I do believe that God has a purpose for me. And if He wants me dead, then that's the way it's going to be.'

Frank was really stirring up a hornet's nest. Everyone was kicking off on him; the only one not saying anything was Al. He sat there with his head down, still a bit rough round the edges. Eventually he looked up. 'You've got to cool it, Frank. Religion, it's a personal thing . . .'

'Of course.'

'So you don't need to shove it down people's throats. Just let it go.'

Tiny put his cue under his arm and applauded the voice of reason. Then he returned to the table and fucked up a spot shot.

The discussion seemed to be over. I watched Al as he left with his folders under his arm to get some work done. Nish went back to his crossword.

Tiny frowned. 'He shouldn't be up here anyway.'

'Who? Frank?'

'No, you dickhead. Al. He's got malaria. He should be tucked up in bed.'

The bar door burst open and Minky barged in with a towel round his waist, his face full of shaving soap. I knew him from Selection. He was one of the directing staff, and in Six Troop. He was over here as the ops sergeant, handling liaison with TCG and all the different police and spook organizations. He looked like that bloke in *The Professionals*, the one without the curly hair. He was almost poster SAS. Or he had been, until now.

'You bastards!' He held up a shaving stick. Whatever was happening, everyone but me seemed to be in on the joke. As they rolled up laughing, he carried on screaming, 'You bastards! *You bastards!*' He ended up throwing the shaving stick at Ken.

Tiny couldn't play his shot he was laughing so much. 'There's prawns in it! Took hours to get them in. He's been shaving with prawn-flavour soap for days and moaning about Gillette changing the ingredients.'

Minky had been stitched up so many times he was completely on edge. He wouldn't even use the toilet block, these days, because he expected the bowl to explode beneath him or the roof to collapse.

36

The next few weeks were busy. On one job, we staked out an area where we knew an IED was going to be placed. A couple more involved us ambushing PIRA weapons and explosives caches, and moving in for a hard arrest when the players came to collect.

We had to be ultra careful about source protection at all times. Ken would often circulate a picture with the warning: 'If things kick off, this is the lad that mustn't be killed.' They were all strategic jobs, working on information that had been gathered – sometimes from careless pub talk, sometimes from informers, sometimes from the sort of gear Ken's patrol had been spreading around that night in South Armagh.

I switched between Frank's patrol and Chris's. I could find myself in a vehicle with Nish or in an ambush position with Tiny or Saddlebags. As in the jungle or team training in the UK, it was all mixing and matching.

Target replacement came high on the task list. We'd hear that someone was being targeted for assassination, and the one of us who looked most like him would step into his shoes. The rest would set up ambushes to stop the hit taking place and then take on the ASU.

Ken had the troop up in the briefing room and told us PIRA's latest target was a well-known political and social figure. The information had come from the target himself. He'd noticed suspicious vehicles following him to his office. He varied his route, but the cars were still there.

'So.' Ken checked his notes. 'The plan is to replace him with a look-alike, and that's you, Al. Up for it?'

We couldn't be ordered to do these types of jobs, only asked. I went on to do it a couple of times in my career and it was scary.

Al didn't even flinch. 'Fine by me.'

Al and Frank would go to the target's house the night before the hit. Frank would get into the back seat of his Saab in the early hours and hide under a blanket. He would have a radio and a G3, and be Al's back-up when the shit hit the fan.

Al would then leave the house as the target normally would, between eight twenty and eight thirty, jump into the Saab and drive about a mile to the Tamnamore junction of the M1, cross the motorway, then head on into Belfast. The rest of the troop would be staked out in three cars ready to take on the ASU.

Everyone was preparing to get out on the ground and Al was having his hair done to look more like the target's. The TV was off and Paul was prepping his kit. I heard Frank mumbling away to himself through the adjoining wall and realized he was praying. I didn't know if it was for him, Al, or the whole lot of us, but he was going for it big-time. I left him to it: that bit was private – you don't burst in and take the piss.

Nish passed by, looking very dapper. Suits and ties were the order of the day. The target came from upmarket Commuter Land. Car pooling was common; three or four suits together wouldn't look out of place.

By 0800 everyone was in position. The three cars were staked out. Ken drove a Lancia, Nish a Renault. Both were three up. Saddlebags was on his own. He'd be clearing the route just ahead of Al and Frank. No drama.

The ops vehicles looked no different from ordinary civilian

ones. Under the bonnet, though, it was a different story: the engines were souped up to cope with the weight of armour-plating in the doors and behind the two front seats, and they had run-flat tyres. As soon as they'd been used on a sensitive job, they were replaced. Tiny had laid claim to the classy-looking Renault with power windows and an electric sun-roof as soon as it had arrived with us, but because he was away on leave Nish had taken it for the job. He made sure it blended in by dumping as much crap as possible in the foot wells and filling up the ashtrays for Tiny's return.

37

At 0830 Ken got on the net to Saddlebags. 'OK, mate, clear it.'

He drove the route the Saab would have taken, eyes skinned. The ASU would have had dickers (observers) out to trigger the Saab away from the house and guide them in for the hit. But Saddlebags wasn't just looking for them. There were other combat indicators. Was anyone on the streets? School kids should be on their way to class; if not, why not? Any side roads blocked by roadworks? Or a broken-down truck to stop the Saab escaping the hit?

Saddlebags rattled off a P (car number-plate) check on every car he saw. The answers bounced back over the net in less than ten seconds: what the make and colour of the car should be, who it belonged to, and if the owner was flagged up as a player.

Al's voice came on the net: 'Just about to leave. There's a Mini at the end of the drive.'

Saddlebags turned round and did a drive-past. 'Roger that. Wait.' He read the number-plate in his rear-view mirror. It was fake. Had it been booby-trapped? Had the ASU gone for a remote-controlled device instead of a hit? Was it just a faulty plate check?

Ken took control. 'All call signs, wait. Al, acknowledge.'

Al gave two clicks of the send button.

Ken was on the net. 'You got anything, Minky?' Remote cameras and other surveillance devices had been placed overlooking the target's house.

'Definitely not. No command wires, nothing rigged up. Your call.'

This was when a ground commander earned his money. Should he call the job off in case there was a device in the vehicle and they had eyes on, waiting to detonate? Or should he take the risk with his men's lives?

Ken took all of three seconds. 'Al, you up for it?'

Al took just one. 'Leaving now.'

It's quite an art trying to look like someone else, especially if they've been targeted.

The ASU would know him very well by now: the way he walked to the car, any little rituals before he got in. Maybe he checked his pockets for his office keys, or maybe he always put his briefcase on the back seat. Al had had only a few hours to find all this out last night, from someone who probably didn't know because it's not the sort of thing you normally think about. The players could have been watching as Al drove off. If things didn't feel right they could simply call it off. It was a long war. That's where 'Fuck it' comes in handy. Just getting on with the job when you know you could be killed at any minute calls for a certain mindset. 'Fuck it' always seems to work.

Even knowing as much as you can about the target, it's still very difficult to walk like a man setting off for work rather than one who knows his head might be in the cross-hairs.

'Fuck it, so what?'

Al had a square of Kevlar resting on the passenger seat next to him. When they started zapping, at least he could try to protect his head while Frank returned the good news from the back seat with his G3.

Saddlebags carried on towards the M1 roundabout where Nish was parked up in the Renault.

Nish got on the radio as the Lancia followed about 200 metres behind the Saab, just like any other commuters.

'I got a dicker – brown Cortina parked up on the roundabout with a CB antenna. The job's on.' Nish wasn't the only one parked up on the roundabout. This was Car-pool Central. They parked, met mates and drove into the city together in one car.

Saddlebags cut in: 'I got a yellow Escort van in the garage forecourt. Definitely two up. They are aware, not dossing. Can't see what's in the back. The rear windows look like they're covered with silver paper, no glass.'

His plate check came back as kosher. That meant nothing. PIRA often held locals hostage while they took their vehicles. What did mean something was silver paper and no glass.

As Al approached the garage the yellow Escort pulled out in front of him, as if heading for the M1 junction.

Frank came on the net and relayed what Al told him he was seeing. Al could be heard talking through clenched teeth to stop his lips moving.

'Intending right.' Their indicator was on, but it could be a bluff.

'Slowing.' The voices from the Saab were cool and calm. Frank had the safety off on his G3, waiting for the contact to start or Al to give him the heads-up.

'Stop, stop, stop. Still intending right. No traffic – nothing to stop them turning. This is it. Stand by.'

Frank shook off the blanket and pushed his G3 past Al's head, ready to brass up the van through the windscreen.

Ken had his foot down. The engine screamed above his voice. 'Closing in.'

Frank was back on the net. 'Stand down, stand down. They've gone right, gone right. Stand down.'

Ken took control as the engine note dropped. 'Nish, the dicker still there?'

Click-click.

'Roger that. Continue as planned.'

Ken dropped back behind the Saab as Saddlebags crossed the roundabout, checking all the parked commuter cars. He passed Nish in the Renault and the dicker in his brown Cortina.

Al continued his running commentary via Frank of where they were and what he could see. Everyone had to have a clear picture of exactly where the Saab was.

Saddlebags continued along the route as the Saab came up to a junction, turned right and headed for Nish on the motorway roundabout. Then the Lancia emerged about a hundred metres behind, and turned.

Nish was on the net a few seconds later. 'Yellow van's back, turning right . . . coming towards you at speed.'

Nish let the van pass and cane it towards the Lancia and the Saab, which had just crossed the motorway. He slipped in behind. 'Stand by! Dicker's on the radio . . . Wait . . . Van turning left . . . wait . . .'

The net was filled with the din of automatic gunfire from the van hitting Nish's car. 'Contact, contact! Wait out!'

It hadn't been silver paper covering the rear windows but sheets of galvanized tin. The two players hidden in the back had dropped them and opened fire.

38

Within seconds Nish was screaming along the narrow country road at eighty plus, fighting every corner.

Cyril opened up with his MP5 through the laminated glass. Eno, who'd passed the Selection before mine, was in the back with an HK53 (the 5.56mm version of the smaller MP5). Elbows braced against the two front seats, he opened up between the other two. Hot, empty cases bounced about inside the car and a cloud of cordite made it even harder for Nish to keep on the road. The two in the van kept firing.

Nish punched through the crazed windscreen. Air blasted in, along with a shower of broken glass. The two vehicles were still firing at each other. Ken screamed for a location but no one could hear the radio.

Nish was finding it hard to close on the van and ram it.

At last they came out onto a main drag.

Nish would have been able to ram them and take them down, if it hadn't been for a group of school kids waiting for the bus. Bags and books lay strewn across the pavement as they threw themselves into ditches or tried to run across the road.

One girl froze like a statue in the middle, still gripping her lunch box. Nish nearly lost control as he swerved to avoid her.

'Paralleling the M1 – I'm on the old main road to Belfast.'

He was on a long straight. Now the Renault could take them.

Eno returned fire again as Nish closed. Cyril was in the foot well, on the net to Ken.

It was good news. 'We're on the same road, ahead of you.'

Ken was in the front and pulled Chris's seat-belt on for him. 'RAM IT!'

Chris hit the gas as the yellow target came into view.

'Can't do it, Ken. We're too fast!'

The closing speed was over 150. Everyone would die. Ken wasn't worried: he would come back into this world as a bull. But Chris didn't have much faith in reincarnation. He spun the vehicle and blocked the road. The Escort screamed towards them, swerving up a bank at the last minute and around them. Chris jumped out of the Lancia and fired bursts into the rear of the van.

Ken pushed his door open and tried to jump out at the same time as Chris, but his seat-belt held him back. Two rounds shattered his door window a split second later. But for the seat-belt, he'd have had the Viking's death he wished for.

Nish managed to avoid the Lancia by throwing his car into a big slide.

'Got him, got him, still ahead.'

Sixty . . . seventy . . . eighty . . . The Renault accelerated and was closing.

The van took a sudden left. Nish hit the brakes, trying to slow enough to follow.

Cyril was on the net. 'Ken, they've turned left, turned left. We can't take 'em.'

Vital seconds were lost as Nish battled to turn the Renault. The van was now back on narrow roads, concealed by hedgerow.

The two vehicles combed the area until they were nearly out of fuel. The army and the RUC moved in to control the panicking locals who just wanted to get to school and work without dying. TCG called the job off.

The van wasn't found until later. The ASU had dumped it in a farmyard, grabbed a hostage, cut the phone lines and continued on foot across fields to avoid roadblocks, before taking another car.

Back at the warehouse, it became clear why TCG had called off the job. An innocent bystander had been killed in the operation. Frederick Jackson had been leaving a timber yard; he was waiting to pull out onto the road as the mobile intercept passed him. One of our rounds had ricocheted off the road and gone through the car door. It entered Mr Jackson's body and exited through his neck. The car rolled back and re-parked itself. He was sitting there for ten minutes before anyone in the yard realized what had happened.

The mood in the bar that night was sombre. Even with hundreds of hours of training, shit could happen. Soldiering wasn't a science. The X factor was the enemy. You couldn't tell them what to do so that they fitted in with your plans. Like Napoleon said, if you planned for A and B the enemy would always do C.

Frank, of course, prayed for Mr Jackson. I listened to him through the wall. 'But what else could we do, Lord? We're here stopping evil.'

Nish, Frank and I had a chat about how much the three of us probably had in common with that ASU.

Even as a Bible-basher, Frank had no problem seeing them as the bad guys. 'They use violence to prevent the democratic process, and they kill indiscriminately.' He shrugged. 'They have to be stopped. Simple.'

Nish raised an eyebrow. 'But I can see where they're coming from. If you'd been born a Catholic here and had to put up with the shit they have, you might be waving an Armalite too. Fuck me, to think it's only an accident of birth that I'm not shooting at Father Frank.'

They were both right. If I'd been brought up in the Bogside estate I would have been in PIRA. But coming from one in South London, I'd ended up in the army instead.

39

There was a lot of hurry up and wait.

Sometimes nothing would happen for a week, although we were always on standby. If something kicked off and they wanted guys on the ground quickly, we even had our own helis parked outside. Tiny was really pissed off that Nish had totalled his pride and joy. Nish thought it was a much better stitch than just filling up the ashtrays and hanging a few bogeys on the rear-view.

During the lulls, there were only so many games of squash or fights you could have in one day. The lads started climbing the walls, especially when Nish tried to get to grips with a few chords of 'The House Of The Rising Sun'.

Frustration was expressed in many ways, but most often in stitch-ups. Minky got over the prawn incident only to have a couple of kippers stuck behind the bars of his electric heater. Nish and Tiny went at it big-time, to the point where I'd be looking under my bed before I got up in the morning in case I was going to detonate something.

It was one of those days. Paul was out doing his own thing, and Frank stuck his head round the door. 'You want to back me in the van?'

'Yeah.' I got up. 'No drama.'

Great. I was going to be shotgun for a job. 'When's the brief?'

'There isn't one. I need somebody to come with me on a shopping trip.'

'Oh. OK.' I picked up my Browning and a couple of magazines. If you weren't on standby, you could just get into a car and drive into Belfast. We were undercover soldiers; we were big lads, with lots of guns. I still couldn't get used to it.

I followed him to the admin van. The dirty old yellow thing was as beaten-up as an odd-jobber's van, which was just the way we wanted it.

'Jump in, you're driving.'

'Where we going?'

'The timber yard.'

'OK.' I had no idea where that was.

I racked back the top slide to get a round into the chamber of my 9-milly. I jumped into the driver's seat, bunged it under my thigh, and checked I had the other two magazines with me. It was a matter of choice, but I always carried three: one in the weapon, two on my belt. If I needed more than thirty-nine rounds, I was deeper in the shit than a pistol could get me out of. Anyway, the idea was to keep out of trouble, not to get into it.

We drove out of the warehouse. 'Why do you need me on an admin run?'

'Cos I'm no longer driving. Not after Tiny.'

The motor-transport officer was obsessed with chips in windscreens and that sort of stuff, to the point of being terminally anal. He was probably after an MBE. Nish had got into a contact and managed to write off a car in about five minutes, but nothing happened because it was on a job. Yet Tiny had scratched a door on an admin run and was fined the cost of the repair.

'So, new policy,' Frank announced. 'I'll drive on jobs, but I'm not going to drive any admin.'

'Oh, right. Cheers, mate – so it's all right for me, is it?'

'Of course. That's what troopers are for.' Frank was grinning from ear to ear. He was in a good mood. I liked him when he was like that.

We drove out of the compound and onto civilian roads.

Frank was still grinning. 'They think I'm weird, you know.'

'Who do?'

'You know exactly what I'm on about.' He opened the window and let a bit of air in. The wagon stank of cigarettes and stale farts.

'You all think my Christianity's some weird kind of madness, but I've got to tell you, mate – we're all mad one way or another. We have a Viking as a boss, there's lads who'll only read about the paranormal, and lads addicted to physical fitness like it's heroin. The only one I know who's normal is Al.'

'Thanks again – what about me?'

'You're not normal. You're SAS. That's all you want to be, isn't it?'

'That's why I'm here.'

'Exactly. What a bunch of madmen we are. And they let us out on the streets every day with these things.' He patted the 9mm under his thigh.

'But Al's OK?'

'Yep, more than OK, the only one with any sense. After all that stuff that went on in the bar a couple of weeks ago, he sat me down and told me I'm annoying people with my attempts to convert them, including him. But like I told him, Christians have annoyed people throughout history. They annoyed the Romans so much they got thrown to the lions. Dietrich Bonhoeffer annoyed the Nazis. Christians have got to stand up for what they believe.'

I glazed over, not wanting to listen to the life story of some German I'd never heard of, especially a Christian one. It was hard enough concentrating on not getting fined for scratching this heap of shit.

'Bonhoeffer – you don't know who I'm on about, do you?'

'If I was that clever I'd be in the engineers.'

'He was part of the plot to kill Hitler. They executed him out of spite, even though they knew the war was lost. He was a fat little bespectacled guy, the sort of lad you'd pick on in the schoolyard. But he believed Christians must fight evil in the world, wherever and whenever they saw it. He said churches are unnecessary. All you need to be a Christian is a Bible.'

'Yours in that Claymore bag? That's your cathedral, is it?'

He nodded. 'I read it every day. You should give it a go.'

I couldn't be bothered to answer. Just get back to the jokes, Frank, that's the boy we want to hear. Like any convert to any cause, he was tearing the arse out of it. I realized that religion itself wasn't the problem. It was the fanatics that scared the shit out of me.

We drove into the timber yard. Frank had a list a mile long of stuff he needed: lengths of 4×2, sheets of plywood, sheets of this and that, glue, all sorts of woodwork shit. I didn't have a clue what most of it was. I'd never done it at school, and I wasn't exactly a craftsman – I was a flat-pack-cupboard-from-B&Q man.

We got back to the warehouse but Frank directed me to the range hut just outside. It was a corrugated-iron set-up that held all the Figure-11 targets we used when zeroing weapons, and all the plywood backings and little squares of paper and paste to glue over the holes so we could use them again.

I thought it must have been range stuff we'd been buying, but as soon as Frank opened the door I saw we were going into what was obviously his workshop. A large kitchen table was under construction, bright white, sprucy wood; all sanded down, ready to be stained. Four chunky kitchen chairs had already had the treatment. The hut stank of paint and freshly sawn timber.

Frank beamed with pride. 'I've made it so the legs can come

off. I'll be able to drive it back to H.' I looked down at the lumps of 4×2 under my arm. 'Fucking hell, Frank – you're going for the whole New Testament package, aren't you?'

He groaned. It obviously wasn't the first time he'd heard that one, but at least I got a smile out of him.

Frank dropped the wood. 'Tell you what, Andy. I'll make you a table and chairs if you read the Bible.'

I dropped my pile of wood next to his and laughed. 'You're not giving in, are you?'

'Don't you believe in God?'

'No. But I'll find out if I'm wrong when I'm dead, won't I? For now, I don't really think about it, mate.'

'Aha – that means you're an agnostic. You can't make a decision because you're afraid. You know that, don't you? That means the door is still open.'

I turned to go as Frank got out his tools and continued the good work of God's family business.

'Mate, the only door that interests me is the one out of here. Do you want me to close it behind me?'

As the new boy, I guessed I was only a natural target for Frank's recruitment drive. I just hoped Nish wasn't planning to ask me to join his band.

40

1 December 1984

We'd heard that an active service unit was targeting a member of the security forces. The informant wasn't sure exactly who the target was, so we were working on a list of possibles in the ASU's area of operations. They'd been keeping themselves busy. A lot of close-quarter shoots had been going down. The players would go up to a front door, knock, then barge in, guns firing, as soon as somebody answered. The targets were mostly RUC or UDR people and the players had always melted away to safety before the police or army arrived.

There weren't enough of us to cover all the potential targets, so we called in a platoon from 2 Para, the resident battalion in the area. Ken's plan was to put one of the troop with a couple of 2 Para lads on each possible, apart from the prime one. This particular guy lived way out in the cuds, just metres from the border, and had been threatened a couple of times before. No wonder he kept a Stirling submachine-gun on the kitchen table while he got the kettle on.

Frank's four-man patrol, including me, would cover him. We would get on target before the rest of the troop took their 2 Para patrols in on theirs.

Boss S was also in Frank's patrol. He'd just recently passed Selection and had been sent over to get some experience. Frank didn't want him on the ground, but how else was an officer going to get to know the ropes unless he was hands-on? Besides, he knew how to shoot. Ken had another heart-to-heart with Frank. Boss S would be on the ground with us and Frank would make sure he stayed with him at all times. He was here to learn.

The fourth member was Eno. He was from the Queen's Regiment, and came up to about neck height on me. He said less even than Chris or Al, and smoked more than Nish.

I listened through the wall as Frank prayed before we went out, even though I couldn't make out exactly what he said. From my side it was never more than a mumble.

The players might already have eyes on target, so to avoid suspicion – and to stop Frank walking across to the house to see if they were going to shoot him – we were dropped off at the target's home at about 11 p.m. We tumbled out of the van like we were old mates as our good friend came to the door and welcomed us inside.

The target, who was in his mid-fifties, had seen it all before. 'I'll get the kettle on, boys. It's a cold night – I can't see them coming out in this.' Even so, he had sent his family away for a few days. His Stirling 9mm rattled about on the washing-machine as it went into spin.

If the players had done their recces, they wouldn't attack through the front of the house. It was one of those places where the front door had never been used. Vehicles and people came to the rear kitchen door via the farmyard. It was unlikely they'd drive in because it was a pain opening the gate. In any case, the border was spitting distance from the kitchen door.

From our armchairs in the warm, dry kitchen, Eno and I had a grandstand view of the courtyard, the cowshed the other side of the hard standing, the dip where a stream ran, and the high ground of the Republic beyond.

The major, Frank and Boss S went into the front room to watch TV. It was important the major kept to his routines. One of the downsides of being a patrol commander on a job like this is that you have to stay with the target. Eno and I would have the first contact.

We turned off the lights and opened the curtains. Feet up on pouffes, weapons across our laps, we watched through the double-glazed french windows. The target was right about one thing. It was cold out there. Ice had formed in the courtyard, and the freezing fog, an Irish speciality, was thickening by the minute.

Our plan was simple. As they came to the back door to the left of us, Eno would give them the good news with his LMG (light machine gun), a Second World War Bren gun, converted from .303-inch to 7.62mm. It was a great bit of kit. I had a G3, along with a couple of high-explosive hand grenades that would do the business with anyone on the hard standing. We would have shot out the double-glazing by then anyway so it would be easy to throw them out and duck behind the wall each side of the french windows.

We watched and waited while the other three caught the football.

Eno leaned over. 'I'm gagging for a fag.'

'Why the fuck do you smoke? It costs a fortune, and you stink.'

'Yeah, but it's a good kick-start. I'll give it up one of these days.'

'What – when you're less stressed than sitting here nice and warm with a brew and a clear field of fire instead of lying out there?'

Eno grinned back. 'Yep, this is the way to go to war.'

'Never tempt Providence,' Frank might have said if he'd been in the room. He came in and told us to stand to. TCG had just been on the net. The job had changed. The duty officer at the RUC police station in Kesh, County Donegal, had received

160

a phone call shortly after midnight. 'This is the Fermanagh Brigade of the IRA: there are blast incendiaries in the Drumrush Lodge, Kesh. The reason for this is that they serve the bastard security forces there.'

41

I knew Drumrush Lodge. It was a restaurant on the Kesh–Beleek road, not far from the Bannagh river. TCG was taking the threat as genuine.

Frank pulled the curtains on the french windows before Eno hit the lights. 'Ken has cancelled 2 Para. TCG wants the troop down at the Lodge – now!'

Ken had already got the rest of the troop together in two cars heading for the Lodge. It was about a thirty-minute drive for them too. We followed Frank into the front room and listened in to Ken on the net. 'All call signs. We don't know if the devices have already been placed. We don't know if it's a come-on for the RUC and they're waiting. We don't know if they have a device to kick off and then wait for a shoot. So let's keep flexible heads and crack on.'

Frank got back. 'Roger that. We're going to take the target's vehicle.' He gave the registration number and colour of the Escort as Boss S checked the maps.

All four of us were soon piled into the target's old van. He wasn't fazed. He'd seen it all before.

Frank drove, Boss S next to him with the map. The weather had closed right in. Freezing fog brought visibility down to no more than about thirty feet. The roads were icy. Our headlights bounced straight back at us, like we were caught in a white-out.

Tiny was driving one of the other cars, with Ken, Nish, and Jocky from Eight Troop. The other contained Cyril, Saddlebags and Al.

As soon as Frank took the Escort over thirty, it fishtailed off the road. Frank corrected the slide and brought down the speed before we ended up in the ditch.

Boss S gave Ken the sitrep. 'We won't make thirty minutes. The ice is slowing us.'

Frank took a corner and the back started to wander again.

'Roger that.'

We only found out later that the ASU had already packed a thousand pounds of ammonium nitrate and fuel oil (ANFO) explosive into nine beer kegs and placed them in a culvert by the entrance to the Lodge. That amount of ANFO would make a five- or six-metre-wide crater and take out anyone and anything in the surrounding area. It was going to be detonated from just over three hundred metres away by two players who were lying in wait for the fog to lift and the RUC to arrive. Their firing point was on high ground, giving a good field of fire and escape route. Some of their mates had taken up fire positions along the link road into the Lodge. They planned to shoot any survivors, and warn the detonation team of any RUC going into the Lodge while the fog was still down.

Minky got on the net. 'We're hearing a blue van, possibly a Toyota, may be part of the job.'

'Roger that.' All call signs acknowledged.

Eno gave voice to what we were all thinking. 'It's a fucking come-on, must be. The information's flowing too easy.'

The Boss was bent over, map reading with a small Maglite between his teeth. 'Down here, turn left. Not far, maybe ten to go.'

Ken piped up from Boss S's foot well. 'OK, all call signs – listen in. We'll block the link road on both sides about one hundred from the Lodge, then move in on foot. This call sign will take the first end. Cyril, move past us and block the other end. Frank, call me when you get here.'

'Cyril?'

Click-click.

'Frank?'

Click-click.

While we made best speed, Tiny was skidding to a halt. Nish and Jocky jumped out and covered front and rear, and Ken stayed with the radio, waiting for Cyril to pass and block the other end before they moved in on target. None of them had a personal radio, and visibility had deteriorated to three metres.

Nish was forward of the car, crouched in a ditch, when he heard a van door slide open in the fog somewhere ahead of him. He climbed onto the road, his HK53 in the shoulder. He was moving forward as Cyril's lights pierced the gloom. He got into a fire position a couple of paces past a five-bar gate. His barrel pointed in the direction he thought the noise had come from. With no visual points of reference, sound became confusing, hard to pinpoint. Stop and listen was the best way. It cut down your noise, so you could concentrate on theirs.

The gate rattled behind him.

Feet landed his side of the hedge.

Nish saw breath condense in the air. Who the fuck was it? Tiny? Jocky? Ken? His weapon was pointing through the hedge. He couldn't pull it back and turn without giving himself away.

He could hear laboured, rasping breath, then the *ssssh-hiss* of a radio.

Nish couldn't do a thing. Cyril's crew weren't yet in place. If he took this guy on now, the rest of the ASU would run – and might even detonate on the way out. One player wasn't enough.

42

We were trying to make distance in the Escort. All we got was a 'Stand by, stand by,' from Cyril. Then: 'We got a Toyota van static on the link road. Driver's door open. No movement. We'll move forward to block the road, then get back and take them on.'

'Roger that. We'll get closer to take any runners. Frank, where are you?'

The car fishtailed once more as Frank hit the gas. 'Five minutes . . .'

Ken and Tiny moved into a cut-off position to catch any runners. Jocky stayed with the car and radio.

They watched the headlights approach and took cover just off the road. Cyril parked up. His team stepped quietly from the vehicle. They checked their mags were on tight and pistols secure in their leg holsters, thumbs pushing down on their safeties to single shot.

All the while, they were being watched by two of the ASU who'd been placing the IED.

Cyril and Saddlebags moved back down the link road towards the Toyota, weapons in the shoulder. They stuck close to keep eye contact. They moved, stopped, listened, trying to work out what was ahead, hoping they weren't walking into someone else's barrels.

Al stayed with their vehicle and threw caltrops across the road, spiked chains that stopped a vehicle by shredding its tyres. If the van or any other vehicle in the trap tried to do a runner, Al would be able to brass them up as they came to a grinding halt.

The two players watched and listened, not sure how many Special Forces were on the ground. They weren't going to move until they had to.

Cyril and Saddlebags heard footsteps coming towards them from the direction of the Toyota. They stopped, let the target come to them.

Cyril took him on with his HK53. 'Stand still! Security forces!' He said it just loud enough to make himself heard, not loud enough to alert the whole gang.

'It's OK, it's only me!'

Whoever 'me' was, maybe he hoped Cyril was part of an army patrol so he'd have time to think of something or get some back-up. I would have done.

'Stand still or I will fire – do you understand?'

The footsteps stopped. Cyril moved forward as Saddlebags covered.

The boy ran.

'Stop! Stop or I'll shoot!'

Ken's team heard the shouts and moved in.

The moment it went noisy, Al knew they needed light. He left his fire position by the caltrops and grabbed a Schermuly flare from the boot of the car.

Everyone on the ground heard the whoosh, like a massive firework as it powered upwards. Most of the flare's effect was masked by the fog, but it caught enough of the running shadow.

Cyril and Saddlebags fired warning shots to the side of him. He carried on running, over a ditch and a fence into a field. They were going to lose him.

The two ASU close to Al knew they had a decision to make.

They stood up and hosed down Al, at exactly the same time Cyril and Saddlebags opened fire.

Al took one round, but spun to face the muzzle flashes. The ASU legged it.

From Ken on the net we heard, 'Contact, contact, wait out.'

We couldn't see what was happening but we didn't need telling. We had our windows down and the weapon reports carried loud and clear.

Ken's team couldn't move forward now in case of a blue-on-blue. They had to stay put and wait for runners, or for Jocky to take down any vehicles. If Cyril and Saddlebags needed help they'd shout for it.

Cyril and Saddlebags had cornered the runner. He'd stopped when he felt the thump of rounds near his feet. Cyril dragged him onto the road and pushed his face into the ground. 'If you move, I'll shoot you.'

He searched him. Saddlebags was covering. 'Al! Plasticuffs!'

They had some in their car.

We were nearly there now. Ken was on the net. 'RV with Jocky. We're going to find the rest.'

Saddlebags wasn't getting any reply from Al so they dragged the player back to the car.

Saddlebags went to the boot. It was then that he found Al lying in a pool of blood.

'Man down! Man down!'

43

Al had taken rounds in the arm and chest.

Saddlebags gave Cyril his HK53 and grabbed the trauma pack from the boot. He needed to stop the bleeding and get some fluid into Al fast.

Cyril got on the net while he covered Al. 'All call signs, man down. It's Al – we need a heli. *Get a helicopter in now. We're losing him!*'

Minky came straight back. 'Roger that, confirm it's Al. Confirm it's Al, over.' They needed to match the blood type.

'Yep, it's Al. Get it in now!'

The net fell quiet for two minutes.

Minky again: 'We can't get a heli up – fog. I'm trying for an ambulance. We're going to get something in for you, wait out, wait out.'

Ken cut in, his voice thick with anger: 'Fuck the weather, I want a heli in now!'

The boy on the floor must have worked out he was in the shit. He jumped up and lunged past Cyril. Cyril dropped Saddlebags's HK53 so he could use his arm to drop him.

He was too late. The boy had melted into the fog, and so had the weapon.

'He's got a 'fifty-three!'

They both went after him.

Saddlebags drew down his pistol. They both fired and the boy dropped.

Ken, like the rest of us, had no idea what was going on. 'Contact, wait out.'

We finally arrived. Frank stopped the Escort and got on the net. 'I'm stopping anything moving out of the area.' He was remarkably cool, considering his best friend had just been shot. But then again, he still had a job to do.

We started to follow up in the area. It was difficult. Night-viewing aids were useless in these conditions; it was all down to the Mark-1 eyeball. If we bumped into any of them, it would be more by luck than judgement.

We'd heard Minky call forward the local unit's Quick Reaction Force (QRF) to cordon off the area. With luck, the players would still be inside the cordon. I was glad we were in uniform: I wouldn't have wanted to be in civvies with a weapon in my hands when the QRF turned up.

Some of their Land Rovers had already skidded into ditches. When the remainder arrived, we could tell by the radio traffic there were more chiefs than Indians. All they knew was that there had been casualties, and there were still terrorists in the area. Every time a tree branch moved it was reported or shot at.

There were bursts of gunfire in the distance. We got on the net every time. We wanted to react to it. Minky came back: 'Stand down, stand down.' It was the QRF, firing at shadows.

Ken was severely pissed off. 'Get this to the QRF – we will contain this area. They are to stay where they are. They are not to fire at anything unless one of us tells them to or they are being fired at. No patrols, no movement; stay in the vehicles. Tell them not to react to anything until they're told.'

Minky said: 'The QRF report movement in some hedgerows by the river. Are any of our call signs down by the river, over?'

Frank didn't waste a second. 'Me and Andy will take that.'

'Roger that. Frank's going down to the river. Ken, acknowledge.'

Click-click.

We lay in the frozen grass getting our bearings as the QRF fired another couple of rounds.

Frank knew what he wanted. 'Andy, get your IR [infra-red] torch and keep three metres in front of me. Flush them out.'

I switched the IR torch on. It would illuminate darkened areas better than the night-sight; it was like using a normal torch, except it could only be seen through the night-sight.

I took a deep breath and played the beam over the hedge as I moved along it, like some kind of high-tech pheasant-beater. But this beater also had a weapon, and it was set at full auto. It was going to be jungle rules: give it a full mag to make sure there's nothing left of them to fight back.

The river on the other side of the hedge was in full flow. Ice cracked under my feet like I was walking on crisps packets. I was in a semi-crouch, safety catch off, butt in the shoulder. I tried not to breathe too hard, kept as small as I could, eyes out on stalks.

Frank was five or six paces behind, butt in the shoulder, aiming along my IR beam so he could take anybody on. Because he was detached, it would be easier for him to react than me.

Blue lights strobed through the fog, catching us like dancers in a disco.

I took two or three steps, stopped, ran the IR beam up and down.

We moved on, stopped, moved on.

Visibility was still shit. There was a commotion in the distance; still more shooting. Running around here somewhere were players who'd just had a contact. They'd be flapping, they'd want to get out of it, and they'd be armed.

At any moment I was expecting to hear a burst of gunfire and to feel the rounds thud into my body. But fuck it, this was what I did for a living. Besides, I wanted to kill them.

We found nothing, and then came the news we'd been dreading. There was no further need for an ambulance, let alone a helicopter.

Al Slater was dead.

44

The fog still hadn't lifted when we drove away in the early hours of the morning. The RUC, the QRF and the sniffer dogs had moved in. The area was sealed off and searched for IEDs, and Bomb Disposal set about defusing the thousand pounds of ANFO.

It was a slow drive back on icy roads. Not much was said, certainly in our wagon, which would have to go back to its owner at some stage. Boss S gave out normal voice procedure as we passed checkpoints, radioing them in to Minky so he could mark the troop's progress. I was cold, and wet from the fog. My eyes stung from lack of sleep and disappointment.

Frank didn't say a word all the way back. Even inside the warehouse, with its glaring, twenty-four/seven lights, everything felt cold and dank. People went about the business of unloading and cleaning weapons, but I had another task. Ken had told me to collect Al's weapons from the job; they were to be made safe and bagged up for the RUC. Then I needed to gather any ammunition he had in his room. We all had hundreds of rounds for our different weapons in our lockers.

Saddlebags and Cyril were up in the briefing room with the RUC. They had to go through the civil process. It was just one of the drawbacks of classifying PIRA as common criminals instead of granting them the political status they craved. And it was important, too, that we were seen to operate within the rules of engagement. Everybody involved had to make a statement after a contact, and weapons that had been fired would be taken away for forensics. It was a fucked-up way of fighting a war, but we wouldn't have had it any other way.

45

There was a strong smell of burnt coffee in the corridor. I opened the door with the Mr Grumpy sign on it and went in. The coffee pot had boiled dry.

Somebody had already brought in Al's blood-soaked belt kit and dumped it on his bed. Frank had volunteered to sort out and pack his personal stuff. I was glad he was doing it and not me. I'd had to do it twice, but twice was enough.

I felt around Al's bits and pieces in his locker as I looked for ammunition. Under a pile of clean socks and underwear, I felt what I thought was a box of 9mm. I pulled it out, and found myself holding a Bible.

Was this the one doing the rounds so the blokes could arm themselves with quotes to get at Frank? It didn't look like it; this one had a dedication to Al on the inside flap. No wonder he hadn't given Frank a hard time, not even in the jungle. He'd been a Christian all along. All credit to him – at least he'd kept it to himself.

I finished gathering up his ammo and started to sort out his weapons. Al had taken an M16 with him on the job, and a 9mm pistol in a thigh holster. I unloaded the M16 first. I pushed down the magazine, and discovered he'd got some rounds off. Up until then we weren't sure if he'd had a chance to fight back.

I bagged up his magazines and turned to the bloodstained leather thigh holster. I pulled out the Browning, removed its magazine, and tried to rack back the top slide to unload it – but it wasn't happening. A round from the burst that had taken Al down had hit the top slide and jammed it in place.

I tagged it with a brown luggage label, ready for the RUC: 'Weapon still made ready – a round in the chamber.' Their armourers would take it down to the range and try to fire it off.

Some of the M16 mags on the chest harness had big holes in them. It must have been a fearsome burst. I was bagging them up as Frank came in. He didn't speak to me, just went to the locker and started his job. He was clearly agitated. He finally turned to me. His jaw was tight. 'What do you think about Ken on the job? I'm not impressed.'

'Frank, we weren't there. We have no grounds to say anything. All we know is what we saw and what we heard – which wasn't much. Ultimately, he was the commander. Al's dead, for fuck's sake. Nothing will change that.'

He was going to say more but I turned my back. Frank was getting on my nerves big-time.

'Oh, my Lord.'

I looked back. He was sitting on the bed, and Al's Bible was in his right hand. He held it up at me.

'I know.'

He then held up a small prayer book in his left, and three or four Christian music cassettes. Frank stared at me. 'I tried so many times to convert him.'

It was as if Frank was in his own world now. 'Why couldn't he have talked about his faith to me – you know, just the once? Why did he have to keep it to himself?'

I tied off another plastic bag and picked it up. 'We don't all try to shove our beliefs down other people's necks, mate.'

Ken's voice came over the intercom. Every room was wired up so we could communicate with each other and the ops room. 'All to the bar now. All to the bar.'

We went over there together. Nobody had showered yet, or even changed out of their wet clothes. Most still had their thigh holsters and all the party gear on. I'd opted for a shoulder holster. I was going to be sitting down: I wanted a quick and easy grab.

Cans and tots of whisky were handed round.

Ken held up a glass of whisky and looked around the room. 'To Al.'

We nodded. 'To Al.'

46

Nish stared at an empty whisky glass.

Frank's knuckles went white around his can. 'At least Al went down fighting. That's what he would have wanted.'

Saddlebags looked up. 'I'm not so sure, mate. I reckon he was just shot, no chance for him to return.'

Frank's head was shaking. 'He fired back, I just know it.'

'Frank's right.'

The group stared at me.

'There were rounds out of his mag.'

There wasn't much more chat. We drifted away in ones and twos. Nish was more sombre than most. Frank began to open up. But it was all about Ken, and I'd seen the bitterness in his eyes as Ken raised his glass to Al.

I didn't understand, never have done, why Frank had it in for Ken. Maybe he just needed someone to direct his anger at, and Ken had been in charge.

As I took Al's kit to the ops room, I thought, At least we all feel a little better knowing that he returned fire. It's a soldier's thing. No one wanted to think of him just taking some rounds and dropping without having the chance to fight back. If that ever happened to me I wanted to be able to fire at least one round back, or even throw a stone.

I briefed the RUC guys about the 9mm, then went back to my room and got my head down. That afternoon I watched *Countdown*, and I failed to solve the conundrum.

A few hours after the shooting, two men were detained by Gardaí near Pettigo when they drove through a checkpoint. The car had been hijacked earlier and the owner was still in the car, at gunpoint. A Winchester rifle and eighteen rounds of ammunition were in the foot wells.

At first light, in a follow-up search of the area of the shooting, explosives were found in the blue Toyota, as well as the nine beer kegs containing the thousand-pound IED at the entrance to the Lodge. A radio and a pistol with six rounds of ammunition were also found near the gate where the body had jumped into the field next to Nish. He didn't have either on him when Cyril and Saddlebags challenged him: maybe he dropped them when he saw the headlights, and thought he'd bluff it back to what he thought was the ASU's vehicle and drive off.

Later that morning, the body Cyril and Saddlebags had dropped was identified as that of Antoin Mac Giolla Bride, a twenty-six-year-old Irish Army deserter.

The Toyota had been hijacked in Pettigo village, County Donegal, at about 9.30 p.m. the same night. The victim said four of the ASU were dressed in combat uniforms. Mac Giolla Bride wasn't.

Two of the ASU had worked at the culvert placing the IED. Two others were up the field on the Kesh side, positioned at the firing point. One of these, allegedly, was Kieran Fleming. Arrested in 1976 when he was eighteen, Fleming was sentenced in 1977 to be imprisoned indefinitely for terrorism offences. After six years in the H Blocks, he had escaped with thirty-seven others in September 1983.

The two at the culvert had just got the IED in position and hadn't even finished setting it when a car full of long-haired civvies turned up. Who would they have thought it was? UDR? RUC? INLA? Or just more smugglers? That was the thing in Northern Ireland. No one was ever sure. There was nearly always a time lag while everyone tried to work out who the fuck everybody else was.

It looked as if Mac Giolla Bride had heard Cyril's car, jumped out of the van and taken cover. He had chosen the same hiding-place as Nish.

Cyril then cruised past the van before turning and blocking the road. The guys didn't know it but they'd parked directly opposite the ditch in which two players were laying the IED.

Then Cyril heard someone walking towards him and Saddlebags. Nish had seen Mac Giolla Bride jump over the gate.

After dropping Al, the IED layers did a runner and kept going until they crossed the border. The two on the hill held their positions. One attached the wires of the device and tried to detonate. He tried several times but failed. Kieran Fleming wasn't a flapper.

I walked into Nish's room.

Frank was in there with him, sitting on Tiny's bed reading a letter. The telly was off. More dirty plates were piled in the corner.

Nish studied Frank's face, waiting for approval. 'You don't think it's a bit too heavy? A bit too much?'

'No, mate, I think it's good.' Frank looked up at me. 'It's to Al's parents.'

Nish shook his head. 'First letter I've written for about twenty years.'

Frank handed it back. Nish folded it and put it in an envelope. 'I needed to say something to them. We're not going to be able to go to the funeral, are we? We're on ops.'

Frank jumped to his feet. 'No, we will go! We will!'

He stormed off. There were guys on standby back in the UK, ready to fly over if numbers were needed. A few of them could easily come over and cover.

Nish licked the envelope. 'Tell you what – Frank's got to wind his neck in. He'll be out of a job and probably a head if he carries on. Ken isn't going to take much more.'

I left Nish to his letter posting and went back to my room. Paul was out. I lay on my bed, waiting for *Countdown*.

Frank stopped by on his way back. He looked a little sheepish. 'Ken has already sorted it. A few of us are going back to H.'

'Good news, mate. I've said I'll stay here. You lads who really knew him need to go.'

He hovered. 'You bored?'

'Yeah, waiting for Carol.'

'Want a book?'

'What you got?'

'You'll love it. Sex, violence, double-dealing, treachery – it's all in there, mate.'

'Go on, then.'

'I'll go and get it.'

Even as he disappeared from the doorway, I knew I'd fucked up. Sure enough, when he came back into the room he had his Claymore bag with him. He pulled out his Bible.

'Don't bother, mate. I'm not interested.'

'Why not? Why not give it a try? Al liked it. If it's good enough for him—'

'It – does – not – interest – me. I – don't – care. You're like a fucking ayatollah, trying to pump it down my neck all the time.'

'Ayatollah . . .'

The book went back into the bag and for a moment I thought he was going to laugh.

'I like that.'

He turned, and left quietly. It wasn't the right time for laughter.

47

Nish and Al had been supposed to be doing their EPC course every Monday. They didn't turn up very often, and it had become a standing joke that whenever the teacher asked them where they'd been, they'd say, 'I'm sorry, sir, I cannot answer that question.'

The Monday after the shooting, Nish handed in Al's calculator and EPCA folder. He also handed in a copy of the *Sun*. The headline read, 'SAS SOLDIER KILLED IN NORTHERN IRELAND'.

The forensic results confirmed what I already knew from the part-empty magazine: Al Slater's weapon had been fired. He'd managed to get off six rounds.

The autopsy report on Antoin Mac Giolla Bride showed that he'd been hit by nine, possibly ten rounds.

The episode was more or less over. There were scuffles at Mac Giolla Bride's funeral on Tuesday, 4 December 1984, when the RUC tried to remove a tricolour from the coffin on the out-skirts of the estate where the Mac Brides lived in Magherafelt, but that, we thought, was that.

A few days later, Nish, Frank and a few others from the troop boarded a Puma that had just dropped off another lot from Hereford to cover for them. They flew back for the funeral at St Martin's Church, where the Regiment has a plot and most of the guys get buried.

Ken didn't come back with the others. He had to hang around for a couple of days to debrief the head shed about Al's death. While that was happening, he obviously got word about Frank having a go at him. Ken stormed back to the warehouse on his return and ordered everyone into the briefing room. He went for it as only Ken could. 'No fucking about now. If you've got a point to make, say it now – put up or shut up.'

To my surprise, Frank got to his feet. He stopped short of blaming Ken for Al's death, but he came very close. None of us really knew why. Perhaps it was because, for all his talk of eternal life, he couldn't deal with the fact that Al was dead.

I knew everybody was encouraged to have a voice in the Regiment, but this was tearing the arse out of it. As I'd said to Frank, how could we judge? We didn't see what they saw; we didn't hear what they heard.

'OK, stop.' Ken had had enough. 'Don't you think I've gone over what happened out there, time and time again? For fuck's sake, the man's dead.'

Frank got up again to have another twopence-worth, but Tiny intervened. 'Enough already, Frank. Wind your neck in.'

Nish got to his feet. 'Listen, I'm right there with Ken. I keep thinking, if only I'd done things differently . . . If only we'd had personal radios so we all knew what the fuck was happening . . . If only I'd fronted Mac Giolla Bride when he jumped the gate . . . If only, if only . . . Maybe this, maybe that. No one's to blame. It's done.'

I knew he wanted to believe that, but one look at his haunted eyes told me it certainly wasn't done in his head.

Cyril was next. It felt to me that he had more gravitas than the rest of us on this job. 'Nish is right. He's dead. There's fuck all we can do. He was a soldier. If you don't like what we do, get out and become a social worker. Debrief over.'

It was. It all stopped. Frank kept himself to himself for the next few days. Christmas came. Frank went away on R&R, and when he came back he dropped the bombshell. He was getting out of the Regiment.

Because of Al getting zapped? Surely not. It had to be religion. Frank wasn't saying. All we knew was that he was going on the Circuit (working for a private security company). He'd taken a job in Sri Lanka with one of the firms, training the Sri Lankan Army to fight the Tamil Tigers, the world's first suicide-bombers.

Nish kicked it all off one night in the bar. 'Come on, Frank, what about you having religion and being on the Circuit? It's just the same as being here, so why aren't you staying?'

Frank remained tight-lipped.

Nish stared at him, and then the penny dropped. 'Oh, fuck, you're going to become a vicar, aren't you?'

'A vicar . . .' Tiny cut in. 'Or, Andy, what did you call him? He's going to become an ayatollah!'

48

The troop was a close-knit group and Al Slater's death hit us hard. It's never easy losing somebody you know, but in the military there's not much time for mourning. I'd known a lot of guys in rifle companies who'd got killed, and those left behind just had to move on. It doesn't mean you've forgotten the guy, but Cyril was right: he was a soldier, and now he was dead.

The jokes came back slowly, but after a while normal piss-taking service was resumed. Tiny and Nish still tried to outdo each other on the stitch-ups, and Minky was still the primary target. He was a big-time boxing fan. He spent hour after hour in the gym trying to knock out the punch-bag or watching bouts on TV. One Saturday night there was a big fight coming up. To stop his enjoyment being sabotaged, he locked himself in his room with some cans of Tennants and a few packets of crisps. Nothing was going to come between him and his ring-side seat.

The bell went for round one, but almost immediately his TV jumped channels. Even from two doors away, I could hear him yelling as he wrestled with the remote control and changed it back, only for it to happen again a minute or two later. What he hadn't factored in was that every room in the troop had the same sort of TV, and therefore the same remote control. As soon as Minky had locked himself in, Nish and Tiny had moved a couple of chairs outside his room and spent the evening holding their remote controls to the glass fanlight above the door and flicking from channel to channel.

The routine went on. Nish's guitar playing got worse than ever, and Ken signed up his Doberman with WeightWatchers. But forbidding the guys to give him sausages was like a red rag to a bull. Everybody started slipping them to him every night, and the thing now virtually lived outside the cookhouse door.

My afternoons were still filled with *Countdown*, then it was dinner, prayers, block jobs, the gym, and a date with the Lager Lovelies.

Meanwhile, in South Armagh, some ASUs were getting very active and hitting green-army patrols full-on. We were chosen to act as plastic ducks. Chris took three of us to set up a really bad OP outside a town where there was a known active service unit. We even pushed a radio antenna through the camouflage net, like something out of an old Second World War film, in case nobody had spotted us.

Frank and Saddlebags had a patrol in position with sniper weapons covering us from 500 metres. Nish and Tiny were in cars with some of the other lads, ready to give warning if a convoy of players came down the road to take us on, and then to counterattack.

There was nothing we could do but sit in the OP dressed as green army, eating dry sausage rolls and laughing at how stupid we looked. We must have looked so stupid that the ASU felt sorry for us because nothing happened. TCG pulled us out after two days. There were other fish to fry.

This time I was on the sniper side, giving cover from high ground across a brightly lit bus station. It was nine o'clock on a Saturday night, cold, icy, the grass crisped up. I had a great field of view through a glass-sided shelter and across to where they were planning to place an IED. They were going to leave it in a van in one of the bus spaces, then leg it.

It was going to be a hard arrest. That basically meant we'd come up against people who would naturally resist, and wouldn't be shy about using weapons. The TCG wanted these guys alive, which meant either they needed to interrogate them or to protect a source. For all we knew, the source, if there was one, might be one of those we were arresting.

Source information was gathered from many different people for many different reasons.

Some did it for money. I never really understood that one, because they would never get any more cash than they could naturally absorb in their lifestyle. That usually meant about eighty pounds a week – otherwise most of them would have gone straight out and bought a brand new car, which might have looked a tad suspicious sitting outside a minging council house. So why run the risk of getting your head drilled, or being burnt alive, for a couple of beer tokens each week?

Some became sources thinking they were protecting their husband or brother – whoever was in an ASU. 'If I tell you what he's doing, can you stop it?'

I had total contempt for these informers.

They were helping us win the war, but they were traitors. It didn't matter what side they were on, I had no sympathy for them when the Black & Decker was plugged in.

Finally, there were touts who did it for ideological reasons. They were highly placed within PIRA, and they gave solid information: the most powerful weapon in any war.

Whatever the reason, this job had to be a hard arrest: it wasn't going to be a walk in the park. If the players had weapons, they would use them. We were all at risk, and so were bus passengers and pedestrians but it can be so much more dangerous to let these things degenerate into a fire fight, rather than actively initiating the contact in the first place and therefore controlling it.

Chris was the patrol commander on the far side of the station. He was waiting with five other guys in the back of a van to hit the IED vehicle the moment it parked.

My job, and that of Nish and the other sniper, was first to give a running commentary to Chris and his patrol, since they were unsighted. We were then to give the standby, and take down any runners, or any bomb-laying backers who came to join in once the thing had gone noisy.

The place heaved with teenagers waiting for the bus to a night out on the piss. Dress code was short skirts, T-shirts, and lots of lily-white plucked-chicken arms and legs. Two sixteen-year-olds couldn't wait to get back to one of their mums' houses, and started shagging each other right there and then. She was classy enough to take her chewing-gum out.

We had dickers drive past the target, then come back on foot. It was all shaping up for a contact.

Then: nothing.

We kept on target until just before first light, when TCG called us off.

It was just part of the job, another variation on hurry up and wait. For every success there were twenty jobs that didn't end in contact. We did another target replacement, this time in an RUC station we'd been tipped off was going to be attacked. Nothing happened. We protected an MI5 agent when he met up with a PIRA source. It passed off without incident.

We got some good news. It was confirmed that Kieran Fleming, one of the players who'd got away the night of Al's killing, was dead. His body had been found in the Bannagh river.

When the two who'd been manning the IED firing point about three hundred metres from the Lodge had run from the follow-up they'd only got as far as the river when Frank and I had started to move along the bank to flush them out. They'd taken to the water to avoid my pheasant-beating. Although it was only twenty feet wide, the river had deep pools and was fast-running. One of the players had reached the other side, but when he'd got out he couldn't find his mate. Fleming had been ripped away in the flood.

His funeral was held two days later. I went along to watch. About thirty people were injured during clashes between mourners and the RUC. Plastic bullets were fired, and it took almost three hours to complete the procession from Fleming's home to the cemetery. When the funeral turned into the Bogside, three PIRA in balaclavas fired volleys into the air as British Army helicopters flew overhead.

I'd sent a lovely multicoloured plant instead of a wreath, and inflated a set of water-wings around the pot. I never found out if they made it onto the display. Al would have liked that.

49

One thing changed for the better after Al's death: Frank stopped trying to be a missionary. Maybe it was finding out that he wasn't the only one among us trying to fight back a tidal wave of devils, and that some people did it without all the song and dance. Or maybe he finally realized his words were falling on stony ground.

I'd also found my role model. Chris was a good lad. He only spoke when he needed to, and I kept reminding myself that I needed to follow his example now that I'd found my place in Seven Troop. I sometimes caught myself doing a bit too much talking now that I'd settled in.

I bet even Ken found him inspiring: Chris still sported the bright blond Viking look Ken must have had when he was raiding the English coastline in a tin hat with horns sticking out of it. He knew his stuff. He was a real professional, and exuded quiet confidence. When he spoke, it always meant something. Maybe that was because he didn't bother getting sidetracked by any of the nonsense that went on around him. Even Frank and his God and Nish and his farts failed to get a rise out of him.

We were all experienced, some had been senior NCOs in battalions, but he handled that and got people behind him.

That was the way I wanted to be. Well, without the sniff before every other sentence.

That didn't mean I cut Frank as a friend or stopped driving the van for him to carry on the family business. It was always good to get out for a couple of hours if there was nothing much on.

We talked about Al's funeral as we drove down to the timber yard one day.

'I've seen a lot of mates die during my seven years in the Regiment,' he waffled, from the passenger seat, 'but this has hit me the hardest. Al meant a lot to me. He thought about the moral side of our work.'

I thought I'd better not tell him about the water-wings.

We talked about military funerals in general. I wasn't a big fan. Normally it's a coffin draped in the Union flag, and lots of 'Jerusalem' and 'I Vow To Thee, My Country'. Rarely a sermon, but often a eulogy from a friend.

Frank smiled. 'Yeah, but I bet you always say the prayers, don't you?'

'I join in on the amen.'

'Don't you even listen to the prayers, Andy? Listen and try to understand what they mean?'

'Of course not. I'm thinking about the man, and how he died. Prayers mean nothing to me, even when the flag's being folded and they get to the burial bit. I just think about the lad. For me, the only significant thing is when the bugler plays the Last Post. And that's nothing to do with religion, Frank – that's to do with the man, isn't it?'

Frank nodded. 'My wife was very upset when Al was buried. She really got on with him. Did you know that?'

'Yes, mate, you told me.'

'She was angry. She thinks most of the people I work with are animals. Al was the only decent one she met.'

'Including me?'

'Yeah, of course. But look at everyone. They're lost, and so are you. Nish just farts for England and hasn't got a thought in his head, and—'

'Come on – Nish?' Frank was wrong. 'What do you think he does with all those copies of *Time* and *The Economist*? Wipe his arse? Or what about taking up the guitar, learning to read music? That's an enquiring mind, mate. I don't see you fighting with him over the *Telegraph* after prayers.'

'If he's got an enquiring mind, why doesn't he use it?'

'He does. It's all a bluff with him, trying to cover up the real Nish. I reckon he feels embarrassed about being clever and a tiny bit privileged, that's all. And maybe he doesn't want to use it the whole time. That's OK too, isn't it?'

Frank was a lot closer to Nish than he was sometimes prepared to admit. Both their fathers had had a drink problem and had made them shit scared when they were kids. And after Al was killed, both seemed to spend more time in their own worlds, slightly detached from the rest of us.

He sat back and put his feet on the dash. 'Maybe. But I just don't feel part of this any more. The Regiment used to feel like my family, but that's changed.'

'So you're replacing it with the Church?'

He laughed. 'Not yet I'm not. I don't have one. I'm still waiting for a white-haired guy to knock on the door and tell me where to go.'

'Then where do you worship?'

'I'm floating around. I've started visiting all the churches in Hereford. Even the Methodists!' He laughed again, but I didn't get the joke.

At least he was lightening up. He told a story of what had happened to him over Christmas leave. 'I knocked on the door of this woman's house – she runs their chapel – and she came out with flour on her hands. I said, "I've just become a Christian, I'm looking for a church." She said, "Couldn't you come back another time and we'll sit down and talk?" I said, "I can't – I'm in the army. I'm going to Ireland in a couple of days and I'm not back until March." I thought that would get me through the door, but she said, "That's all right, I'll still be here." '

'Will you go back when she's finished her baking?'

'I think I might be allergic to flour. I'm going to carry on trying them all.'

It was a light-hearted moment, but I couldn't help thinking that all he was doing was marking time with us until he found something better. That was what it felt like, anyway. 'Frank, do you really want to leave, mate?'

He thought for a while. 'Yeah, I'm ready to move on. God's going to take care of me.' He nodded a bit too vigorously. I didn't believe a word of it.

50

We got the warning order for a job in three days' time. A PIRA weapons hide had been discovered. Int had it that a new ASU was planning and preparing for a hit on an RUC station. The troop were to put in a reactive OP (observation post) and hard-arrest the players who came to collect.

ASUs would only go and pick up their weapons at the very last minute. Often they aborted – not because they'd found out they were going to get hit, but for stupid reasons like somebody having a flat tyre and not making the RV on time.

Sometimes the dickers would look at the target and decide not to take it on because a particular policeman hadn't turned up or there were extra police on duty or, just as suspicious, fewer. To them these were all combat indicators. They were paranoid about us hitting them. If they noticed anything unusual that they hadn't picked up on their recces, they'd bin it. It was a long war; they could wait.

All we could do on this particular job was set up an OP and keep eyes on the hide until the ASU turned up, or the Tasking and Coordinating Group (TCG) pulled us off target. The plan was that Chris would take in a four-man patrol on target the first night and set up an OP. It had to be really close so the patrol could see exactly what was going on, and be able to react quickly once the players had opened the hide – otherwise everybody would be running around in the dark and there'd be a gangfuck. Chris's patrol would stay the first four nights, and then Frank's patrol, including me, would take over for another four – and so it would go on until TCG said to stop.

The two patrols met in the briefing room and Chris, the overall commander, gave a quick sniff and started to give out the orders.

The main problem we always had on this sort of job was working out who was actually carrying out the weapons pick-up. Sometimes an ASU might send out dickers first as cannon fodder, young teenaged lads who'd just walk past the hide and see if there was a reaction. These lads wouldn't even know it was a weapons hide, they'd just be told to walk a route – and they'd do it because they wanted to be in with the big boys. Sometimes they'd actually be told to empty the hide and dump the weapons in a skip or somewhere the ASU could pick them up in safety.

ASUs operated a cell system very much like the French resistance in the Second World War. All information was contained. Even if one of those young lads got lifted, nine times out of ten all they'd know were the names of a couple of other people in their cell. They wouldn't know where the weapons were, who their supplier was or even what the job was. Only one or two people had that in their heads, and would only reveal the details at the last minute. Lifting dickers might compromise not only the job but their lives. They might have been told to empty the hide, and they'd get excited and play with the weapons. As soon as that happened, we had no option but to go noisy.

Chris gave the order, therefore, that we would wait until whoever got onto the hide – whether it was a couple or the whole eight-man ASU – had physically got the weapons and mags out of the ground and it was obvious that they were the ones preparing for the job. The giveaway might be their age or whether they were loading the weapons rather than just playing with them.

There had been a fuck-up in 1978 that no one wanted to repeat. John Boyle, a sixteen-year-old Catholic, was exploring an old graveyard near his family's farm in County Antrim when he discovered an arms cache. He had told his father, who'd passed on the information to the RUC. The next morning Boyle decided to see if the guns had been removed and was shot dead by two Regiment guys who'd been waiting undercover.

Frank got to his feet. 'No. This is supposed to be a hard arrest. You're giving them the opportunity to present a threat. We don't wait until they load up, we arrest them straight away.'

Everybody, myself included, went ballistic. 'Come on, Frank, for fuck's sake . . .'

I knew exactly what I was going to do, whatever Frank said. If they had weapons in their hands and were just metres away, I was going to hose them down. Simple as that.

Things got heated. Most of us believed Frank could be putting other people's lives at risk here. This wasn't about us doing God's work against evil-doers, this was about a four-man patrol taking on anything up to twelve Provisional IRA.

Chris just stood there: water off a duck's back. He was the boss and this was what we were going to do.

After he'd finished the orders, I took Frank to one side. 'Listen, mate, I'm with Chris on this one. I'd rather be judged by twelve than carried by six.'

Frank had calmed down and even smiled. He sat back on the sofa. 'It's not always as black and white as that. I'm not going to kill them. We're there to arrest. We'll do that before they get their hands on any weapons.'

'Then you'd better make sure you take the right decision at the right time, or one of us will get dropped.'

He looked at me very calmly – too calmly for my liking. 'God will guide me, don't worry.'

I left him, and did worry. Not about the job – fuck it, if it kicked off on the ground, we'd deal with it. I worried about Frank. God and our kind of work didn't mix easily. Al had obviously found the right balance for himself. I didn't think Frank had.

Yet, for all that, I admired him for the way he stuck to his principles. It must have been tough to have a conviction that went against the grain of an organization he loved. I knew that, deep down, he didn't really want to get out. He was cutting off his nose to spite his face, and it annoyed me. But, as he'd said, Christianity had been pissing people off for years.

The job was cancelled the afternoon before Chris took the first patrol out. Maybe TCG decided the job wasn't worth it, maybe the head sheds were worried about Frank. We never got to see what Frank would do when push actually came to shove, but by then, I felt, the final nail was already in his coffin.

51

There was a bit of edge between Chris and Frank after the reactive OP job that never happened, but Frank didn't force the issue. Then he was taken off ops for a while to run the desk while Minky was away. The focus of the piss-taking now shifted from his religion to his past as a signaller.

The whole army ran on the tribal system. It bred loyalty and a feeling of belonging that never left you. You could take the boy out of the Green Jackets, but you couldn't take the Green Jackets out of the boy . . . And that was the way it had to be. No one should forget where they'd come from – unless they were a signaller, of course.

By March we were all back in the UK. After a couple of weeks' leave, we were getting ready to go to Oman. Apart from Frank: he was getting ready to go.

I couldn't see the sense of not fighting to keep him in: the Regiment was always keen to recruit good men, and it invested a fortune in training them. Just getting a trooper like me to the point at which I had patrol and entry skills cost more than it did to train a fast-jet pilot, yet when we said we were going to leave, no one asked us why or tried to change our minds.

Frank was an experienced corporal who was about to be made up to sergeant. He may have bored us rigid about God making his decisions for him but he was still one of the best when it came to planning and preparation. And I couldn't help feeling the whole God thing was a phase, maybe even an escape from something.

And he'd brought a hell of a lot to the party. Until he single-handedly opposed the policy, signallers were only allowed to do a three-year tour with the Regiment then had to return to their units. Not only did Frank get the policy changed of scaleys only being allowed to do one three-year tour with the Regiment, he was responsible, too, for the Regiment changing the way they used pistols in CQB (close quarter battle), bringing their standards of combat shooting to a new level.

Frank had come back with phenomenal pistol skills after an exchange tour with Delta Force in the States. Delta had taught him the Weaver Stance, a method developed by Deputy Sheriff Jack Weaver during freestyle pistol competition in the late 1950s. It was adopted by the FBI, then the US military.

'The Weaver' allowed you to shoot much faster and more accurately. Instead of standing square-on to the target with both arms out straight, you stood side-on with your firing arm out straight and the other bent and pulling back. The isometric tension produced by pushing *out* with the stronger hand while pulling *in* with the weaker provided excellent recoil control when the weapon was fired.

Getting old and bold to accept this new Yank method was hard, but the results spoke for themselves. Frank stood his ground, as he did on everything, and got it accepted. Thanks to him being as much of a pain in the arse about the Weaver Stance as he was about his God, troopers could now double-tap a head shot over five metres with four inches of barrel. If Winston Churchill had been around, he might have said that never had so much been owed by so many to just one born-again ginger-haired nutcase.

If you decided to leave an infantry battalion, where a soldier's training would have cost about three quid and a Mars bar, the CO would have sat you down and said, 'Stop, think about it. Think about what you're doing . . .' The Regiment's response seemed to be 'There are thousands who want to take your place, so see yer.'

Then again, maybe they know that from the moment there's doubt in your mind it's time for you to leave. Mentally, you've already gone.

52

We held the traditional auction of Al's kit. Even lads from other squadrons came along to the Paludrin Club, our Naafi in the Lines. Whatever his family didn't want was on display. Chris conducted the proceedings.

There was everything from a pair of socks to the air tank from his diving kit. People buy at stupid prices. The cash either goes to the next of kin or, if it was the dead guy's wish, towards a squadron party. Most of us, including Al, had written it into our will, and had also set aside five hundred quid to foot the party bill.

Al's parachute went for hundreds; I landed up with his Barbour jacket for something like four times what it would have cost in a shop – and I didn't even wear waxed jackets.

There was one more ceremony to be performed. During an evening down town Frank was presented with a glass tankard and a nine-inch statue of a trooper in freefall gear. 'Here you go,' Chris said, with a sniff. 'See you around.'

Everyone asked Frank about the Sri Lankan job he'd lined up, but mostly what they wanted to know was: 'Why are you getting out?' He fielded every question with the usual platitudes.

On our second day back from leave, Frank came into the

Lines to collect his kit. Each squadron had its own block, but the combination of industrial carpet tiles and meshed-glass fire doors provided a unifying theme. The living accommodation consisted of one-man rooms with white Formica cupboards, a sink, a bed and a couple of shelves; there were showers and toilets at the end of the corridor.

The bottom floor of B Squadron's block was mainly for lads who lived out but needed somewhere to store their kit. People cycled in or ran, had a shower, got dressed. The singlys lived on the top floor, but usually not for long. This was Thatcher's Britain. Everybody was encouraged to get out and buy a house, and Hereford was probably the only place where a soldier could do that. Special Forces pay was good, and you knew that, fingers crossed, you'd be based there until you were forty.

My room faced Frank's across a corridor. I was sorting out my gear for Oman, and he was packing his plywood MFO (Movement, Forces Overseas) box. I was going to give him a hand bunging it in the back of his estate car.

It was about eight o'clock and everybody else was out for the night. I looked at him in his tracksuit as he minced about inside his locker. 'Frank, this Sri Lankan job, it's not exactly godly, is it? You could stay here and do the same thing, couldn't you?'

He didn't look up from his packing. 'Ah, but I can't stay, can I? I want to move on and find a church, remember?'

'Man can't live by bread alone, eh?'

'Yep, you got it. I've still got to pay the mortgage, and the kids are going to need shoes. Maybe I'll go to college when I'm sorted, study theology.'

'Become that ayatollah?'

He stood back from his MFO and smiled.

I nodded at the beret and the other stuff in his hand. 'You won't need that stable belt now, will you?'

The new-style belts were much thinner than the old ones, and the metal buckle with the winged dagger was tinnier.

Being a new boy, that was what I'd been saddled with.

It disappeared into the box with everything else.

'Are you leaving because of Al? Is that what this is about?'

He shook his head. 'I told you. I don't belong here any more. Something else is filling my life.'

'Ah, right. And you're still immortal, are you?'

'We all are.'

'So that night Al died, how come you sent me ahead to flush them out of the hedgerow?'

I thought at first that God hadn't given him the answer to that, but I was wrong. 'Because I wanted to be the one to kill whoever killed Al.'

He then went off on one about Ken, the job that night, and why Al shouldn't be dead.

Fuck this. I felt all right being part of the squadron. I'd been there nearly a year now and my feet were firmly under the table. I'd proven myself. Besides, I'd been a sergeant in the infantry before I'd come here. I'd already killed, had already had to make hard decisions on operations.

'Frank, I've got to tell you – everybody always has a better plan than the one that's going to be used. Why? Because they know it's never going to be put into practice, so they can say what the fuck they like. They can gob off till the cows come home that their idea is better. And you know what? It gets even better with hindsight – the plan that never has to be used.'

I found myself ranting, because he was wrong.

'The fact is we all need a leader. Ken was the boy that night. He was there making the decision, one way or the other. You're just angry and frustrated, mate. You're angry with Al for being a Christian all along and not telling you. You're angry because he's dead. You may even be angry because you and your God couldn't save him. But you really need to get over it.'

Frank didn't answer. He turned away.

'So, you giving me that stable belt, or what?'

After several long moments he fixed me with his cornflower blue Bambi eyes.

'No.'

53

April 1985
Oman

We landed at Seeb International, just outside the capital, Muscat. I was excited about the three months that lay ahead. The whole squadron was going to practise desert warfare, and the Ice Cream Boys would be working beneath clear sunny skies. There was a lot of operational stuff like HALO (high altitude, low opening) to be done, but Nish was generally talking up the fast glide, the freefall part of the trip.

Most of the squadron had been to the Middle East before, whether on operations, team jobs, or training someone else's army. They were at home here, and I was finally feeling at home with them. I saw a lot of Nish's friends.

We stood around on the tarmac waiting for our transport and trying out our new sunglasses. You don't get country briefs when you go away: you're expected to have done your own homework. I'd found out that Qaboos bin Said al-Said had overthrown his father in 1970 with a bit of British help, and had ruled as sultan ever since. The population was about three million, and the borders stretched over a thousand kilometres. It was a big old place.

Oman was bordered by the United Arab Emirates to the north, Saudi Arabia to the west, and Yemen to the south. The Arabian Sea lay on its eastern coastline, which faced India and part of Iran. The northern coast beyond Muscat, the Musandam peninsula, dominated the Strait of Hormuz, a major political and economic flashpoint in the Arabian Gulf. It was through here that the bulk of Middle Eastern oil flowed daily to run the free world's economy. Capture the Strait of Hormuz, and you could hold the Western world to ransom.

Up north were the vast, rugged mountain ranges of the hot, parched interior, but down in the south, between the sand seas, we were on the same longitude as Bangalore. They even had a monsoon season.

It hadn't taken much to discover the big things here were oil and natural gas, for which the leading customer was Japan. Or that it was a totally Muslim country, although the sultan was liberal. Alcohol was for sale, and in the cities women were allowed to wear Western clothes.

The Regiment had been founded in the deserts of North Africa in the Second World War and operating in Oman for years. Technology might have come on in leaps and bounds, but the principles of desert warfare hadn't. There was this stuff called satnav knocking around, but nobody really trusted it. The military had been using it since the late seventies, but the equipment was bulky and needed lots of power; great if you were on a warship, but not so handy on foot or in a wagon. Smaller satnavs were being developed for Special Forces, but they were still the size of house bricks. Their batteries ran out far too quickly, and the equipment constantly malfunctioned. It wasn't soldier-proof so got regularly smashed. It would never catch on. The best navigation aids were the skills the lads had relied on in the Second World War, when all they'd had were stars, compasses and piss-poor maps.

It wasn't long before the Omani Army turned up with a fleet of British-made Bedford four-tonners and we rattled off into the interior. In the middle distance, huge mountains pushed up against a perfectly clear blue sky. I'd been half expecting sand dunes and Lawrence of Arabia, but this terrain was hard-core. Elbows and knees would get torn to shreds out here.

54

We pushed along a single-track tarmac road across a vast rocky plain that stretched for miles in every direction. Sixteenth-century forts, built by the Portuguese when Oman had played an important role in the slave trade, rubbed shoulders with villages of mud and straw.

After an hour we came to a tented camp in the middle of nowhere. It was protected by wire fences, and looked just like the set of *The Great Escape*. Schwepsy was going to love this. He could play prison guard.

For the first three days we bedded ourselves in. The old hands had seen it all before, but as far as I was concerned even unpacking a .50-calibre machine-gun and mounting it on a Land Rover was new and exciting. The only thing I wasn't happy with was the early-morning temperature. It took the sun a good twenty minutes to get the place warmed up. I must have lizard DNA.

Tiny quickly developed a routine. The moment he woke, he sat up in his sleeping-bag in our twenty-man tent and shouted, 'I'm bored. Where's Frank?'

He wasn't the only one who missed having him around, if only to take the piss.

'He had to go.' Nish summed up the situation from his bed

one morning. 'Frank's trouble is that he's a complicated mixture of happy warrior and embittered pacifist.'

Tiny wasn't too fussed about what Frank was. He still had the second half of his routine to perform. He'd get up, stick his head out of the tent flap, and look back, surprised. 'Turned out nice again!'

It made me laugh every time, but perhaps that was because he wasn't calling me a crap hat any more.

Paul missed *Countdown*, but I reckon that had more to do with Carol's perky consonants than the mental exercise.

Some of the scaleys missed their workouts so much they rigged up a makeshift gym. They hit the punch-bag stupid every afternoon, then did several hundred chin-ups and went for a run. Ken tried to join in, but the scaleys didn't roll out the welcome mat. They knew it was only a matter of time before he got bored with the bag and was challenging them to a fight instead.

The banter was non-stop. They were scaleys and we were blades or Jedis. The Force was with us. So was the food. A couple of local lads kept us in chapattis, while the cooks knocked up the rest of the scoff on their number-one burners, which flared like rocket jets along a narrow trench capped with huge dixies.

Most of the talk as we shook out was about freefall. The big one was CRW: not the Counter Revolutionary Warfare Wing, but Canopy Relative Work, the trick of flying your canopies towards each other and linking up.

'We need to get the troop stack going,' Nish announced. 'We need a holiday snap.'

Everybody groaned.

'No, we can do this. It'll be a laugh. We get someone to fly base. The second lad wraps his legs into the first lad's rig lines, then slides down them until it looks like he's standing on his shoulders. And so on. We'll have the whole troop stacked by the end of the trip, easy!'

It might have been easy for him, but they hadn't taught me anything like this at Brize Norton or Pau. All I knew was that the more guys joined the CRW stack, the slower the forward speed became, but the faster the descent. That was why the best jumper joined last.

Nish stretched out on his camp bed. For once he wasn't smoking; standard operating procedures (SOPs) didn't allow it under canvas. He pointed at me. 'New boy goes first. Just keep on your heading and I'll come in to you.'

Harry, the Royal Marine Adonis, burst in. '*Raus! Raus!* Ve hef found an escape tunnel.'

I didn't have a clue what he was on about. We followed them out to the perimeter wire, where Hillbilly was balancing a pair of upside-down jungle boots on the edge of a man-sized hole that went down about three feet. A sign above it, made out of a Figure-11 target, said, 'Eight Troop's escape tunnel.' Hillbilly was Six Troop, but he was probably the only one who could spell. We took bets on how long it would take Schwepsy to spot this and send down the Alsatians.

Harry rounded up the guys from the Mountain Troop tent. He wanted them to pose for a sign of his own that he'd hung above the main gate. It said: 'Stalag 13'.

We watched as he lined them up along the wire. They had to dangle their wrists through, and stare longingly towards the mountains. The sad thing was, the dickheads probably couldn't wait to get out and climb them.

55

Once we'd shaken out, it was time to get on with training. We were going to work first with our support weapons – the 81mm mortar, .50-calibre machine-gun and GPMG in its sustained-fire role. I knew the GPMG and .50 cal like the back of my hand after my years as a rifle-company infantryman. I also knew about the capabilities of the 81mm mortar and how to call them in for a fire mission. I'd just never fired one.

Ken sent me to join the mortar training group, and it turned out we had a bit of a head start. Nish had been in his battalion's mortar platoon back in Para Reg days, so he became No. 1 in Seven Troop's mortar team, Paul was No. 2, and I was No. 3. That meant I started off lugging the ammunition and putting my fingers in my ears when the thing went off, but I soon got to learn how to set the thing up and aim it.

The 81mm was still the backbone of fire support in any infantry battalion, lobbing as many as twelve rounds a minute about five kilometres. It could be man-packed in three loads, but mortar detachments were normally vehicle-borne. We piled everything into the Land Rover 110s, including more ammunition than my old battalion would have been allocated in about ten years, and moved out into the desert to play.

Like everything else we did, the sessions were fantastically un-army. There was nobody standing behind you insisting on safety checks and correct procedures. All we did was load a 110 with kit, drive into the desert and have a cabby.

We wasted no time keeping up the image of the Ice Cream Boys. We were in shorts, trainers and sunglasses, and out came the bronzer. 'I hate firing mortars in sand,' Paul moaned, as he brushed his arms. 'Sticks to the Ambre Solaire.'

Chris was our mortar fire controller. Each troop had one on the line, and each troop had a tube. We set the four tubes up about fifteen metres apart. The MFCs gathered in a little cluster behind us, under a bunch of old Martini parasols, and waffled away like a bunch of washerwomen. Chris had chosen well. He just barked the occasional fire-control order, then sat back with the others among the piles of ammunition and iceboxes loaded with food and drinks.

The mortar's range was set by the angle of the barrel and the amount of energy supplied by a series of explosive charges. Plastic rings of propellant a bit like horseshoes were wrapped around the stem. There were seven to start with; the more you left on, the further it flew.

What it does at the other end depends on the type of round: high explosive, smoke or illume. The HE fuse can be set for air burst, against enemy out in the open; delayed, when the round penetrates before detonating; or instantaneous, when it explodes as soon as it hits.

Nish and Paul could do all the jobs blindfolded. Even in a pair of running shorts and with a cigarette hanging from his mouth as he hunched over the optic sight, Nish didn't put a foot wrong. Then he'd laugh it off, as if none of it really mattered. His meticulousness seemed to embarrass him.

56

After three days of hosing down the desert, we were getting on-scheme and it was time for a competition. We built a series of sangars about a kilometre away. They were essentially trenches with rock protection around and above them, just like the Adoo had had. The object was to drive along in your 110, stop on command, jump out as a three-man team, assemble the mortar, fire, and score a direct hit with rounds on a delayed fuse. All the firing orders would come from your own troop MFC, ice lolly in hand, basking in the shade of his Martini parasol.

As we arrived with the mortar tube, base plate and ammunition, Chris started off with a fire mission. 'Immediate action!'

The guys waiting their turn sat back, jeered and threw rocks at us.

Paul threw the base plate to the ground, grabbed the aiming post and ran about fifteen metres towards the target while Nish married the mortar's ball joint into the socket at the centre of the plate. I held out the bipod for the barrel to rest against and closed the retaining collar around the tube. Nish attached the optic sight, lining it up with the aiming post to gauge bearing and direction.

I pulled the large green plastic cylinders of ammunition, welded together in pairs, from their metal containers, stacked them on top of each other and undid their caps.

Rocks and insults were still heading our way big-time. 'Come on, you dickheads, get on with it.'

Chris shouted the fire order: 'Direction – one six four.'

Nish adjusted the sight. 'Direction – one six four.'

Chris peered into his little handheld computer. 'Elevation – one two two eight.'

Nish spun the dials. 'Elevation – one two two eight. Number one – ready!'

There was a volley of rocks.

Chris removed the ice lolly from his mouth and checked his handheld computer. 'Two rounds, charge three – stand by!'

It was my turn to scream. 'Two rounds, charge three!'

I pulled out the first round, ripped off four rings of propellant and threw them into the empty ammunition box, passed the round to Paul and prepared the next. He removed the safety pin and put it into the plastic ammunition cap to keep tally.

I jammed my right foot onto the base plate to steady it, we threw two rounds down the tube to bed it in and Nish re-adjusted the sight accordingly.

'Enemy troops in trenches!' Chris was getting positively expansive.

That meant I had to twist the fuse at the point to 'Delayed'.

'Six rounds – fire!'

We loosed off one every five seconds.

There was a chorus of jeers as all six dropped around the sangar but not one went in.

I started to clean the tube as Boat Troop ran down from their 110, set up and fired their two bedding rounds.

They scored a direct hit with the second round of their six. They jumped up and down, and made sure we knew everyone outside Boat Troop was a wanker. Later, Mobility and

Mountain also failed to get a hit, so Boat Troop won. Not a prize, they just won. That was what it was all about.

During the next couple of weeks, while we were playing about with the .50 cal and the GPMG, Ken managed to get hold of a Huey from the Omanis. The pilot came and picked us up whenever he could.

When you jump from an aircraft, the slipstream throws you out and you've got something to fight against. Jumping from a helicopter is the same as jumping off a building. You feel yourself gathering speed, but there's no initial resistance to work with. I found it very hard to get myself stable until Nish took me aside after the first couple of jumps. 'Just imagine you've got a big beach ball in front of you and you're trying to wrap yourself around it so you can slip it a length.' He grinned. 'Bend over it and really try and give it some. That curved shape as you hump is what gets you stable.'

Nish wandered around with an I-don't-give-a-fuck attitude, but actually he did. He'd been extremely sharp on the mortars, and was almost godlike when it came to jumping. The weird thing was, he didn't seem to give a shit about himself. He cut his hand one day, but didn't deal with it. 'I'd better clean that up later,' was all he said, but he never did. I was gaining the impression that, as well as being embarrassed about his intelligence and education, he didn't like himself that much.

After four or five goes at shagging the giant beach ball, I was getting stable straight away, grabbing air and sorting myself out. I felt like a kid who could suddenly ride his bike without stabilizers.

We drove out into the desert on the last day to RV with the Huey. We set fire to a pile of tyres and diesel oil to give us smoke, then jumped with civilian sports rigs. The lads all had their own, and Nish had brought me his spare. They were smaller and lighter than military ones; they just had to carry a body and no equipment. As a result they were faster, and you could spin around and play about a lot more in the air.

I had to learn how to pack them. The RAF controlled military parachuting, and never let jumpers pack their own chutes. Again, Nish showed the way. He told it simply, so I learnt quickly. He wanted to bring on people like me. Nish was fascinated by flying, not just freefall. He wanted to understand the theory and mechanics of it, and the heli pilot would end up spending just as much time on the ground, explaining how the thing flew, as he did in the air.

We got a last jump in just before the sun went down, and packed the rigs again in the light of the burning tyres. Nish sorted the lines that led from the rig up to the canopy. He turned to Chris. 'You know what, mate? I miss Frank. It's fucking weird without him. What about you?'

Chris just gave a sniff. 'No, not really. He's gone. Fuck it.'

'No, mate. Feels different, feels different.' Nish shook his head. 'I miss Al even more . . .'

57

One of the scaleys slipped on some rocks and broke his ankle – either that or Ken finally got the chance for a little contact sport. Nish was unfortunate enough to be the one walking past the squadron HQ tent when the sergeant-major needed an ambulance driver for a trip to Muscat.

We got wind of it before the casualty was even in the wagon, and handed Nish a king-size shopping list. 'And try and get a cool box.' Tiny counted out some rials. 'Fill the fucker with ice cream and beer.'

A few hours later, Nish burst back into the tent. He was all smiles but empty-handed.

'Where's the cool box?'

'Get this – they pay for blood. I just gave two pints. I'm a bit dizzy, but so what? It's over thirty quid a pint.'

Tiny was already on his feet, and it wasn't to demand his rials back. 'We get tea and biscuits?'

'Even better. Chocolate digestives.'

Done.

We went to inveigle the head shed into letting us trundle into the city and do our civic duty. Nish still looked pale but nodded so hard I thought his head would fall off. 'It's organized. The doc's waiting for us . . .'

We grabbed two dusty wagons. We weren't exactly in show-room condition ourselves. Our hair was so matted it stuck up almost vertically. We might have ended up quarantined at the hospital as a health hazard, but for thirty quid a pint it was worth the risk.

We bumped across the desert to the metalled road. Schwepsy sat in the back beside me. After a moment or two I realized that he was vibrating with excitement, and not just about making a big cash withdrawal from the blood bank.

'We rigged it up, you suckers!'

He was bursting to tell us about the 81mm shoot. Boat Troop's mortar team had placed a round in the trench the night before and attached a lump of PE (plastic explosive) to it, then they'd run a command wire to the base plate area and covered it with sand. Schwepsy hadn't taken out the safety pin on their second round. He'd just counted the round down to target, then detonated the one already in the sangar. All that time and effort just to win. We all wished we'd thought of it.

Bastards . . . But it didn't take us long to get our own back.

We were lining up outside the donor room, waiting for the needles to be jammed into our arms. Schwepsy had stopped laughing as soon as he'd smelt hospital. He edged further and further back down the queue.

Nish was first in, and came out three pints lighter than he'd started the day. He clutched his arm and looked like a ghost. 'Tell you what, mate, those needles – they're big 'uns. More like six-inch nails.'

All of a sudden, Schwepsy wasn't so sun-tanned.

Everyone caught on: each of the lads moaned and groaned more vigorously than the last as they came out of the giving room.

Schwepsy swayed. But he still went in. The lure of cash far outweighed the fear.

Fast glide was next on the menu. We'd be practising both

HALO (high altitude, low opening) and HAHO (high altitude, high opening).

If you were jumping HALO, you were already above the location where you were going to operate. You jumped, fell, and opened the canopy as low as possible to avoid radar and minimize time in the air.

With HAHO, you used the canopy as a means of travel. You jumped out at, say, 30,000 feet, deployed the canopy, and used the winds and thermals to take you to where you needed to be. The canopy had a natural speed of about twenty knots, so if you had a fifteen-knot wind behind you, you travelled at thirty-five. HAHO called for extreme-weather clothing and oxygen equipment to survive temperatures as low as minus 40°C, especially when a fifty-mile cross-country descent could take more than two hours.

We flew south to Rustaq. The terrain down there – mainly sand and brush – was much better to land on than a frozen field in the UK. There was a whole spectrum of experience on display, with the now not-so-new boy at one end of the spectrum and Nish at the other – but luckily for me, the troop traditionally started from scratch on a fast glide, then worked its way up.

We jumped clean fatigue – no equipment, no weapon, no oxygen gear, just the parachute – initially from 12,000 feet. The sky was filled with guys tracking, arms back in a delta, steering towards each other so they could link up and fall as a group.

Keeping together in the air wasn't just a crowd-pleaser. You avoided mid-air collisions and ensured you hit the ground together as a patrol – usually tactically, at night, and carrying your own weight in gear. Nish was the master of the art after his time in the Red Freds. The best of what I learnt, I learnt from him.

The first time we landed, he took me to one side. 'Forget what they taught you at Brize, all that rigid star-shape shit. You've got to be flexible. Bring your arms and legs in more.

Use your body; don't use your arms. It'll come, mate, it'll come.'

He lay on his belly in the sand and arched his back. He was dirt-diving, something we all did as we practised our relative work. His arms weren't straight out from his sides like I'd been taught. They were bent, with his hands almost in front of him. His wrists were limp. 'You want them to sway with the wind. Use the stuff, don't fight it.'

Some days we spent hours lying on two-foot by two-foot flat trolleys, practising relative work. You'd get on, arch your back, then propel yourself around with your feet, fine-tuning the linking moves. It wasn't a free-for-all: you flew relative and waited your turn to join in. The most important man was the pin. He was the one who had to fly stable-on-heading so the others could fly to him and stand off until it was their turn to join. The pin wouldn't be the best jumper – he normally brought up the rear. Small wonder, then, that I got nominated for pin and Nish was last.

We spent a couple of days doing nothing but fun jumps. We'd somersault, flip, track, spin, experiment with different ways of grabbing each other. We even did some pin checking, flying over your victim so you were in the vortex immediately above him as he fell. That would make you drop on top of his rig, and you'd both go unstable and tumble. It all helped you to get a feel for the air.

I soon found myself getting into the Ice Cream Boys' swing of things. Each time we landed, we ripped off our jumpsuits and stood around in shorts, boots and shades as we sorted our rigs. We took turns riding a couple of motorbikes cross-country to the nearest medieval settlement in search of ice cream.

The next big challenge was to stop the stuff melting during the thirty-minute return journey. It was Nish who came up with the idea of soaking a couple of Arab *shemags* in water and wrapping them around the plastic box bungeed to the back-rack. As we caned it back across the desert to our C-130, the evaporating moisture acted as a makeshift refrigerator.

58

Most countries don't take kindly to military aircraft encroach-
ing on their air space. They'll scramble an intercept, and if the
pilots don't like what they see they'll hose you down with air-
to-air missiles. On the other hand, commercial 'friendlies' blip
across their radar screens every day of the week. A lot of our
jobs would therefore start with freefalls from military aircraft
flying along commercial air lanes, or from the cargo holds of
commercial jets belonging to colluding airlines. They'd nearly
always involve relative work, and almost never be clean
fatigue.

We eventually started jumping with weapons and full kit,
including a Bergen strapped to our arses. It was a whole new
ball game waddling to the tailgate; the extra weight also
restricted your leg movements in the air and made your body
sit up as you fell. Even so, you could still do relative work – as
long as you packed the Bergen right. Leave just one of the side
pouches open and symmetry was lost. The air caught it and
you spun like a corkscrew.

It only took one fully laden jump for Nish to start fuming. As
far as he was concerned, this wasn't the way to jump with kit.
'It's safer on the front. It helps you fall, gives you a lower centre
of gravity.'

But the crabs' manual said that was the way we had to pack it – on the back.

He argued non-stop with the RAF instructors. 'The whole planet banned this years ago – it's unsafe.'

They didn't budge. The manual was gospel.

The RAF pissed on our parade even more as the week wore on. They'd decided that equipment could be dropped in a big, bulky MFO box, the kind of crate Frank had been packing that day in Hereford. They'd rigged it up with a parachute designed for heavy equipment drops, and insisted it would work.

'All you have to do is jump out and fly relative to it.'

Nish took a suck on his cigarette. 'Which means we can't do any relative work. It'll be like Wacky Races trying to keep with this thing.'

Tactically, it would be a pain in the arse following it, because nobody would have control over the box. Not even the box would have any control over the box; that was why aeroplanes weren't box-shaped.

'Trust us.'

'Jesus fucking Christ,' Nish muttered. 'Two words you never want to hear from the air force.'

They took us to the truck upon which it was proudly displayed. The parachute rig was fitted with an automatic opening device (AOD), exactly the same as ours. As it encountered a specific level of barometric pressure (at whatever height you set), the AOD would pull the pin from the rig and let the canopy deploy.

We used them if we were jumping with equipment at night. It didn't take much to have a mid-air crash when you were tracking in the dark. If two heads collided you might knock yourselves out. The AOD would bang out your rig for you, even if it wasn't guaranteed to save you. As you spun and tumbled, the canopy might become tangled, or the lines so twisted it couldn't fully deploy.

We tried a daylight jump with the RAF's new toy and it just wasn't happening. The box fell at what seemed like more than terminal velocity and skidded across the sky. It was almost impossible to follow.

The moment we were on the ground, we gave the box a good kicking. Tiny tried opening it to see if it contained anything worth having. It was just filled with bricks and general rubbish as ballast. He wasn't impressed.

The RAF insisted we try again. 'Practice makes perfect, lads.'

The MFO box was mounted on a conveyor with stainless-steel runners, ready to be pushed into space. The opening height for the AOD was set at 3,600 feet this time. As soon as we were at 12,000, the loadmaster leant over and pulled the 'cherry' – the red plastic safety catch – from the AOD. We did the same with ours.

Nish sat and brooded over it. He seemed to be in his own little world.

As we neared the drop point, Saddlebags and I got up and stood by the bundle. No waddling: this time we were jumping clean fatigue.

While everyone else jumped with racing jockeys' goggles – much smaller and with vents on both sides – I still had the standard-issue monsters with no ventilation, so I had them lifted as usual, to clear the condensation. Next trip I was going to make sure I had a Gucci pair, to go with my own rig.

We got the 'ready' and 'set'. On the 'go', Saddlebags and I pushed the bundle off the tailgate and followed it out, tracking down fast and steep, but it was a lost cause. The fucking thing somersaulted and scudded across the sky, like a suitcase falling off a roof-rack on the fast lane of the M25.

Nish came screaming past us like a bolt of lightning, arms swept back. At first it looked like he'd crashed straight into the box, but he managed to get alongside it and gave us a thumbs-up before pushing himself away and dumping his canopy with the rest of us at 3,600.

Saddlebags and I looked round for the bundle. It wasn't above us. We looked down.

The canopy hadn't opened.

It plummeted towards the desert floor.

By the time I'd sorted myself out and joined the CRW stack, bricks and debris were strewn in a huge circle all round the point of impact. Such a nice box. What a shame.

We landed within twenty metres of each other and Nish was laughing his bollocks off. By the time we'd stuffed our rigs into their bags and were waiting for the transport, he still hadn't stopped.

'That's enough of that fucking bundle jumping, eh?'

In the middle distance, the C-130 came in to land.

'How did you do it, Nish?'

He grinned. 'Spare cherry. When I tracked in, I stuffed it into the AOD. Safety catch back on. I'd better go and collect it before the crabs turn up.'

59

Nish mightn't have been too happy with things, but I was. This was the stuff of recruitment posters. Sometimes I'd be floating under the canopy as the C-130 landed on the desert strip below me. Sometimes I'd be eyeballing the little Portuguese forts and watchtowers on the hillsides, looking like something out of the Crusades. History was all around me. I loved this game.

We moved on to jumping with oxygen, from 18,000 feet, then 24,000, going higher and higher. Unfortunately, gas has a tendency to expand as you climb, and where Nish led, we followed. The back of the aircraft stank like a drain; everybody farted uncontrollably.

You had to make sure your teeth were in good nick for the same reason. Any air in a tooth cavity would expand. It wasn't unheard of for teeth to explode. Guys had also been badly injured when they flew with blocked sinuses.

Until the last minute, we were breathing oxygen supplied by the C-130. Two RAF jumpmasters moved around with orienteering torches attached to their heads, glowing a dim red so as not to destroy our night vision. Each had an umbilical trailing from his face mask, and their hands moved instinctively to make sure it didn't get snagged or detached from the oxygen supply.

The inside of the aircraft was totally unpressurized, so masks had to go on at 12,000 feet. And the higher we went, the colder it got.

One particular night, we were jumping from 24,000 feet. I checked my alti, one on each wrist. They weren't the old Lancaster-bomber type now but small plastic commercial ones. Like pretty much all sports gear, they were much better than standard issue. We were just below jump height. The command came to rig up. Because of the noise, the jump-masters did this by holding up A4 flashcards and illuminating them with their red head torches. These were always presented in a set order to cover all the safety checks.

I pushed my Bergen behind my legs and put my boots through the shoulder straps, attaching the hooks on each side of it to my rig's harness. I was carrying in excess of a hundred and fifty pounds now. Besides my parachute, I had twenty-four pounds of GPMG rigged up along the left-hand side of my body. The main butt was detached so it didn't stick up above my shoulders and get in the way of the canopy lines, and secreted in my Bergen, along with four hundred rounds of ammunition, weighing another twenty-four pounds, spare batteries for the patrol radio and, of course, my own kit.

We detached our oxygen masks from the main console and switched to personal bottles. They held just twenty minutes' worth and were attached to a belly-band.

We got the order via flashcard to stand. The Bergen hung upside-down from the bottom of my rig. I tightened the shoulder straps around my thighs so I would be able to use my legs to fly. With so much weight hanging off me, my back wanted to arch. The main jumpmaster talked to the flight deck on his head mike, and the tailgate yawned open. Even though I had a helmet on, I heard the massive rush of air, and then a gale was thrashing at my jumpsuit. Far below, just the odd pin-prick of light punctured the inky blackness way in the far distance.

The aircraft pitched left and right and gained and lost height continuously as the pilot lined it up towards the drop zone. We were formed up in two lines just short of the tailgate. I was number three in the left-hand line. We got the order to move, and the two lines leant into the weight before waddling forward like ducks. I had to grip the back of Tiny's rig for support.

The front lads, Nish and Chris, got their toes right on the edge of the tailgate. We braced ourselves as the aircraft swayed from left to right and the wind tugged.

The jumpmaster commanded the final pin check. I ripped open the Velcro flap on the back of Tiny's rig to eyeball the steel ripcord pin that kept his canopy in place. Easier said than done in the dim red glow – and by now my oxygen mask was soaking wet inside and my goggles were starting to steam up.

Tiny's pin looked good. It was positioned correctly and there were no obstructions to stop it being released from the rig. When Tiny pulled his handle, the steel wire would in turn pull the pin cleanly from the rig and open up the flaps that hold the canopy inside it. Under pressure from a spring, the drogue chute would be forced out of the rig and grab air. The drogue, in turn, would pull out the main canopy and lines attached to the rig.

I hit him on the right shoulder to let him know. I got the same from Paul behind me.

The two jumpmasters were now fixed to the fuselage via a webbing strap and stood on the edge of the tailgate gripping both Chris and Nish to stop them falling as the aircraft lined up on target. They soon thrust two fingers in the front guys' faces, and yelled. Nish and Chris semi-turned and did the same to the two men behind, and it went down the lines.

Two minutes!

It had to be a yell. You can only just about hear it above the wind rush and the din of four screaming turboprops and, of course, we were wearing oxygen masks.

I pushed up hard against Tiny as the aircraft rocked from

side to side. Beyond the open tailgate, there were no longer any pinpricks of light as reference. The sky and ground were one and the same.

I stared at the jump light consoles to the left and right of the tailgate. The two bulbs were unlit.

My goggles had steamed up again. I kept my left hand on Tiny, and with my right I lifted the lenses to let some air in.

'Red on! Red on!'

The red jump lights blazed each side of the tailgate.

Every one of us turned and screamed it to the guy behind him, in front, to anyone who was listening.

'Red on! Red on!'

The red lights changed to green.

Everybody screamed together: 'Ready . . .'

'. . . set . . .'

We rocked back in unison.

'. . . go!'

We pushed to the tailgate in a fast waddle, each guy propelling the one ahead. Tiny disappeared instantly into the blackness and I tumbled out behind him.

The aircraft's slipstream picked me up and took me with it. I felt huge relief as the weight came off, but I was upside-down and still being buffeted around in the slipstream. I spread my arms and legs and arched my back. Immediately, I flipped over into a stable position.

My goggles demisted instantly. Moving your head is about the only thing during freefall that doesn't affect your stability. I looked around, trying to spot other bodies in the pitch black.

It was going to be a two-minute freefall. I had just 120 seconds in which to find someone to link up with, and to try to make sure I didn't crash into anyone or they did to me. I knew they were just a few metres away as I stared into the darkness, but I still couldn't see a thing. The exposed skin on my face wobbled under the pressure of falling.

Some of the stars above me were blocked off for a second as someone tracked left to right above me.

My body jerked as someone gripped my arm and pulled me towards him.

Then another pair of hands from the darkness broke my right-hand grip to join in.

We held each other's jumpsuits, not knowing who was who, lengthening our legs to push ourselves closer together.

At 4,000 feet, we shook each other's arms, let go, turned, and tracked away from each other quickly to get some distance before opening.

I checked my luminous alti, and pulled the right-hand handle at 3,600.

The rig wobbled a little from side to side as the drogue pulled out the main canopy.

I waited, but got no bang from a frying-pan. It was more of a dribble as I got pushed upright; there wasn't any force. I was hanging in a sitting position.

60

My hands shot to the steering toggles. I ripped them off their Velcro and pumped both down rapidly in an effort to expose the canopy and help it grab some serious air. Sometimes they needed a couple of tugs to unfold.

Nothing happened. I knew I was still falling too fast. I looked up. It was too dark to see anything. I might have had a big bundle of laundry above me.

I looked down. There were no points of reference, just the rush of wind. I didn't need to check my altis to know I was well below 3,000. I had about thirty seconds to go before I hit the ground.

I couldn't think of anything else to do but scream, 'Shiiiit!'

As if that was going to help.

I kept on plummeting downwards. I stood a good chance of crashing through someone else's canopy and taking us both out.

I had to cut away.

I'd never done it before. I didn't want to do it now. But I'd run out of options.

I let go of the steering toggles. One hand went for the red cutaway pad on my right, the other for the reserve handle on my left.

I couldn't stop myself screaming again; as I grabbed I banged out my right arm as fast and hard as I could to cut away the main chute at the risers.

Immediately I fell even faster.

I was almost in a sitting position because of the Bergen, and it was starting to drag me backwards. I didn't want that. The emergency rig was on my back.

I yanked the left handle across my body. I could feel the risers of the reserve moving up and then – *bang!* – frying-pan time.

This wasn't a square canopy, just a basic round one. I had no control of it – not that I gave a fuck at that precise moment. The big problem was: it was so much smaller than the main canopy and I was carrying so much weight that I was still falling too rapidly. I had some other things to do.

I didn't waste time checking my alti. I had to release my Bergen or I was going to break my legs when I landed – at the very least. It was still down by my arse, attached by the two hooks to my harness. I pushed down the release arms and the bundle dropped the fifteen-feet length of its retainer rope. When I heard it hit the ground, I'd have a split second before my boots did the same. Then, with my feet in a proper parachute landing position, just like they'd taught me on my static-line course, all I could do was accept the landing.

The Bergen thumped into the ground. Then, feet and legs together, shoulders in, teeth clenched, chin tucked into my chest, so did I.

I came in like a bag of shit. I grabbed a few lines and pulled them in to make sure the wind didn't catch the canopy and drag me along the desert.

All done, I just lay there for a few blissful seconds as my goggles steamed up once more. It was pitch black. I couldn't hear or see a fucking thing.

I undid my rig, laid the GPMG to one side, undid my Bergen, de-rigged everything and bagged it up. I dug around for a head torch and tried to get my bearings. Without the ability to steer to the drop zone, I'd probably drifted miles off-course.

I got out my Firefly emergency beacon and sparked it up. It gave out rhythmic bursts of high-energy light. Sooner or later somebody would find me.

It was about twenty minutes before I saw the welcome lights of a wagon. A little while later, a four-tonner pulled up. Nish was driving. Paul, Chris and Tiny were also aboard.

For once, Nish wasn't grinning. Normal service was resumed, though, once it was established I was OK. 'There you go – fucking crap hat.' Tiny lifted my rig for me. 'It's gonna cost you.'

Have a malfunction, I discovered, and it was a bit like getting a hole-in-one. The Milky bars were on me. I thought, Shouldn't it be the other way round?

Nish stuck an arm around my shoulder. 'Listen, mate, no one packs a malfunction into the main so you can practise. You just have to wait for them to happen. You're going to have many more.'

He helped me with my gear and as we put it on the back of the four-tonner, he said, 'I bet that was the way Al would have wanted to go.' He looked away. 'If only I'd checked that guy jumping over that gate . . .'

Tiny shook his head in exasperation. 'Nish, for fuck's sake, stop. He's dead. Leave it.'

But, increasingly, Nish couldn't leave it. The fun and piss-taking were a smokescreen, a layer of bullshit to cover up the bad feelings. He would walk out into the night saying he wanted a smoke, but it was obvious he wanted to be with his own thoughts.

I think he really did blame himself for Al's death. He didn't need to, but nothing we could say would change that.

61

With just a couple of weeks left in Oman, the OC, whose name really was Rupert, got all sixty of us into the HQ tent to explain a new squadron rotation system. There was going to be a composite troop over the water. It would be made up of guys from each squadron, and the tour lasted a year. At some stage, everybody would have to get it under their belt. But what they were looking for now was experienced guys to step up to the plate.

I knew I stood no chance. I was too junior. I had my infiltration skill, but still lacked a patrol skill.

Nish and Hillbilly were bouncing around, but Schwepsy kept pretty quiet. He was thinking about getting out. He wasn't alone. The Regiment was like a feeder to the private security companies. Nobody got judgemental about it. If you'd been in for a while and a good job came up, you just had to do the maths. Schwepsy had told me that when Frank left.

It wasn't the first time I'd heard talk about the Circuit: the handful of really good outfits that had contracts all over the planet, for bodyguarding, advisories, on-the-ground fighting, you name it.

A lot of the guys had left after Operation Storm and gone straight back to highly paid jobs in Oman, training the army to keep the Adoo at bay down south, though the choice option at the moment was the one Frank had in Sri Lanka. The Tamil Tigers were getting seriously sparked up, and there was bound to be a lot of work. People were trying to find out how much Frank was paid, and how long-term it was likely to be.

I was very happy where I was. The squadron was going to split up soon and zoom off all over the planet on team jobs, ops taken on by small groups, maybe four, maybe a troop, possibly as many as twenty or thirty. Nine out of ten times they'd be working for the Foreign Office, 'maintaining the UK's interests overseas'. Some would be fighting, some training other Special Forces groups, some sorting out the locals, then going to fight alongside them, perhaps trying to stop an insurgency or start one.

Some already knew what team jobs they were going on but didn't say, and nobody asked. Op Sec (operational security) was important. You only needed to know what you needed to know. Three who didn't know yet were Hillbilly, Nish and me.

Hillbilly sat on an old 81mm ammunition box later that night while Nish stretched out on his camp bed, debating whether or not to go over the water. A hundredweight sack of pistachio nuts stood on the sand between them. The waffle turned to team jobs in general. Nish knew exactly what he wanted. 'Anything in RWW would do me. I'd rather start a war than try to stop one.' He spat a mouthful of shells in Hillbilly's general direction.

I joined in. 'How do you get into RWW? How does that all work?'

Hillbilly did the same trick with the shells. 'You don't get in – they come for you. Nice work if you can get it. But first, me and Big Nose here, we're going over the water.' He shoved Nish away from his nut stash, then leant over and picked up the bag. 'It'll be a laugh.'

'I don't know about that.' Nish's expression had become serious. 'It'll be a chance to hose down a few more of those bastards who killed Al.'

'Nish, shut up.' Tiny put down his book at the other end of the tent. 'It's OK. It's all right, mate.'

Schwepsy appeared, his Aryan locks freshly washed and combed for an SS recruitment poster shoot. 'Guess what?' He helped himself to a fistful of Hillbilly's pistachios, cracked a couple open and spat the shells over Nish. 'Frank's back in H.'

Tiny was busy scratching himself. 'What happened?'

The pistachio-fest gathered momentum. Schwepsy turned to talk to Tiny. I was on the bed opposite so he spat the shells at me. 'Dunno.'

Nish sparked up: 'Probably overdid the ayatollah stuff, shoving it down everyone's neck. That's what's happened – he got binned.'

'Who knows? Who cares? Sounds like a cracking job, though.' Schwepsy bent down and grabbed the bag from Hillbilly. 'You two going over the water?'

Hillbilly shrugged. 'Sure, why not?'

I sat there like a spare prick at a wedding. It was like they were all getting ready for a great party and I hadn't been invited.

Tiny looked at me. 'I know exactly where you're going. Once you've done that scaley course, all crap hats go to F Troop. You'll be back to the jungle, mate.' He gave a chuckle and climbed into his sleeping-bag.

I thought: Fuck me, if he's that happy about it, I have to be worried.

62

Hereford
August 1985

We bummed around for a couple of weeks back in the UK, then everybody went their separate ways. Most went on team jobs; I was trying to get my head around Morse code.

By the end of the ten-week course, I'd be expected to knock out twelve words a minute, minimum. Out on operations we had to be able to communicate with each other – and with Hereford – to encode and decode, use all the encryption radios and make our own antennas. But when satellite comms were down and everything else went to rat shit, the faithful old dots and dashes would still come through. Everything we sent would be beamed to 'receivers', scaleys who lived in an underground bunker surrounded by satellite dishes and machines that went ping. It would be decoded and disseminated. But it always went to Hereford first.

Three weeks in, I could manage about one word every ten minutes. I went down town one Saturday afternoon for a breather. Coming out of McDonald's with a bag and a carton of Coke, I bumped into Frank.

He looked genuinely pleased to see me.

'All right, mate? How's it going?'

The smile slipped. I guessed things weren't going too well.

'Fancy a pint?'

We headed for the Grapes, an old haunt of ours.

'I heard you were back.'

'And I suppose they're all saying it was for preaching the gospel too loudly . . .'

Music banged away on the jukebox. The air was thick with cigarette smoke. Every table was packed with Saturday-afternoon shoppers having a quick steak and kidney pie and chips.

It was a pint of bitter for him, lager for me.

We had to stand inches apart because of the noise. The cornflower blues had lost their sparkle.

'The whole country's just one big minefield. I went there to train, but they wanted me to fight the Tamils – and for no extra money. It wasn't about Bible bashing; it was about not getting my legs taken off for no good reason.'

I got stuck into my Kronenberg and let him carry on bumping his gums.

'I learnt my lesson over the water. And, besides, what the company was paying me was just a third of what the Sri Lankans were paying them.'

'They did spread the word that you were Bible-bashing . . .'

'They would, wouldn't they? They wanted an excuse to get rid of me. I went to a church in Colombo, but that was all I did. I was stitched up.'

'What are you going to do?'

He turned back to the bar, suddenly deflated. 'I don't know.' His tone became aggressive. 'I'm on the dole. Can you believe it? I never asked for anything in my life. They said, "What do you do?" So I told them. Know what job they offered me? Where we just met up. McDonald's. Can you believe that?'

'There's definitely no work? You been that badly stitched up?'

'There's some bits and pieces of bodyguarding about. I'm looking.'

'Look, mate, if you need some cash, I haven't got much, but—'

He lifted a hand. 'It's all right. I've got the dole, and they've given me milk coupons for the kids. That's enough humiliation for one week.'

I racked my brains for the odd word of comfort, but I wasn't the world's best at emotional conversations. We just stood there and did a bit of synchronized gulping.

'You know what, Andy? I think I'm still numb.'

'It can't be a good feeling, getting stitched up like—'

'No, no, no – from leaving the Regiment. It feels like there's nowhere for me to go. I miss the drive into camp every day. I miss the lads. You're the first I've seen. There's just no sort of . . . *clarity* . . . out here. It frightens me.'

'That's because you're a happy warrior and an embittered pacifist.'

Frank's eyebrows nearly disappeared into his hair. 'You been eating dictionaries?'

'Nish's words, not mine. It's how a lad called Graves described his mate, Sassoon. Not the hairdresser, another poet.'

'Well, I'm not Sassoon the poet, I'm Collins the unemployed.'

'You saying you fucked up, getting out of the Regiment?'

He put his empty glass on the bar, and the fire came back into his eyes. There wasn't even a flicker of uncertainty. 'No, not at all. I'm off for a piss.'

I watched the world's biggest liar head off towards the toilet and got another couple in.

63

Airport Camp, Belize
December 1985

Torrential rain pummelled the corrugated-iron roof of the Nissen hut. I felt like I was inside a giant snare drum. The MoD hadn't stretched to air-conditioning in the sweltering heat and humidity of Central America, but they had forked out for some Christmas tinsel and streamers, so we knew they loved us really.

My kit was packed on the floor ready to go. I was going to be back in Hereford in time for Christmas. The weekly RAF Tristar was about to land from Brize Norton with the mail and new bodies. The old ones were heading back to the UK the next day. I had an appointment at Woolwich military hospital. Not Ward 11, Snapper's old hang-out, but to find out what was wrong with my right leg.

I'd been here four months without injury, then done something to my knee on my last patrol along the Guatemalan border. I didn't know what or how, but in the jungle even a simple cut can become a serious problem. Fungi, parasites and exotic diseases battled to prevent your body healing. Within days, the joint had swollen up like a football. When I bent it, pus oozed out, and I could hear the fucking thing creak. Before long I was having trouble moving it at all, and had to be cas-evac'd out.

The rain eased and the drumming subsided. I lay there thumbing through back copies of *Time* magazine. 'SO FAR, SO GOOD,' said this week's cover. 'With candor and civility, Reagan and Gorbachev grapple for answers to the arms-race riddle.' Inside, I read about a bloke called Terry Waite who was flying to Beirut to try to free some hostages: 'An Anglican lay associate, Waite was drawn to the Church, he has said, for "its passionate coolness, its mixture of authority and freedom".' I made a mental note to remember that for next time I saw Frank. He was looking for a church; it sounded like this guy had it sorted.

It was all a bit happier than last week's cover: 'COLOMBIA'S MORTAL AGONY – A volcano unleashes its fury, leaving at least 20,000 dead or missing.'

Maybe *Time* alternated good weeks with bad; the issue before that one had 'HERE THEY COME' over a picture of Charles and Diana. The blissfully happy couple were on their way to Washington for a three-day visit. I could imagine the security frenzy.

The sound of punches and grunts took over from the drumming. A kit bag hanging from a tree outside the huts had been turned into a punch-bag, and Des Doom was giving it some serious stick. He was PVRing (taking premature voluntary release). It cost a couple of hundred pounds to break your contract, but then you were free to go. The trouble was, he'd only been in the Regiment four years, and had been taken off team jobs and sent to Belize for the whole duration of B Squadron's tour as a punishment. He was severely bitter and twisted about it, forever taking it out on the bag. I wondered whose face it was wearing today; he had a fair number to 'talk to'. They all suffered from NBPE – not being punched enough.

I didn't know what he was going to do when he got out; Des

kept his cards close to his tattooed chest. But I was sure it would be as solid as a tank.

The only training facilities apart from the kit bag were some weights – a couple of catering-size baked-bean cans, filled with concrete, either end of an iron bar. After he'd made them the entertainments officer had obviously needed to catch some Zs.

Nish and Hillbilly were over the water. I'd had a letter from Hillbilly to tell me about a two-up, two-down in H that was going on the market after Christmas. The couple was splitting up. The male half of the relationship didn't know this just yet, but the female half had decided not to marry, so they'd be looking for a quick sale. Hillbilly was turning into one of Thatcher's golden children, often buying and selling property before it was even built. He would put down a deposit, and because new builds in Hereford were usually oversubscribed, he'd sell on his reservation to the highest bidder.

The owners of the two-up, two-down weren't the only ones going their separate ways. Nish had split with his wife and she had gone to Cheltenham with their son, Jason.

As a PS, Hillbilly said Nish had progressed from 'The House Of The Rising Sun' to 'Duelling Banjos' and it had been driving him deaf and mad. He'd banished Nish from the room they shared and made him practise in the sauna.

Harry was on a team job somewhere. He was thinking about getting out as well. He wanted to climb Everest, and the only way he could do that was to leave. Unlike other regiments, the SAS didn't grant their soldiers funds or time off for adventure training. It was particularly tough on Nine Troop guys, because they all got mountain lust sooner or later. Instead of pot plants and pictures, Harry's house was decorated with 1930s yoke-style ice crampons and old wooden skis. I couldn't make much sense of that. If I got some walls to hang things on, I'd go for something a bit more interesting than my old parachutes.

Des landed a final flurry of punches and the compound fell silent.

64

Guatemala had been making claims on Belize since the eighteenth century, and F Troop was part of the UK battle group stationed as a deterrent against incursions. There were four guys on aircraft crash standby with the Puma helicopter crew at any given time. The rest of us were out patrolling the border.

I craved that time away from the camp. Garrison life was boring, and neck-deep in bullshit. All there was to look forward to, apart from heaving the baked-bean tins, was tea and toast at 1100 in the sergeants' mess.

We went in four- or six-man patrols, dropped by helicopter, and spent ten to fourteen days on the look-out for Guatemalans.

The maps consisted of vast areas of closely packed contour lines, which were hills, covered in green, which was jungle. There were no proper roads, and very few tracks.

High humidity combined with sweltering heat meant that in theory there was a definite limit to how much kit a man could carry; the maximum should have been around 15 kg, but it could be much more. Mess tins were thrown away, because they were pretty useless things anyway. All that was needed was a metal mug, and a small non-stick frying pan, ideal for boiling rice in.

The most popular weapon to take into the jungle was the M16 or the M203 version that had a 40mm grenade launcher attached under the barrel. They rarely needed cleaning, so we didn't have to waste time and energy trying to keep our weapon in good condition.

One guy never used to touch his M16 at all, out of principle. He said, 'I know that it's going to work, I know that the weapon's reliable, so I don't need to clean it.' And the fact is, if you squeeze the trigger and it goes bang and a round comes out of the end, that's all you want.

I loved our contact with the locals – when it eventually happened. Every time we walked into a village near the border they would scatter. The Guats used to come over the river and steal their women at gunpoint, and to the villagers one set of jungle camouflage looked very much like another.

The kids didn't care if we were Guats or Brits: they just hoped we were there to give them something. They didn't understand us and we didn't understand them, but we had some good fun. The rest of the time they ran around between the huts, or on the small football pitch that was the pride of every village.

Some of these places were just starting to get generators, and visits from American Peace Corps volunteers. Like modern-day missionaries, these fresh-faced twenty-year-olds were bringing in hygiene and preventive medicine, and the lot of the villagers was improving – or so the volunteers said.

The fact was they had lived like this for thousands of years. And now they had new illnesses, a new culture – and religion. The kids now wanted to wear Levi's and smoke American cigarettes instead of spending their lives surrounded by wallowing pigs and scrawny chickens. As soon as they were old enough, they left. You couldn't blame them, of course, but I sometimes wondered whether the price they paid was to have the soul sucked out of them.

There was a commotion in the corridor.

'F Trooooop!'

I'd have recognized that voice anywhere. Tiny had perfected his Snapper impression over the years. He'd come out for a few weeks to cover the changeovers.

He shoved his head round the door, pointed at my fat bandaged knee and laughed. 'I told you you'd hate this place. Some good news, though. Frank's on the Circuit.'

65

Frank must have thought the old guy with the white beard had sprung a miracle. If he'd gone without a job any longer, he'd have been forced behind the counter at McDonald's after all.

He'd been hired by one of the security companies to train up a protection team in Athens. The principal went by the name of Vardis Vardinoyannis.

'Richest man in the Aegean.' Tiny spread himself out on the bed opposite mine. 'Owns Motor Oil. Always under threat, always protected. Extremists have already dropped his brother.'

If Vardinoyannis was that much of a target, no wonder they'd snapped Frank up. He was one of the best shots the Regiment had ever produced.

He hadn't been doing himself many favours over the summer. He'd tried out all sorts of religious groups in his quest to find a replacement for Seven Troop. He even sang in a happy-clappy band in the shopping precinct on Saturday after-noons. Lots of the guys had seen him, and that sort of news travels fast. I supposed you couldn't fault a guy for praising the Lord in public with a smile and a couple of tambourines, but I wondered if he knew how much he might have been denting his prospects.

Tiny had made himself comfortable. 'Can you imagine him with the protection team? All those big black handlebar moustaches, and then suddenly up pops this little mop of ginger.'

The image made me smile, but it meant this Greek, or who-ever was advising him, was pretty smart. Anyone planning a hit on the principal wouldn't pay much attention to Frank. The handlebar moustaches would draw their fire.

That's why female bodyguards were so highly valued. They simply don't look like part of the protection package. But she's not carrying the principal's sandwiches around in that brief-case: it's a Heckler & Koch MP5K that can be fired from the carrying handle; or maybe the whole briefcase is made of Kevlar as a ballistic shield.

BGs had to be pro-active, too, not just waiting for an attack but always anticipating one. What if a car rammed our vehicle a bit further down the road there? What if someone opened up from the crowd just feet away? You had to think like that oth-erwise you were the rabbit in headlights. The Seven Ps came into play with a vengeance.

Good VIP protection wasn't about a lot of heavies looking hard and picking their teeth with stilettos – that's just the show-business version. It was about the stuff you didn't see. It was about making sure that every detail of the principal's movements – where he was going to be, what he was going to do, when he was going to do it – was kept out of the public domain.

Family details, work locations, all that sort of information had to be kept tight. Vehicles had to be secured at all times so no devices – explosive or tracking – could be placed on them. Where did the post go to be checked and verified before it was handed to the principal? It wasn't just letter bombs they had to worry about: gases could be used in a postal attack. If the principal had a drink in a pub, the VIP protection team had to make sure that the glass came home with them, or was washed there and then; poisons could be designed to target a particular human using a sample of their DNA.

Everything had to be protected. If you missed one small component, your principal could be dead.

A businessman was targeted for months on end in Lebanon, but his security was excellent. He never went out without a team, and they always varied the route. The terrorists couldn't get near him, and the vantage-points from where they could see into his compound were too far away for a long-distance shot.

His PA lived outside the compound, in another part of the city. She drove to work in a Citroën 2CV and parked in the admin compound. Gent that he was, her boss came out every morning, regular as clockwork, and helped her inside with her briefcase.

One night, while the 2CV was parked outside her apartment, the players rigged it up with an IED. They trained binoculars on the compound from two kilometres away, and as soon as he went out to open the door for her they kicked it off. They were both killed instantly. All it had taken was just one chink in the armour.

Tiny propped himself up on one arm. 'You'll never guess what else. He got baptized in the Wye before he went away. Big marquee job on Bishop's Meadow.'

The river bisected Hereford. Bishop's Meadow was a park on its banks, with a shingle shore. Frank and his wife had literally taken the plunge. The church rigged up a big tent and turned it into a three-ring circus. Crowds came to see this baptism in the middle of town. Even Central Television was there.

66

Hereford
April 1986

Six weeks of X-rays, injections and physio later, the football around my knee joint deflated without the doctors having had a clue what had caused it. Maybe something had bitten me. There was a week or two more of bruising and creaking, but then I was back in business.

I was promoted to lance-corporal. The extra pay came just in time for me to be able to afford the house Hillbilly had told me about. It was a Westbury starter home: two gas fires on the ground floor, no central heating, and walls so thin I could hear my next-door neighbours flush the toilet. I didn't care: it was mine. Only a matter of time, I said to myself, before I fulfilled my boyhood dream of a place with an acre of land and its own moat.

Chris had already faded from the troop by the time I got back from Belize. By March I was running around Hereford, not doing much except training and wondering if Hillbilly had known that the previous owner of my house was about to walk away because he was shagging her, while the rest of the squadron was running around all over the planet on team jobs.

In June 1985, South African forces had carried out a raid on Gaborone, the capital of Botswana, and twelve alleged ANC members were killed in their sleep. The South African government claimed that ANC guerrillas used it to launch attacks inside South Africa; there had been several mine blasts, which had killed white farmers near the border. The Botswanans said that they did their utmost to prevent ANC military activities inside its borders. They turned to the Brits for help, and I was told to learn Swahili.

I joined Eno, whom I'd met over the water, and about half a dozen others down at the education block each day. The course tutors were a mixture of guys from the Education Corps who were only four lessons or so ahead of us, and two Anglican missionaries who spent more time reminiscing about the good old days than they did teaching us the language.

I didn't mind: it was fun. And I was getting a second patrol skill. If I passed, I'd get extra pay. Every penny helped. The asking price on the house had been twenty-five grand, but the big-time negotiator from South London had haggled it down to twenty-four and a half. To save on bills I still hadn't had the gas reconnected, and boiled water for brews with a hexi burner in the stainless-steel sink. The kettle came from my room in the block.

My furniture consisted of a microwave, a telly, a small stereo, a chair, a bed, and a china ornament of a cat the previous owner had left on the mantelpiece. I didn't need a radio. The party wall became a speaker when my neighbours listened to Radio 4. I bunged all my washing in the laundry at camp, and survived on food from work or cartons of egg fried rice that I collected from the town in my ever-decaying Renault 5. For all that, I was happy. I'd become one of Thatcher's children.

Nish and Hillbilly were still over the water, but I was hearing strange things. Nish kept having run-ins with the head shed over there, and his wingman, Hillbilly, kept having to fend them off. Nobody was too sure what it was all about.

Maybe it was Nish's incessant guitar playing. Maybe he and Hillbilly just didn't like the command structure. There were always problems in a troop made up of guys from different squadrons who hadn't grown together.

Things wouldn't have come to a head like that in Seven Troop. It was small; everybody knew each other; everybody had a voice. Every troop was like that, except the composite over the water. For whatever reason, it sounded like one of the operations people, the guy who was doing the equivalent of Minky's job at the time, had it in for Nish, and Nish wasn't exactly turning the other cheek. He'd been given a couple of chits as warnings: a third strike and he'd be out. I couldn't understand it. This wasn't like Nish. He was far too intelligent, articulate and funny to let himself get into those kinds of arguments. I hoped his wingman could sort it out.

I hadn't heard much about Frank now he was in Athens, so I was really pleased to bump into him again. I was halfway through the six-week Swahili course and wandering round with a fistful of vocab cue cards, mumbling away to myself like an idiot, when he shouted to me from the other side of the road. We landed up in the Grapes again.

Frank looked a lot better than he had last time, and insisted on buying. 'It's all right.' He tapped his jacket. 'I've got some drachmas left over.'

'About time.'

We chatted about various people he hadn't seen for a while, and the big topic of the moment, the nuclear reactor that had exploded at Chernobyl in the Ukraine. Wales and the area round Hereford were thought to be vulnerable to fallout.

'You still on the Athens job?'

'That's all finished.' He handed the barmaid a tenner. Music blared. One or two other lads gave the Bible basher a nod of recognition. 'I had fun in Greece but it was time to go.'

I didn't ask why. The BG world was very fickle. You could

get binned because the principal didn't fancy the smell of your aftershave. Or you had a job for life because he liked playing chess with you.

Frank didn't look at all worried. He had other things on his mind. 'Guess what happened while I was in Athens, though? I finally got to talk in tongues.'

'Oh, right . . . I didn't know you were trying.'

'Yeah, for months. I was going to the Pentecostal Church here, and failed dismally. I was beginning to think I was being punished for some sort of sin in my past.'

I shrugged. There were probably a few to choose from.

'Then all of a sudden one Sunday I opened my mouth and words I'd never heard before came spilling out.'

'I know that feeling.' I held up my cue cards.

'Not Swahili, you twat. I was speaking in tongues. I was talking to God.'

'That's all well and good, mate, but he ain't going to pay you for it. Why don't you give Terry Waite a call? Sounds like he could do with some close protection while he tries to get those Yanks out. And you could do the tongues stuff together, eh? You wouldn't even need an interpreter.'

I started doing a bad impression of a TV evangelist waving his arms at the sky.

It got a smile out of him. 'I don't think he'll be into tongues. He's an Anglican. But, anyway, I've got another job.'

He put his glass back on the bar. He'd seen the expression on my face. 'I was surprised they'd let a Bible basher back on the Circuit as well. It's with Ralph Halpern, the guy who runs the Burton chain.'

I wasn't sure who he was talking about, but Frank couldn't wait to fill me in. 'Britain's most highly paid executive. He's on a million a year plus.'

A radical splinter group of the PLO had issued threats against Europe's top Jewish businessmen, and Halpern didn't want to take any chances. Because no specific threat had been issued against him, he didn't qualify for Special Branch protection. He had to hire his own.

Frank looked smug. 'I was only going to be there for two weeks but they kept me on.'

The music was starting to bounce off the walls. Frank moved a bit closer. 'We're moving to Bobblestock. I'm a yuppie now. Earning good money. Company cars too – BMWs and Mercedes. Things are going great.'

Bobblestock was one of the new estates springing up around the town. Hillbilly probably held deposits on all of them.

'Good stuff. So, still no regrets about getting out?'

He took a bit too long to finish his pint, put down the glass and wipe his lips.

'Nope. Not one.'

67

The Swahili bit the dust for one reason or another, and we started our squadron build-up to take over the team, part of which meant being on standby as back-up for the troop over the water.

The landscape had changed over there. From 1976 to 1983, only nine PIRA players had been shot by the Regiment, but we were taking the war to them, these days, and they were standing their ground. They had plenty to fight with. Once they'd been starved of weapons and ammunition, but now they were awash with Armalites, Semtex, and even heavier stuff like RPGs, machine-guns and flame-throwers. The thank-you letters were being sent on a regular basis to other terrorist groups like the PLO, and rogue states such as Libya – as well as to thousands of naïve Americans.

The Yanks fell hook, line and sinker for the PIRA public-relations machine's portrayal of the island as something akin to the 1950s John Wayne film *The Quiet Man*, with Black and Tans raping and pillaging the poor helpless locals on a full-time basis. PIRA somehow managed to link their brand with shamrocks, leprechauns, fiddles and Guinness, and the dollars poured into the Noraid bucket like they were going out of style.

Even so, during a period when the 12,000 soldiers in the green army only dropped two PIRA players, the twenty-man troop had accounted for eighteen. Ken's choreography of the information war was reaping benefits, without a doubt.

One of the lads from A Squadron was getting married in Hereford and a lot of the others wanted to fly back for the stag night and wedding. I was one of six guys who volunteered to stand in. We flew over in a couple of Pumas, and as we came in to land at the back of the warehouse it felt a bit like coming home.

It wasn't difficult to find Nish. I followed the wavering electronic chords of 'Duelling Banjos' to the same old block, and found myself standing outside Al's room.

I hammered on the door and called Nish's name.

Several megawatts of amplifier fell silent, and were replaced by a very aggressive 'Fuck off!'

He hit another chord.

I banged on the door again. 'Nish, let me in.'

'Who the fuck is it?'

'It's me – Andy. Let me in, for fuck's sake.'

A key turned in the lock, but the door didn't open.

I let myself in to find Nish's room in its usual shit state, but what really worried me was the shit state of Nish. His eyes were glazed. He was in a rage. He looked almost possessed. There were dents in the plasterboard wall and his right hand was bleeding. Blood was smeared over the guitar.

He sat down on Al's old bed.

'What the fuck you doing, mate? You all right?'

He tipped a cigarette from the pack and placed it with difficulty between his fourth and little finger. His normal smoking fingers looked like a pair of freshly grilled sausages. He'd probably broken them on the wall.

'I suppose so. Just getting wound up by that cunt.'

'Who? Hillbilly?'

The smell of sulphur caught in my nostrils as he managed to

light a match. 'No, that fucking sergeant.' His hands shook with anger.

'Where's Hillbilly?'

'He's had to go to TCG. That's why I've locked the door. Without Hillbilly standing in the way, I'm going to drop the cunt.'

Blood trickled down his hand as he smoked, first onto his wrist and then the dark blue duvet. Things had been going downhill. One of the sergeants was rumoured to be on accelerated promotion and that meant that as long as he didn't fuck up within the next few years he might even get a commission. It meant he was playing things by the book, and that wasn't good news for Nish. Nish didn't play things by the book.

'Why don't you just wind your neck in, mate? You've only got five weeks left of this tour.'

They'd had another run-in just before I arrived. Nish being Nish had taken the piss out of him in the briefing room. They'd started arguing, and Nish nearly dropped him. That explained the dents in the walls. Nish had adopted the Des Doom recipe for stress relief.

'Why don't you turn that guitar down a couple of decibels? He's going to come down and bollock you again, and it'll all kick off. You'll just drop yourself in the shit. You touch him, mate, and it's you that's fucked, no one else.'

He covered his face with his hands. Smoke leaked out between his bloodied fingers. 'I know, I know. Fucked up, isn't it?'

He lowered his hands and smiled.

That worried me most of all.

'You've got to calm down. Just a few weeks to go and you're back. Tell you what, I'll get some brews in, and you stop playing that fucking thing. You're shit at it, anyway.'

He nodded, but his eyes glazed over again as he lay back on Al's old bed.

68

I walked down the corridor to the Burco and saw the sergeant hovering outside the accommodation. He was waiting for the guitar to start up again.

I waved. 'All right, mate? I'm just fixing me and Nish a brew. You want one?'

I didn't know him; I just knew of him. I had no idea why he'd been picked out for accelerated promotion, and I didn't really care. All I cared about was Nish.

He hardly gave me a glance.

Hillbilly got back about an hour later. He took one look at the blood on the walls and turned on Nish. 'What the fuck have you been up to now?'

His hair was a bit longer, and he was wearing a black-leather bomber jacket, denim shirt and jeans, but otherwise he looked exactly the same. He gave me a nod as he sat down next to Nish. 'You've got to cool it, mate.'

A bit later, Hillbilly beckoned me into the corridor. 'Listen, I'm going to get the stupid fucker out for a drink. He's retreating deeper and deeper into himself in here. But I've got to stay with him. If he drops your man, he'll get RTU'd (returned to unit). You coming?'

All three of us went into the bar. It was Saturday night,

and most of the lads who weren't at the nuptials had gone to see the Tasking and Coordinating Group crew. The sergeant was at a table in the corner. The place had been gentrified. They'd progressed from cans of Tennants to proper glasses, and there was even a draught tap. We ordered three lagers and stood at the bar munching peanuts. Nish lit cigarette after cigarette.

Nish looked calm, but he wasn't. Close up, I could see he was sparked up. He'd changed since Oman. And what was all the shit with using Al's room?

Hillbilly introduced me to the new game in town: 'not a pub crawl so much as a Republican crawl'. He and a few of the others had started going into Belfast and having a pint in the hard-line PIRA pubs – 'It has to be a pint, no halves, that's cheating' – and walking out. They had a list and were ticking them off one by one, like kids with an *I-Spy* book. 'We went into Andersonstown last week and had a couple. Nish here stood right next to First Battalion, didn't you, mate?'

The Belfast Brigade of the Provisional IRA covered the largest of the organization's command areas. Founded in 1969, along with the formation of the Provisional IRA, it was historically organized into three battalions: the 1st Battalion based in the Andersonstown/Lenadoon/Twinbrook area of west Belfast; the 2nd Battalion based in the Falls Road/Clonard/Ballymurphy district of west Belfast; and the 3rd Battalion organized in nationalist enclaves in the north (Ardoyne, New Lodge, Ligoniel), south (the Markets/Lower Ormeau) and east (Short Strand) of the city. Hillbilly and co were playing a big boys' game.

Nish smoked and listened. 'Tell you what – we'll have a game of pool in a minute.'

'Yeah, good idea, mate, let's do that.' I emptied my glass. 'Mine's a pint. I'll go and set them up.'

The pool table was in the corner furthest away from Sergeant Fast-track and his cronies. As I set up the balls, I glanced back at the bar. Nish was taking his socks off. Hillbilly stared at me with a helpless look on his face.

Nish put his trainers back on and shoved his socks into his jeans pocket. The two of them came over and I flipped a coin. Hillbilly was going to kick off.

We finished what passed for a game, and Nish stubbed his cigarette out on the floor. He pulled one of the socks from his pocket, picked two balls off the table and pushed them down into the toe. His eyes were fixed on Sergeant Fast-track.

Hillbilly grabbed his cue and turned it horizontal to restrain him. He tried to push him behind a pillar and out of sight. 'Fucking calm down, mate – give us the balls. You're going to kill somebody with that. Calm down . . . Look at me . . .'

Nish didn't respond.

'Get Fuck-head out of here, and quick.'

I rattled over to Fast-track's table. 'I need some help. You've got to show me Jimmy's weapon rack . . .' I tried to sound like the keenest new arrival on the block. 'Come on, you've got to show me. Nobody's told me where the weapons are. Nobody's even told me where the ops car is. What happens if we get a call-out?'

He looked me calmly up and down. 'You're not on the standby team, are you? Otherwise you wouldn't be in here, would you?'

Out of the corner of my eye I could see Hillbilly still trying to get some sense into Nish.

'Oh, all right, for fuck's sake.'

He got up and off we went. He took me to the armoury under the briefing room, which I'd been to hundreds of times before. He showed me all the racks, we went through the protocol, and then he showed me the ops car.

'Satisfied?'

I made all the right noises.

He went back to the bar and I headed straight for the

accommodation block. Hillbilly had steered Nish home, and he was stretched out on his bed.

Hillbilly emerged into the corridor. 'He's got me really worried, you know. He specified this room – it was Al's, wasn't it?'

'That's Al's bed he's sleeping in.'

'All I can do is look after him, Andy, but it's no fucking picnic. We need to get him back to the squadron.'

69

I was driving past the armoury one evening about six weeks later when I spotted Nish. I'd heard he'd been back from the troop four or five days, but he hadn't shown his face at the squadron before he went back over the water to finish his tour.

I stopped the Renault and rolled down the window. 'Oi!'

He turned, but he wasn't wearing the kind of expression I'd hoped for now he was back.

He wandered over and hunched down beside my wreck, studying the wires hanging out of the dashboard before pulling the cigarette from his mouth. 'I've been stitched up. They're going to bin me.'

'No, mate. Not a chance.'

'They just have.'

The day he'd come back, he'd gone to the squadron office, but was told there was a problem. One of the intelligence officers over the water had sent a message that an unauthorized civilian had dropped Nish off at the warehouse.

'It wasn't even at the warehouse.' Nish took a lungful of smoke. 'It was way down in the main camp.'

He'd been given a week to write his defence before going in front of the CO. The week had ended today.

'You won't believe this. The woman concerned, the "unauthorized civilian", was with me at an RUC do. She's got clearance – she works for the RUC. She didn't even know I was in the Regiment. I told her I was a scaley.'

She'd offered to drive Nish back because it was pouring with rain. 'It wasn't a breach of security – she never went near the warehouse.'

I'd never seen Nish serious for more than five minutes. Now we were into double figures.

We all had our cover stories over the water, and they varied according to the circumstances. Maybe you'd been working at the airport or you had something to do with British Telecom. You always needed a feasible cover story to give you a reason to be where you were, whether it was at a roadblock near the border or having a drink in a bar. It didn't stop there. Every time you met someone new, man or woman, in a café, at a filling station, no matter what was happening, you'd run a P check on their name and car plate.

If they had any terrorist history, or any connections with players who had history, they would have been flagged and we would be told about it. We would also be told where they lived and worked, if they were married, if they had kids. P checks were not only meant to protect us. You never knew what might turn up. It could be the first step in the cultivation of a new source. Even if you hadn't talked to them, you filled in a Casual Contact Report.

'You don't have to justify it, mate. You're many things, but you're not stupid.' This just didn't smell right. 'What's going to happen? RTU?'

'Yep, for a year.'

That wasn't so bad. 'That'll be gone in no time.'

'Nah, I've binned it. I've PVR'd.' He smiled, and there was a glimmer of the old Nish, but it was just a veneer. 'I've never been particularly comfortable with authority figures, especially officers.'

'What now?'

'Don't know. I've always wanted to fly. Maybe—' His eyes shone. 'I've always wanted to beat the highest freefall record . . .'

The cigarette described an arc across the sky and he went into another world. 'Twenty miles high – that's three and a half times higher than Everest. It's a vacuum that high – no sound, right on the edge of space. I'd accelerate faster than the speed of sound before dumping the canopy. Fucking great.'

'Don't you need a space suit and a helping hand from NASA to get that high?'

'S'pose so.'

Nish came back down to Earth for a moment. 'I'm going to dump my kit at Hillbilly's.' He stubbed out his cigarette and stood up. 'I've still got Jason's school fees to pay. I can't let him down. I'd better start thinking about getting a job, hadn't I? But, first, I'm going down town. You coming?'

I went, along with plenty of others. None of us could believe how he'd been dealt with. By the end of the evening, Nish was sitting in a depressed heap. It wasn't just the alcohol. 'I've fucked up, PVRing. Even driving out of the camp was a night-mare. That's me, I'm history.'

There was no way he'd go back and beg. Once you'd made that decision, you had to stick with it.

'You know what? I've even got a letter from the CO, con-gratulating me on the last couple of jobs. For all the fucking good that did me.'

70

Life went on – and I wasn't sure the sergeant ever knew how grateful he should have been for that. He'd had a narrow escape from Nish's sockful of spot balls.

Frank was still with Ralph Halpern, only he was *Sir* Ralph now. Nish was BGing for the comedian Jim Davidson. Hillbilly had introduced them and they'd become good mates after Jim had done a couple of shows for us at the Paludrin Club. The three of them were peas out of the same pod, working hard and playing even harder.

Jim had had a bad reputation in some quarters, but he'd always been there for the Regiment. He was one of the very few people who never asked for money when putting on a show for the military. Even the cost of going into operational areas came out of his own pocket. He was on the board of a number of army charities, and had personally raised hundreds of thousands of pounds for them.

For all that, he had a lot of ups and downs in his personal life, and I was never too sure who was looking after whom. But by the sound of it he and Nish were having a great time, and it seemed like Nish was getting back to his old self.

They were having a party at Hillbilly's one night, and Hillbilly had nipped into the bedroom with some girl while

Nish guarded the door. Hillbilly's girlfriend walked up the stairs and asked where he was. Nish knocked loudly on the bathroom door. 'You in there, mate?'

Hillbilly jumped out of the first-floor window. The girl he'd been with climbed out, grabbed the drainpipe, and swung herself onto the next sill. She came out of the bathroom just as Hillbilly ambled up the stairs with two pints of milk he'd nicked off the neighbour's doorstep. 'Just popped down the garage for supplies . . .'

So, things seemed to be back to normal for the pair of them.

I was a sniper on the counter-terrorist (CT) team. We used the PN 7.62, with Lapua ammunition, handmade in Finland. The weapon of choice for close-range work was the Ticker, a .22-calibre three-burst rifle that had a suppressed barrel and gave accurate head shots at anything up to about sixty metres. The weapon got its name from the gentle ticking sound it made as the working parts slid into place when it was fired.

A burst of three .22 rounds into the head dropped the target like liquid – and at the same time, their small calibre meant they didn't pass through his skull and drop any Yankees standing behind him.

Every available bit of downtime was spent on the ranges with these weapons. We needed to be sure that when we took a rifle from its case after hours of travelling and bouncing about, we could place a round in the chamber, take a head shot from the standing position at 200 metres, and hit the centre of mass – which, on a Hun-head target, was the little circle on the nose. One round, one kill, that's what it was all about. Unless it was a Ticker, of course, in which case it was one burst, one kill.

71

Life on the team got even more interesting when I was called into the squadron office and told I was going away with RWW for a couple of weeks.

'Why me?'

'Don't ask, just go.'

Hillbilly had been given the same message as soon as he came back from over the water. He told me it felt like all his Christmases had come at once, which pretty much summed up how I felt. I was still a junior, still a lance-corporal. RWW was way beyond my experience and skills.

With two guys from RWW – the 'Wing' – we set off in an Escort estate for Larkhill, the Royal Artillery camp on Salisbury Plain.

One of them was a Jock I'd come across a couple of times in the Lines. Andrew only spoke about three words a day, and when he did you could only understand him if you were close enough to watch his lips move under his sandy moustache. The accent was impenetrable.

'You're going to learn how to operate Blowpipe, the shoulder-fired ground-to-air missile system,' he announced, as he checked the road map, using up a week's word ration in one go. 'It's a heap of shit.'

You needed a degree in physics and the ability to process about ten different things at once. I'd never been good at the tapping-your-head-while-rubbing-your-stomach-and-hopping-up-and-down-on-one-leg trick when I was a kid, and deploying Blowpipe was like doing all that while using a typewriter and counting backwards from a hundred. Blindfolded.

Once you got the launcher on the shoulder, and it was a heavy bit of kit, you had to keep the sight picture on the target the whole time. That meant following it with the missile launcher on your shoulder. You'd kick off the missile, then have to guide it manually via a thumb joystick. In other words, a target could only be taken on when it was coming directly towards you or going away from you.

'We had them in the Falklands. Out of ninety-five fired, there was only one kill.' Andrew had a sudden burst of verbal diarrhoea. 'Blowpipe? A hosepipe would have done better.'

After two days of trying to master a weapon that was soon to be scrapped anyway, we switched to Stinger, the American equivalent. Not only was it lighter and easier to operate, but the electronics were far more sophisticated and the warhead deadlier. Its sensors locked onto the heat signature of the target; you fired it and off it went. The only vaguely complicated thing you had to do was a thing called super-elevation, to give the missile time to come out of its housing on its kick motor and drop a fraction before the main motor fired up and took it skyward.

Stinger was a brand new bit of kit at the time of the Falklands. In fact, it was the weapon's combat debut. British forces had been equipped with half a dozen of the things, but the only person who had received proper training on the system, an SAS trooper who was due to train other troops, was killed along with 21 others when the Sea King he was aboard crashed into the sea on 19 May. He was carrying all the Stinger training manuals at the time.

The Jock had first-hand experience of how good it was. A

patrol from D Squadron, with Andrew in command, was on some high ground on the morning of 21 May as a squadron of Pucará attack aircraft screamed in to zap our ships. He had just a few seconds to read the instructions and fire. Luckily, the Americans always used cartoons in their instruction manuals, and despite missing the page about super-elevation, Andrew let one go and down came a Pucará. The pilot ejected safely and walked back to Goose Green, which was still in enemy hands at this time. The Argentines surrendered the next day without another one being fired. It wasn't for want of trying. After Andrew's bull's-eye everyone wanted a go, but nobody was familiar with the weapon's recharging procedure. Stinger's score for the conflict was therefore: Fired 1, Killed 1. Ninety-five times better than Blowpipe, then – and the same rate as a sniper should achieve.

I wish I'd been there. As I discovered later, Andrew always took his teeth out on jobs because they were so expensive he didn't want to lose them or get them smashed. And he always wore bright red braces under his combat gear. He must have hoped that if he was captured, everyone would assume he was Coco the Clown.

He was a good lad. Towards the end of the course I sometimes got as many as ten words in a row out of him. I eventually asked him what I was doing there.

'The Wing might need some help later on, and you've been recommended.'

I sat there feeling quite pleased with myself. 'Recommended? What's the job?'

Andrew sucked on his Embassy. 'If you're on it, you'll find out, won't you?'

Eventually I did.

Following the Russian invasion of Afghanistan in 1979, the SIS and the CIA had begun covertly backing the Mujahideen with training and arms. The West didn't take too kindly to the idea of Soviet troops massed that close to the Gulf oilfields.

At first the training was basic and carried out in safe-houses in Pakistan, but by 1982 the SIS was infiltrating Afghanistan. Things went badly wrong, however, when one of our teams ran into an ambush. The Brits escaped and made their way back to Pakistan, but the items they left behind presented the Soviets with a massive propaganda coup. Passports and other incriminating documents were paraded at a press conference. Whitehall denied it had anything to do with them, and some lads suddenly PVR'd quite soon afterwards.

72

The Regiment got more heavily involved in Afghanistan when I was sitting in the Malaysian jungle after Selection. They helped the Mujahideen with their communications and control systems, but soon found they couldn't risk teaching them the 81mm mortar or heavy weapons. The Russians would descend the moment they heard them firing.

The solution was to bring Muhammad to the mountain. We'd round up about thirty at a time and get them out to Pakistan. Then we'd throw them on a C-130, and have a two-week trip to one of the little islands off the west coast of Scotland.

The groups would spend a fortnight firing heavy weapons while chatting tactics on how to take down the Soviets' comms and how to hit their major command so it lowered morale. At the end of their stint in Andrew's back yard, we'd put them on the C-130 with a packed lunch and a can of Fanta, get them back into Pakistan, then over the border to put theory into practice.

Everything was going very nicely until the Russians deployed their Hind gunships. Basically an airborne artillery park, the Hind was the most formidable helicopter in existence. It turned the tide again. By the mid-eighties, the

Americans were flapping big-time. The Kremlin needed to be taught a lesson.

Ronald Reagan suddenly hailed the Muj as freedom fighters, but the only way they could win this war was by making the Russians pay such an unacceptable manpower cost for the occupation that public opinion turned against them and the army started to rebel. Simply put, that meant killing and wounding as many Soviets as possible, and fucking up their infrastructure in any way we could. Just about anything was a legitimate target.

Before that could happen, the Hinds had to be eliminated.

The Stinger was the obvious solution. The trouble was, it was so good at knocking things out of the sky that the Americans suddenly got reluctant to let go of them. The risk of them falling into the wrong hands was just too high. So we were tasked with teaching the Muj how to use Blowpipe instead.

Unsurprisingly, after our sessions with Andrew at Larkhill, it wasn't long before we discovered that it really was a piece of shit. The sky was still full of Hinds. The Americans had to relent. They opened the toy cupboard and broke out the Stingers.

The training had to begin all over again. The west coast of Scotland reopened for Mujahideen short breaks and the C-130s resumed their shuttle service.

The kit started to filter into Afghanistan via covert convoys, but the shifty fuckers weren't using them. The Stingers were far too nice and shiny, and the Muj were saving them for a rainy day.

It was then that we had to get our hands dirty. We ambushed, attacked, blew up and killed anything that carried a hammer and sickle.

Inevitably, it was only a matter of time before the story broke that the Brits were supplying Stinger missiles and lads were in-country. The Soviets went ballistic, but the government was able to deny everything.

The Stingers did tilt the balance a little. We helped make Afghanistan the Russians' Vietnam. Eventually they'd had enough. One day, they just got in their tanks and their few remaining Hinds and crept out of town.

By now the Mujahideen had turned into really well-trained fighters. All they'd lacked in the beginning was battlefield organization. We had taught their junior commanders, the boys on the ground, how to deploy their lads a lot more effectively – and their weapons as well. They had learnt not only command and control, but how to plan and prepare operations, use explosives, and control the fire of heavy weapons and artillery to the best effect. One of the junior commanders who had passed through our hands was an Arab freedom fighter who'd come over to fight the Soviets in the name of Islam. His name was Osama bin Laden.

Some of the tactics used by the Taliban against NATO troops today are reassuringly familiar. If our guys are ambushed, they know exactly where the Tali cut-off and machine-guns will be placed – because it was we who taught them in the first place.

We withdrew soon after the Russians, and the Muj started kicking the shit out of each other again. Fifty thousand people were killed in Kabul alone during the civil war that followed.

The Taliban finally won in 1996, and they ran the shop until late 2001. Then, after 9/11, the USA came calling with a few thousand tonnes of bombs so the Northern Alliance could enter the city and take over for the US forces that were 'liberating' the country. And the show goes on.

Even today pallet loads of Stingers are unaccounted for. They could be lying in somebody's cave, still waiting for that rainy day, or they could be in Iran, being busily reverse-engineered. The US and UK governments are still shitting themselves about them, and with good reason. A transport aircraft dropped with more than a hundred troops on board would make for the mother of all Prime Minister's Questions.

73

November 1986

Nish was off to Buckingham Palace to receive the Queen's Gallantry Medal for his part in the target-replacement job that Al had volunteered for. At the same ceremony Al was to be posthumously awarded the MM, just two short of the VC.

I knew it would be a good day out for him. I'd been to Buck House myself to receive the MM when I was a Green Jacket. I felt pissed off with the Regiment, though, when I saw Nish back in camp being issued with No. 2s, best dress uniform. It felt like all of a sudden the head shed wanted him back for a day or two because there was something good on – or maybe they just didn't want him turning up in civilian clothes and the Queen asking him why.

Nish looked really happy to be back. In fact, he was radiant. He was starting to look like his old self again.

But as we chatted away in the team's crew room while he waited for his corporal's stripes and SAS wings to be sewn onto his No. 2s, the mask slipped. 'I've been out of the Regiment nearly four months and there hasn't been a single day I haven't regretted leaving. I miss you lads, and I miss the life.' At least he wasn't in denial like Frank still was.

SEVEN TROOP

He scuffed the ground with the toe of his plimsoll. 'Can't stop thinking about Al. If only I'd fronted Mac Giolla Bride, he'd be coming along to the Palace with me.'

'Mate, it's too late. As we've said all along, it's done. He's dead.'

A couple of days after the investiture, I was amazed to see Nish strolling around the camp with the CO like some sort of royal visitor. Guys were doing double-takes wherever the pair went.

I met up with him in the pub that night.

'I'm back in!' He beamed. 'God save the Queen!'

The invitation had said Nish could bring two guests to the Palace, and he'd invited his mother and his son, Jason, who was now eight. They took their seats and Nish took his in the line-up. He was last of about fifty.

'The Queen arrived dead on time and chatted to each of us for a minute as she gave us our award. It took an hour for her to get to me.

'She said, "Is your family here?"

' "Yes, ma'am, I've brought my mother and my son."

' "They must be very proud."

' "Yes, ma'am."

'She asked me about where we'd done the job; apparently she used to go fishing there as a child. She said she was sad that so much had changed. Then she asked, "What are you doing now?"

'I didn't want to say I was BGing a comedian, so said I was between jobs.

' "You're no longer in the army?"

' "Unfortunately, no, ma'am."

' "Are you intending to go back in?"

' "I seriously hope so, ma'am."

'According to my mother, we chatted for another five minutes – she timed it.

'Then the weird thing. As we were leaving, a group of senior

273

head sheds came over and asked me why I'd left the Regiment. I told them, and one of them said, "Well, do you want to go back in?"

'That was that, and I thought no more about it. Jim Davidson had arranged a big piss-up in Bristol with all the girls from his show. We got so hammered that when Hillbilly phoned I could hardly hear him.

' "What the fuck have you done now?" he was saying. "The RSM's trying to get hold of you."

'I said I'd call him tomorrow when I was sober, but Hillbilly said it had to be that night. The RSM had left me his home number!

'I phoned him and he said, "The CO's been speaking to me and he wants the answer to a question. Do you want to come back in?"

' "Yes."

' "All right, come and see the CO tomorrow." '

He beamed again. 'The rest is history.'

'That's fantastic news, mate – when do you start? You coming on the team?'

The smile slipped. 'There's a catch. Story of my life – so near and yet so far. The deal is that I have to go to Twenty-four Troop for a year. If I do that, I can come back to Seven.'

Air Troop, G Squadron, was known as the Lonsdale Troop because all they wanted to do was fight each other. It seemed a small price to pay, considering he'd got into the swing of it over the water. The year would fly by. And maybe they'd move him sooner after a few hundred renditions of 'Duelling Banjos'.

I started doing the build-up for a team job with Hillbilly. Things started to feel as though they were back to normal.

'I won't miss the two-in-the-morning calls.' Hillbilly grinned. 'He used to phone and say, "This is Clarissa, say hello to Hillbilly. Oh, and who's this the other side of the bed? This is Fifi. Say hello to Hillbilly." '

Three months later I was sitting in the Paludrin Club having a pie and a mug of tea when in walked Andrew from the Wing. He motioned me over to a quiet corner.

'I've been offered a job on the outside.' The sandy moustache twitched as he rolled up some Golden Virginia. 'I'm looking for lads.'

'What is it?'

It had to be something to do with the Firm, the SIS. Andrew had been doing nothing but work for them for about the last three years.

'I can't say just now, but you interested?'

'Mate, I'm sorry – I've just been picked up and can't get out of it.'

'Where you going?'

'The Det.'

14 Int, Walts, Dickheads, Operators, Spies, Men in Cars, Murderers, Assassins – the Det had many names, depending on who you were and which end of their weapons you were standing, and Eno and I were their newest recruits.

The job would last two years, and we had no say in the matter. We were going, and that was that.

74

Until 1972, information-gathering responsibilities in Northern
Ireland had been split between MI5 and MI6. Both organizations worked to their own agenda, and the intelligence was
piss-poor as a result. The army took the decision to set up its
own secret intelligence-gathering unit, which was given the
cover name '14th Intelligence Unit', or '14 Int' or the 'Det'
(Detachment) for short.

Male and female recruits were taken from all three services
and put through a course that lasted six months and covered
techniques of covert surveillance, communications and agent-
running. They were trained in part by the Regiment at a camp
near Hereford, but that was where the connection with the
Special Air Service started and finished.

To us they were Walts (Walter Mittys), and the Det was the
last place any of us wanted to go. It wasn't that long since
the Det had wanted a Regiment lad to go and hide in
Dungannon, watching people go in and out of a betting office.
The OP was compromised by kids and the lad got away,
but the Det wanted him to go back the next day and do
exactly the same thing. One of the officers of the Det was
overheard saying, 'It doesn't really matter if he gets
compromised because he's not one of us.' Ken heard

276

about this and sorted it out in his usual persuasive manner.

Now two guys from each squadron were being approached to go, and most were saying no. In the end the CO called in all the squadrons to give us the good news. 'The Det is something that you will do. The skills that they've got, we must have back. We're starting to lose it, yet we're the ones that developed it. One way or another, we'll regain that skill. It's all part of becoming a complete soldier – we need complete soldiers.' You either loved him or hated him; there was no in-between.

There was a lot of bad feeling. A vigilante mob from D Squadron went around threatening anyone who put his hand up to volunteer. Eno and I kept ours down, so I was just a little concerned when I got approached by Andrew in the Naafi.

Just a few days before his job offer, Eno and I were called into the CO's office. 'You have two options,' the CO said. 'You either go over the water for two years, or you go nowhere. You volunteered for the Regiment, you volunteered for operations. This is an operation. If you're refusing to go on operations, you're not staying in the Regiment.'

The first person I bumped into on day one of the training package was Tiny. 'I'm on the training team.' He grinned. 'You can call me "Staff" and I'll call you "Walt".'

The instructors were a mixture of Regiment and people from the Det who were back from over the water for a couple of years.

Everybody was given an alternative identity, keeping the same initials and the same Christian name, and something similar to our real surname so we didn't forget it. Working under an alias, we'd always sign our name in a way that reminded us of what we were doing – perhaps it was a pen of a striking colour, or one that we kept in our right-hand breast pocket rather than the left.

We learnt the skills of covert entry to look for information, weapons and bomb-making equipment, and of leaving so that no one had any idea we'd been there. We would be working against players who were switched on. If we fucked up, everything would be compromised.

We learnt how to follow a man and his family for weeks to find out what their routines were, where they went, who they did what with, trying to establish a time when we could get into the house.

Did he go to a social club every Saturday night with his wife and kids? Maybe he got back, on average, at about midnight, so we had between eight and eleven to get in, do our business and get out. But that wasn't good enough. If it was July, it wouldn't get dark until half ten. So you might have to wait a couple of months or until he went away to visit his parents for the weekend or maybe took a week's holiday on the coast.

He had to be under surveillance all the time, to ensure that when he did go to the club with his wife and kids, his wife didn't leave early to put the kids to bed, or if they were on holiday, that they didn't come home early because the weather was crap or the kids were ill.

We had to learn how to use all sorts of cameras, including infra-red equipment that would enable us to photograph serial numbers and documents – and photographs. We had to take in Polaroid cameras as well, to take pictures of the tops of tables and desks, to make sure we left them exactly as we found them. We had to make sure we never left sign. If it was wet and muddy, we had to take our shoes off and put others on. We couldn't just run around in our socks. If the floors were tiled, the sweat on our feet might leave marks.

Our voice procedure on the net became very slick. We had to be able to give a complete running commentary without moving our lips. In Northern Ireland, somebody was always watching; you could never forget third-party awareness.

There had to be complete honesty on the ground. There

wasn't any space for bullshit; if you fucked up, you had to put your hands up and say so straight away.

By the end of the course we could break into any kind of vehicle, house and building. There were no other operators anywhere in the world with the degree of knowledge that came from a combination of surveillance, technical attack, covert CTR (close target recce), and methods of planning and preparation, plus the skills we had already learnt in the Regiment.

I realized how fortunate I was to be a 'complete soldier', and I could see now that those who'd volunteered to do this initially were the enlightened ones – and that had to include the CO. I was able to do all the kinetic stuff with guns and explosives, but now I could also stand back and become the grey man, gathering information, making appreciations, planning and preparing covert operations. After all, the most effective weapon in any war is information. It's not the guns: they're just useless lumps of metal unless you know where to get in, and how, and can point them at the correct target.

75

By the time Eno and I got on the ground in Derry, the second largest city in the Province, the pair of us looked and acted like locals. I even had the Kevin Keegan perm that was all the rage. To be fair to the others on the course, we'd had a head start. We'd both been raised on London housing estates, and neither of us was shy about gobbing off.

I was now a full corporal in the Regiment, and loving every minute of my job. I liked nothing more than spending an evening breaking into players' houses, or roaming the streets looking for targets. And, unbelievably, I was being paid for it.

The whole purpose of the Det was to gather information about terrorist active service units, their weapons, hides and known associates, so we could pre-empt attacks, make arrests, and save innocent lives. This was done in a wide variety of ways, from putting OPs on their hides and following the players who used them, to planting surveillance devices inside the weapons they'd cached and letting them take them away.

'Jarking', the planting of miniature transmitters inside weapons and equipment, more correctly known as 'technical attack', had started in the late seventies. The idea was that the devices would be activated when the weapon was picked up, and the terrorists' movements could then be monitored. By the time we were on the Det, more sophisticated devices had been developed, which not only allowed the location of the weapon to be tracked but also acted as microphones, enabling us to listen to PIRA conversations.

It was inevitable, of course, that PIRA would discover its weapons were being jarked, no matter how clever we were at disguising our work. These people weren't idiots: they had scanning devices. We were all playing the same game: they knew that the weapons were being tampered with, they knew that their buildings were bugged. They would use counter-measures, which we would try to counter-counter.

Another important part of the job was the identification of potential sources. A player might have younger brothers or, better still, older sisters. The women were more emotionally intelligent, and often desperate to do something that would help their brother. Sometimes we could be close enough on OPs to listen to sisters begging their brothers to stop before they got killed. We could then work with them, explaining that we might be able to protect their family member if they told us what he was up to.

I felt quite comfortable wandering our patch, but it took me a long time to find out why I got so many nods from the Strabane locals. It was bandit country down there near the border, with more weapons than Dodge City. A couple of PIRA lads had been zapped just before we arrived, and tensions were high.

We had to break into a particular player's garage, but the area was well lit and overlooked by houses. We'd have to be on-target for at least thirty minutes if we tried to defeat the locks, so the only answer was to copy his keys.

The RUC set up a vehicle checkpoint on the road he took to work. These mobile patrols were a regular occurrence around the city. They operated plate checks for twenty minutes or so, then moved on to do the same thing somewhere else. They ran an everyday P check, and of course he came up as a known player. He was pulled to the side and taken for questioning while his car was searched. When the keys came through, we'd have just a few minutes to take impressions before he got suspicious. In any event, we'd have to do the break-in within a couple of days. Nine times out of ten, as soon as a player had been separated from his keys even for a few minutes, he'd change all his locks. As I said, they weren't stupid.

I caught a glimpse of the guy while he was being searched, and I couldn't believe it. Maybe I was an Irishman ... I certainly had one as my identical twin brother.

76

We needed to coerce a high-ranking player into becoming a source. He had close links to Sinn Féin and the Provisional IRA – or Sinn Féin IRA, as the Protestants liked to call them. If you'd broken this boy in half you'd have found the tricolour running through him, like 'Blackpool' through a stick of rock.

The player was high profile and well connected, so the decision was made to stitch him up and use him. By now I was a team leader. We placed surveillance on him for a month. We found out who he met, who he telephoned, what they talked about, what he liked to eat, where his wife had her hair done. None of it revealed anything useful.

They were squeaky clean. Not even a private video of him and his wife playing doctors and nurses. He regularly attended Sinn Féin meetings, rallies and lectures, but they were all perfectly legal. What would have been nice was evidence of a massive overdraft because he was addicted to drugs, gambling or hookers. There was none of that, so we had to get creative.

Northern Ireland was, and still is, a deeply conservative

place – no matter what side of the religious divide you're from. To be outed as homosexual would have been bad enough, but as one with a fondness for underage rent-boys? A social nightmare – and illegal. They would have marched down to his house and burnt him out.

The plan was simple. We'd go into the house and plant something compromising when the opportunity presented itself.

It was two weeks before he took his wife to a Saturday-night fundraiser in Strabane. We'd made duplicate keys on the last visit. Another team kept a trigger on them for the night, and our earpieces buzzed as we listened to the news of how many sugars she was having in her tea and how long it took him to have a piss. By the time we left, the evidence was tucked away among his union magazines and volumes of Irish history, and we'd arranged his subscription to a specialist magazine published in Amsterdam.

The following morning, my team were on the ground in our cars, ready to take him. An RUC mobile patrol of two armoured Land Rovers was also standing by, with a couple of guys from TCG in the back. They were going to set up a vehicle checkpoint on the road ahead, once we'd worked out which way he was going.

An RUC and army search team was on stand-by in the security force base at the other side of the river. A rifle company would move in and cordon off the area while the rest of the guys conducted house-to-house searches. To keep it authentic, these lads would have no idea what they were looking for, but they were thorough. They'd find the gay porn under the marital bed and we'd tip off a journalist or two.

We had no idea where the target was going as we followed him but the lads in the Land Rovers were listening in, and the vehicle checkpoint was in position. He got pulled, and his car was searched; so far, standard stuff. He was then shoved into the back of one of the Land Rovers. I could only imagine his shock at seeing the two TCG lads sitting there in jeans and T-shirts. I wished we'd had cameras as well as microphones.

We were parked outside a Spar shop four hundred metres away, waiting to hear him accept defeat. The pitch was simple: you come over and start working for us, or by the end of the day you'll have been exposed as a gay-sex pervert. Just think about all the problems you'll have with Sinn Féin, the IRA and the unions, let alone your wife and family: you're going to be fucked.

The pitch was hard, yet sympathetic. We wanted to be able to work with this guy. He listened to it all, and then he said: 'Go ahead, I don't care. Everyone will know it's not true. And in any event I'd rather be known as a gay pervert than say one word against what I believe. I'll tell everyone what you've done today, and they'll side with me because I'm true to the cause. So go on, let's see who comes out on top.'

I couldn't tell if he was bluffing; it certainly didn't sound like it. But it didn't matter: he'd won.

He was released, and no searches were carried out. He probably went straight home and found the planted evidence himself. The job was a complete failure, but none of us minded. The guy had to be admired. There wasn't even a hint of treachery about him. And despite all the information we got from sources that did save lives, they still gave me a bad taste in my mouth. No matter what side you're on, no one likes a traitor.

Hillbilly called a few days later. He was going away with RWW (revolutionary warfare wing) on a fastball. There wasn't even time to pack. He didn't know how long he'd be out of circulation. 'Keep tabs on Big Nose for me, will you? Look's like he's getting stitched up again. The CO's not letting him come back to Seven Troop.'

77

We had information that some weapons were going to be taken to a house in the Bogside. Two players would come and collect them for a shoot on British soldiers.

It was nearly last light. Eno was in an Astra up on the high ground of the Creggan. The brown-brick terraces were gloomy and depressing. The smashed street-lights and abandoned cars added to the effect. There wasn't a blade of grass to be seen, just patches of churned-up mud. The sky was shrouded by coal smoke belching from every chimney. After a night fucking about here you could smell it on your clothes.

The weapons had been jarked and he was waiting for a beep. I was backing about four hundred metres away – out of range of the jarks but close enough to give support.

It was raining. The locals had their heads down against the wind. The estate was on the high ground of the city and a strong one always rattled through.

I sat low in my Fiesta. My feet were blocks of ice. My hands were tucked under my thighs. My head was freezing too, but at least my Kevin Keegan mullet kept my neck warm.

The fingers of my right hand were wrapped round a pistol. The Creggan and Bogside estates had been Catholic strongholds for centuries. The Bogside used to be exactly that, a bog.

The Catholics camped there during the siege of Derry in 1689, then moved up here, to the Creggan, to get out of the shit.

Three weeks ago, a soldier in cover on the corner of the street just ten metres from where I was sitting had taken a round in the head. The street painters had already been out and filled the street corner with a picture of a PIRA sniper firing from the kneeling position. *Brits come up here if you dare – but don't expect to go back down.*

'Stand by, stand by. They're moving.'

The beeps had gone off in Eno's earpiece.

This wasn't the time to jump up and start moving, but to check no one was looking or passing by before I turned on the engine and rolled out.

Eno followed the signal down the hill towards the Bogside, just a hundred metres from the old city wall. I backed him as he soon found himself behind a blue Escort, two-up. The P check came back clean.

They drove into Cable Street, on the edge of the estate.

Eno pulled in. He'd done his bit. The Bogside was closed to vehicles; this was probably as near as they could get to the drop-off.

'Stop, stop, stop. Just past the Sinn Féin office, on the left. Passenger door open, lights still on.'

I was already parking my Fiesta and dumping my car pistol under the driver's seat as the Escort turned into Cable Street. It was blocked off at the other end to protect the Sinn Féin office from drive-by shootings. As casually as possible, I locked my car and started walking towards Cable Street.

'Delta's foxtrot.'

I could see Eno's Astra parked up in front of me, next to the massive murals commemorating the death of hunger striker Bobby Sands in 1981, alongside freedom fighters with their raised fists clenched around M16s. They were probably painted by the same guys who'd just been busy up in the Creggan.

Eno was keeping the trigger on the Escort, so I had a running commentary from him on what was happening round the corner.

'Big sail bag being taken out the boot. Engine still on, driver still complete. That's the bag out, wait ... wait. Closing boot ... boot closed. Bravo One's foxtrot towards the estate. Black leather on jeans. He's aware.'

I turned and saw the bag-carrier check behind him before disappearing into the warren of the 1960s housing estate.

'Delta has Bravo One. Temporary unsighted.'

The Escort backed out of Cable Street and Eno was on the net telling the desk. The car wasn't important now. The sail bag was.

The Bogside's architect, if there was one, must either have been a fan of scary movies or high on LSD. It was a maze of two- and three-storey tenements interconnected by dark alleyways. Some alleys led to others; some just came to a dead end.

I kept telling myself I belonged there. You must always have a reason to be where you are. If you don't feel it emotionally, you don't look as if you feel it physically.

I had well and truly bedded in. I was a local. I didn't have a shave until Friday night. I wore market jeans and cheap trainers.

It was getting dark. The few street-lights that still worked flickered on. Kids shouted and screamed as they chased a football through the puddles. Scabby dogs skulked in doorways. I passed a corner shop, an old freight container with a heavily padlocked door.

The kids stopped playing football and stared. Children as young as five or six got paid as dickers.

I'm going to see a mate, that's why I'm here.

They didn't know who I was. They wouldn't be thinking: there's a Special Forces soldier or a Det operator. They'd just be thinking: Who the fock's he? Has he come down from the Shantello or Creggan? Or has he come over from one of the Protestant estates the other side of the river – is he here to shoot someone? They looked as nervous as I felt.

I bluffed it. I stared them out.

Who the fuck are you looking at?

I had my hands in the pockets of my parka. One thumb was on the pressle of my comms set.

'Bravo One still temporary unsighted, checking.'

It wasn't a problem. I would also hear the bleeps once I was in range. I wanted to find the weapons, not the player.

I didn't know what time it was. I wasn't wearing a watch, in case someone came up and asked for the time. With an empty wrist, you could just shrug and keep moving.

Eno wouldn't leave the car. He was backing me now: he might need to ram it through a barrier to come and get me out.

78

I came into some sort of square. I got a faint signal. Adults were looking at me as well now. Faces were pressed against the glass in one or two kitchens, trying to see through the condensation.

The whole of Derry was made up of tribes. Those faces didn't know me, and this was a war zone. Just about anything that was unknown and moved could be a threat.

I looked right back and stared them out.

Who are you looking at? Get back to boiling your cabbage.

I still had a faint signal. It got stronger as I walked.

A couple of male voices had materialized behind me. I wasn't turning back to look. Why should I?

I kept walking. If they challenged me, I'd front it out. My accent was just passable in short bursts. But why should they challenge me? My mate lived on this estate. There was no hesitation in my stride – I made sure of that. After all, I had every right to be here. I knew where I was going. I turned left down the next alley to see if they carried on following.

Shit, dead end.

No way could I just turn round and come out again. It would look unnatural. I'd seemed to know where I was going, so why would I suddenly get it wrong, unless I didn't know?

The mumbling voices stopped at the mouth of the alley. The fuckers were checking me out.

Think: you have to have a reason to be here!

I faced the wall of the dead end. The ground was littered with dog shit, old Coke cans and a burnt mattress.

The voices still murmured to each other. It was easy enough to guess the conversation. 'What the fuck's he doing down there? What's going on?'

I unzipped my jeans and went to take a piss, but it wasn't happening. I started counting. How long does a piss take?

Eno was in my ear. 'Delta, radio check. Delta, radio check.' He hadn't heard from me. He was readying himself – did he come in on foot, or stay in the car?

One hand still on my cock, I double-clicked the pressle with the other.

'Roger that – you're all right.'

I wasn't all right. I didn't know if I had a drama here or not. I had a weapon, but if I had to shoot these guys it was a long way back to the car. There just weren't enough rounds in the magazine to deal with the opposition that would pour out of every doorway.

It was all going on behind me, and I couldn't turn round to see. If I did that, it really would kick off.

'Have you got a mayday?'

A mayday signified something less drastic than a contact. There was a problem, but it didn't mean you were going to draw down and give away your cover.

I double-clicked. It was a possible mayday.

'Roger that. You still got the trigger?'

I could just hear the beeps in my ear.

Click-click.

'Roger that. You want me foxtrot?'

No clicks.

'Roger that. Do you want me standing by in the car?'

Click-click.

'Roger that. Engine on.'

The lads were still behind me. They weren't going to come down the alleyway, but that didn't make me feel any better. It was still the fear of the unknown, of not being able to look behind and see the scale of my problem. It scared me more than anything else I had experienced. It was all to do with not having control.

Thirty seconds had passed. I zipped up and turned. The guys had gone. I walked to the end of the alley. The only people in sight were kids on rusty old bikes.

I turned left to carry on with the job and was soon walking past the player. He was empty-handed and heading out of the estate.

As the cabbage-cookers checked me out and kids threw cans at the dogs, the signal got stronger.

Click-click, click-click.

Eno did the talking for me. 'Stand by, stand by. You have the bleeps.'

Click-click.

I carried on walking. I exited on the other side of the estate and followed the back-streets to my Fiesta.

I mumbled, 'I've got thirty-one, thirty-three, thirty-five . . .'

Job done. The weapons were in one of those houses. We both had to lift-off now because we'd been exposed. Other lads would already be on their way in to get a trigger.

For our contribution, Eno and I were awarded a medal. The investiture was formal, of course, but I didn't have any trousers. We were just running round in jeans and trainers. I certainly didn't have a tie, and there wasn't any time to buy anything.

I turned up to the ceremony in a borrowed pair of thick-serge RUC uniform trousers, a pink casual shirt and an RUC clip tie. At least my shoes were clean. I spent an hour polishing them, something I hadn't done since battalion days.

It was only on my way there that I realized I hadn't had a

shave. It didn't really matter. It wasn't as if the Queen was going to do the presentation. That honour fell to the guy in charge of the Det. And it wasn't as if they were real medals. Eno and I had both won the Army Spy, Class 1. It was cardboard wrapped in silver foil, tarted up with a bit of ribbon and a cartoon of a sleuth with a magnifying-glass.

It was a great night, with something to eat and a couple of beers in the Det. Funnily enough, I felt just as proud as I had when I'd got my MM from the Queen – possibly more so. I was getting this one from my peers, even if they were Walts.

None of our work was ever attributed to us. There might have been a passing mention of a bomb factory in the local paper, or some assault rifles being unearthed in the Bogside during a routine army search, but nothing, of course, about the three months of undercover work that had gone into tracing the ASU, sourcing their equipment, finding where it was all collated, and where it was moved for assembly – which could be anywhere from a derelict warehouse to somebody's garden shed.

No mention of the army then being given a tip-off and told to search a whole row of houses.

79

20 March 1988

I sat in front of a TV with the rest of the Det, watching helicopter footage of an IRA funeral that had taken place in Belfast the day before. The eye in the sky had fantastic optics. It was there so we could identify every mourner without risking anyone on the ground.

Caoimhin MacBradaigh had been killed three days before by an Ulster Defence Association (UDA) gunman in Milltown cemetery as the three-member ASU slotted by the Regiment in Gibraltar were being buried. Michael Stone had gone in there with a pistol and hand grenades, killed three people and injured sixty others. He was chased to the motorway and beaten up by the crowd, then rescued and arrested by the police. Catholic Belfast was inflamed.

The FLIR (forward-looking infra-red) footage showed us a grey-scale screen with a bird's-eye view of MacBradaigh's procession. Hundreds of mourners crammed the narrow streets.

Then, inexplicably, a silver VW Passat headed straight towards the cortège. It drove past the Sinn Féin stewards, who tried to direct it out of the way. Instead of just turning, the

Passat then mounted the pavement and turned down a side road. The camera operator stayed with it. Was it another Michael Stone-style attack by the UDA?

The side road was a dead end. The Passat turned around, but by the time it got back onto the main road that, too, was blocked by taxis.

It tried to reverse, and was then swamped by bodies. In full view of the world's TV cameras they jumped all over the vehicle, rocking it and smashing the windscreen.

The driver tried to climb out of his window as more black taxis moved to box him in. He fired a shot into the air and the crowd fell back. But only for a moment. The hard core surged again, armed with wheel braces and anything else they could grab. One of them wrenched a stepladder from a photographer and rammed it through the windscreen.

Two men were eventually pulled from the car, punched, kicked, and dragged into a nearby sports ground where they were stripped and searched.

The poor bastards were then thrown over a wall and shoved into the back of a black cab. The jubilant driver waved a fist in the air.

They were driven to Penny Lane, off the Andersonstown Road. Two PIRA stabbed them in the back of the neck before executing them with shots to the head and chest.

As PIRA scattered, a priest appeared. The image of him administering the last rites to the naked and mutilated bodies was to become one of the most enduring of the war.

Only a handful of us in the room knew that the priest, Alex Reid, was already deeply involved in peace negotiations secretly taking place between Downing Street and Sinn Féin.

From start to finish, the incident had lasted no more than twenty minutes, but we all knew we'd never forget it. The dead men weren't UDA coming in for the attack. They were two army signallers: Derek Wood, who was twenty-four, and David Howes, who was twenty-three.

Al Slater as a training corporal, Depot Para, 1982.

Waiting for a helicopter pick-up, Belize, 1985.

Right Helicopter resupply on the Saudi/Iraqi border, 1991.

Below D Squadron controlling prisoners after an attack.

Above Half-squadron admin day in an LUP, Iraq, 1991.

A raiding party returning over the border from Iraq.

Left My 'multiple' posing before a foot patrol, 1979.

Below Posing in the Shantello Estate, 1987.

Below Medal day at North Det.

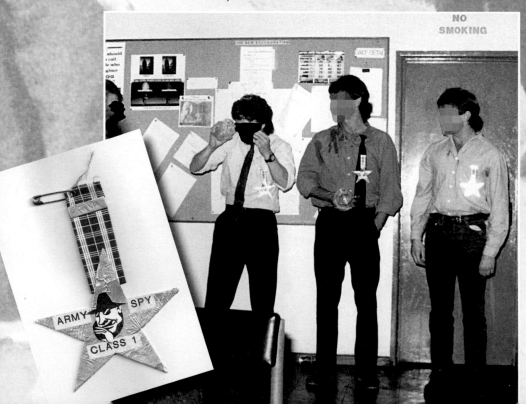

Left Author with Kevin Keegan perm, Derry.

Below A night in at North Det.

Left Author without perm, giving a set of orders for a job.

Below Father Alec Reid administers the last rites to one of the two soldiers murdered at Milltown.

Above RGJ, 1981 – earning our air assault wings with 101st Airborne at Fort Campbell, Kentucky.

Below With coca growers in Colombia, 1989.

Above Sergeant Vince Philips on exercise in Brecon.

Right Nish between moments of madness.

Below The two sides of Frank Collins.

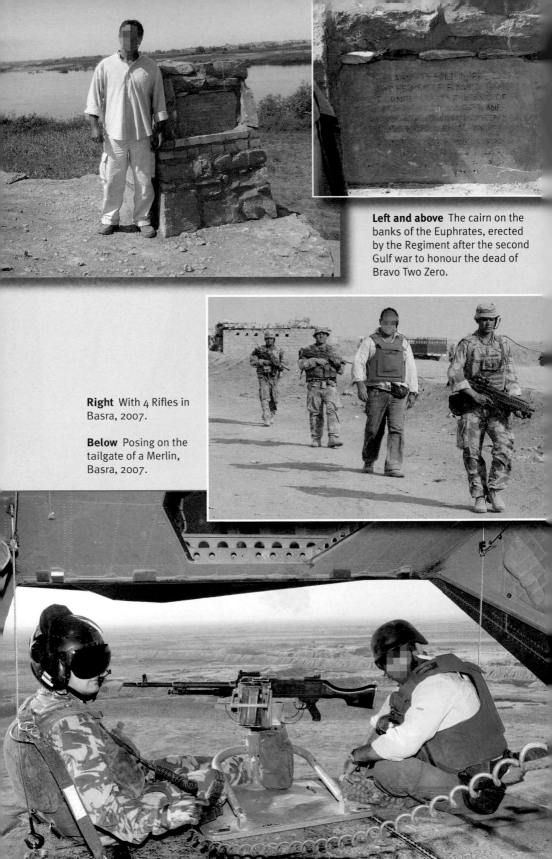

Left and above The cairn on the banks of the Euphrates, erected by the Regiment after the second Gulf war to honour the dead of Bravo Two Zero.

Right With 4 Rifles in Basra, 2007.

Below Posing on the tailgate of a Merlin, Basra, 2007.

Later that day, PIRA issued a statement saying that the Belfast Brigade IRA claimed responsibility for the execution in Andersonstown of two members of the SAS, who had launched an attack on the funeral cortège of their 'comrade volunteer, Kevin Brady' (the English spelling of Caoimhin MacBradaigh).

I knew them, but they weren't SAS, and they weren't Det operators. They were signallers at Headquarters Northern Ireland. Wood should have been taking the new lad, Howes, to a security base in North Howard Street to show him a communications transmitter, which he would be servicing for the next couple of years. Howes had just been posted from Germany to take over from Wood, who was almost at the end his tour.

The two corporals should never have been anywhere near the funeral. Support guys were supposed to stick to defined, constantly changing routes. Wood would have been told, 'Today, the red route.' And that was the route they should have taken.

I never understood why they ended up in that street. They would have known the funeral was taking place. Everyone did. There was a strong sense of tension and anticipation in the area. It was out of bounds to everyone, even the green army. Maybe they just got lost.

They didn't know how to handle themselves when things went wrong. That wasn't their job. They were technicians. And even if they had been SAS, sheer weight of numbers would still have overwhelmed them. The only difference would have been that instead of only one round being fired from a thirteen-round mag – and into the air, at that – there would have been thirteen dead men lying on each side of the car before they got lifted.

Harry Maguire and Alex Murphy were convicted of the murders and sentenced to life. There was a sad postscript. It emerged during the trial that if PIRA hadn't been so illiterate, there was an outside chance Wood and Howes might have been spared. Howes's ID card said he was based in Herfod. Herfod wasn't Hereford: it was a British military garrison in West Germany.

In 1998 Murphy and Maguire were freed as part of the Good Friday agreement, after serving just nine years.

80

September 1988

Twenty-four Troop didn't work out for Nish. The CO went back on his promise to let him come back to us after twelve months, so he quit the Regiment and went on the Circuit. He'd just got back from Rio, where he'd been standing in for some-one on a BG job, so I needed to be in Hereford. I'd promised Hillbilly I'd keep an eye.

I was called back from Derry to the warehouse, where Minky was waiting with a brew in the crew room. 'They roped you in as a Walt as well?'

I went across to the Burco and fixed myself one. 'Where's Eno?'

'Still out, mate.' There was still no smile, still no acid reply about him only becoming a Walt over everyone else's dead body.

Something bad had happened.

'Nish?'

'No, mate. Hillbilly.'

'What happened?'

He shrugged.

My first thought was that somebody should go and tell Nish. I really didn't want to do it over the phone.

The fastball made sense now. The Khmer Rouge had driven several million Cambodians, desperate to escape the killing fields, across the border into Thailand. The enormous refugee camps that had sprung up were a huge financial drain on the Thais, and an even bigger source of social unrest. The only way they could get the refugees to return to Cambodia was to replace the Khmer Rouge.

Ordinarily the world's policemen would have stepped in, but the CIA and their associates were finding it almost impossible to obtain political clearance for black operations, these days. The new Freedom of Information Act made it harder to keep the skeletons in the cupboard, and American public opinion wouldn't have stood for planes laden with body bags coming back from South East Asia all over again. They offered the Thais money and intelligence, but no other support.

That was where we came in.

They could have helped the Thais launch a conventional attack, but that would have risked a very expensive and open-ended commitment. It might also have provoked a reaction from the Vietnamese, who had their own Cambodian agenda. They had invaded in 1979 and installed their regime in Phnom Penh, but most of the rest of the country was still in Khmer Rouge hands.

A secret training camp was set up near the border, and over the next few months Hillbilly and a number of others flew out to Bangkok, met with the Cambodians, then went forth to generate mayhem.

The operation led to the Khmer Rouge's very first military defeat. Whitehall was able to 'maintain the UK's interests overseas' and the Cambodians were able to build on that success; by September 1989 they had forced the Vietnamese to withdraw. That, with the Soviet retreat from Afghanistan in February of the same year, signalled the end of the Cold War.

Minky went to give Eno the bad news and I finally made

contact with Nish. I hadn't heard him so upset since the night Al was killed.

'I knew he was due back in the next couple of days . . .' His voice cracked. 'I just left a message on his answering-machine to give me a shout as soon as he got in.'

His breathing became more laboured. I pictured him gripping the phone in one hand and a fistful of cigarettes in the other.

I didn't know how Hillbilly had died, or even where. The official version was that he had been found in his hotel room.

Nish was none the wiser. 'All the squadron would say is that he was on a team job and had a heart-attack. But I ain't buying it.'

Nor was I. Heart-attack? The boy didn't do drugs or steroids, and was mega-fit.

'You all right, mate?'

He wasn't crying, but he was close. 'Yeah, fine.'

We never did find out how Hillbilly died, and I suppose we never will. I'm certain about one thing, though: it doesn't take six weeks to get a guy's body back to the UK if he's died of a heart-attack in a hotel room.

Eno and I had a can or two the next day. I muttered Frank's line about the tiger and the sheep. That was about all we could do. We couldn't even go to the funeral in Hereford when Hillbilly's body eventually came home because we were still on operations.

Nish managed to pick himself up, and headed off to Swaziland with Harry. They'd joined a task force of ex-Regiment and Intelligence Corps guys set up to combat the rhino and elephant poachers. They identified the dealers, unmasked corrupt officials and trained the anti-poacher units. When Harry asked if he was up for the job, he jumped at it. It was right up his street, and I guess it helped to fill the vacuum left by Hillbilly's death.

Schwepsy was also out and about. He was well established on the Circuit, which meant that not too many days would go by without somebody somewhere being called an 'orrible little man.

Des was finally allowed to get out after the Belize punch-bag disintegrated and there was nothing left to pummel. He and his family were in Washington DC. He was BGing Saad Hariri, the son of the man being tipped as Lebanon's next prime minister.

Saad was in his early twenties and went to Georgetown University. The family didn't like high-profile security. They wanted close protection, but subtly provided – a Regiment speciality. Des could look good in a Turkish brothel or the White House, as long as he kept his tattoos under wraps. They'd scare the shit out of the First Lady.

Frank wrote me a letter while I was still over the water to say he was praying for Hillbilly and he was as glad as I was that Nish wasn't on his own. Sir Ralph Halpern had been in the limelight: we'd all been reading the red tops and loving every minute. 'Five Times a Knight', as he was now known, had been catapulted from the financial section onto the front page after his girlfriend, Fiona Wright, had sold her kiss-and-tell memoirs. I'd asked Frank for the low-down, but he wasn't telling.

He said life was really good. He was working a week on, a week off, and still driving flash company cars. He'd joined the congregation of All Souls at Langham Place, and was no longer doing the happy-clappy thing. My Terry Waite joke had led him to the Anglican Church, and he wanted to become a minister.

I couldn't imagine Frank in a dog collar. He still only ever wore Rohan trousers, a checked flannelette shirt, and a knitted tie.

'Why the tie, Frank?'

'Because when I buy a train ticket people treat me differently.'

You had to be happy for him. Like Des, he was living his dream.

The letter ended with an invitation. Frank, ever the optimist, wondered if I'd like to come to his ordination, whenever that was going to be.

81

March 1989

None of the troop I'd first met in Malaysia was still around. They'd all been killed, had got out, or were away on long-term jobs. After training the Det, Tiny had disappeared onto Planet Spook. Chris had gone to the Wing, then back over the water to run the troop.

Saddlebags had become an instructor, running Selection. Same as anywhere else, once you'd gone, you'd gone. The new faces took over.

The day after I got back from Northern Ireland, a team of us were scrambled to Cyprus. Terry Waite's little trips to Beirut hadn't quite worked out the way he'd hoped. He'd been chained to a radiator for two years and it looked like we'd have to go in and unfasten him. The plan was a smash-and-grab: the helicopter pilots were giving us fifteen minutes on the ground to shoot our way in, do the business, and bundle him aboard. In the end, we had more stand-tos than brews as we hung around in an RAF hangar, and were finally sent home. Maybe it suited the powers-that-be to leave him where he was.

I was glad Frank hadn't taken my advice and asked Waite for a job: he might have ended up sharing a radiator.

I hadn't seen much of the Ginger One. While I'd been over the water, he'd been all over the shop. He'd fallen out with Sir Ralph and moved on to Mohamed Al Fayed. But Sir Ralph still owed him a bonus. Bizarrely, he had an opportunity to confront him about it while he was on the Al Fayed team. The Burton boss was in his gym, having swapped Fiona for a running machine. Frank went at him like a righteous terrier and chewed him into submission. He got his cash. If he ever did become a minister, I pitied his parishioners. When he brought out that collection plate, they'd be handing over their houses.

I got back from Derry a 'complete soldier', finished a three-month demolitions course, and was then sent to learn Spanish. At least I knew why this time. A new team job had been running in Colombia for the last six months. G Squadron were there at the moment, and two B Squadron troops were set to take over.

The cocaine trade alone was worth twenty billion dollars more than the combined wealth of McDonald's, Microsoft and Kellogg's. The coca leaf grew like a weed all over the Andes, but Colombia was where it all came together. You only had to look at a map to see why. It joined Central America to South America and had hundreds of small airfields and harbours within reach of both the eastern and the western seaboard of the USA.

Colombia was one big coca warehouse, and its thousands of square miles of rainforest were peppered with primitive drug-manufacturing plants (DMPs) where the leaves were processed into paste and then white powder. They were thrown up from bits of wood and palm, and easy to camouflage.

The Medellín and Cali cartels were awash with money. At one stage, Pablo Escobar, the leader of the world's most powerful drugs cartel, offered to pay off the country's national debt if the Colombian government just left him alone. Their private armies had every weapon on the planet: heavy weapons, RPGs, heavy machine-guns, ground-to-air missiles and helicopters. Cubans and former Israeli Special Forces trained them. There were fire fights at every level of the drug business, from dealers on the streets to pitched battles against the anti-narcotics police or security forces. In Colombia, the drugs war really was a war.

With twenty thousand drug-related murders a year, it had become the most dangerous place on earth. The most frequent cause of death for a Colombian adult was gunshot wounds. It was a social problem, but it required a military solution.

82

The Regiment had trained with America's Drug Enforcement Agency (DEA) and the US Coast Guard, and run operations inside the UK to thwart IRA attempts to raise funds through drug-dealing. Margaret Thatcher offered to help, and the Regiment became part of what was called the First Strike Policy. Stop the manufacture of drugs at source, the theory went, and they wouldn't end up on our streets.

The strategy was to attack the drug-manufacturing plants in the same way we would an enemy airfield. The objective was to destroy both the pilots and the aircraft. Technology is easily replaced; skilled humans aren't. And the more chemists and technicians we could take out, the better. A new DMP could be set up in two or three days; it wasn't so easy to get hold of the people to operate them.

The job was top secret. No one was to know what was going on, or where we were flying when we left Brize Norton one Sunday morning. The reason we couldn't tell anyone, we discovered, was because Downing Street wanted the *Sunday Express* to have an exclusive. 'SAS IN COLOMBIA' was splashed all over their front page the day we left. The picture showed some G Squadron boys kicking in a DMP door.

Our new staff-sergeant appeared. Gaz was just short of six

foot, with wavy brown hair. He was so fresh-faced he looked like a fourteen-year-old with stubble – and, recently divorced and immensely sociable, he was bent on reliving his youth. Gaz was tailor-made for B Squadron. Even the sergeant-major called him Champagne Charlie. He wore Armani suits and Jermyn Street shirts; if Hillbilly had been alive, the town would have been a nightmare with the two of them on the prowl.

Gaz was an ex-Green Jacket, as were his brother and his dad. And they'd all either been in the Regiment or were still. Everybody wanted to be best mates with him: with his family connections, he was SAS royalty. It was only a matter of time before his mum turned up for Selection too.

Gaz had left the Regiment for a couple of years. He'd departed as a corporal and immediately been given a troop on his return. Some of the guys in the squadron were bumping their gums because he'd PVRed to become an outboard-motor salesman, then jumped two ranks when that didn't work out.

Outboard-motor salesman? I couldn't believe they fell for that story. Apart from anything else, it was such a bad one.

Gaz was one of the guys who'd suddenly resigned from the Regiment in '82. Soon afterwards, Russian helicopter gunships had started falling out of the skies all over Afghanistan.

83

We started training the anti-narcotic police shortly after we arrived in Colombia. We had a ten-man patrol each, and took them through every facet of jungle warfare – surveillance and counter-surveillance, aggressive patrolling, OPs, close-target recces and demolitions. They were all right, those lads, considering they were just doing it to feed their families. They didn't really want to be out taking on the cartels, and we sometimes had to coax them into working.

Once we'd spent a month training them up, each two-week patrol was tasked to cover four square kilometres of rainforest. When they found a drug-manufacturing plant, they'd carry out a CTR and plan an attack. The other three patrols would RV with them. But they were nearly always unsuccessful.

The problem was that we had to radio every operational detail to Bogotá, and that included the timings and taskings for the helicopter gunships. They would keep out of hearing distance until we attacked, then be on target within two or three minutes to take out any runners. The DMPs were often sited by rivers so the lads could have getaway boats at the ready; some even cut a landing zone (LZ) out of the rainforest and had a heli standing by. It was the Hueys' job to hose them down.

But Escobar's boys had thought of that. Palms were greased and the helis overflew the DMP minutes before we attacked. As soon as they heard the rotor blades, everybody would leg it. We destroyed the empty camp, but that didn't mean much.

It wasn't our only problem. The ANP (anti-narcotics police) weren't too keen on camp attacks. To make themselves feel better, they wrapped coca leaves round sugar cubes and sucked them the night before. By the time we'd positioned them at the start line, they were ready to sing and dance all the Broadway hits.

Then Gaz took control of the Bogotá situation. He was the only person we were in touch with. When we found a DMP, our comms went directly to him. He would tell everybody else where to go and what to do at the very last minute. We also took control of the ANP situation. Once they'd gathered at the troop RV we made them our prisoners, and ensured they didn't smuggle in any coca leaves or sugar after we'd checked their kit.

The strike rate went through the roof. Chemists and technicians were getting dropped big-time. We'd hit a camp, kill as many as we could and melt back into the jungle while the media were helicoptered in to photograph a handful of smiling Colombian policemen.

For all our successes, the ocean of drugs was so vast that whatever we did was just a raindrop. You could only restrict the trade; you couldn't eliminate it. The drugs barons' billions bought them too much insulation.

After every couple of patrols, we headed off for a day or two of R&R. Bogotá was probably the most exciting city in the world. There was nowhere else I could think of where grand-scale lawlessness met such a tidal wave of drug money head-on. The war wasn't only in the jungle: it was here on the streets.

The big appeal of Bogotá, as far as we were concerned, was the food. We lost a huge amount of weight on the pig swill we were given in the jungle so we'd spend a couple of hours in the shower at the Dann Norte or the Cosmos Hotel, then head down to one of the restaurants in the embassy district.

That particular Saturday, we were hoping to catch Carl Williams taking the world heavyweight title from Mike Tyson on a bar TV. The next day, we were going to watch a bullfight in the old part of town. The bullring was the size of Wembley. The steaks weren't much smaller.

I was clean, freshly shaved and smelling frou-frou. I picked up my 9mm and shoved it down the front of my jeans. We were out on a social, but in that part of the world you didn't leave home without one. I shoved a spare magazine down the side of my shoe and folded over my sock to keep it in. Gaz did the same.

The pavements were bustling. Blacked-out Mercedes swept along the potholed roads, narrowly missing the kids who lived like feral cats in the craters where the sewers had collapsed. Their skin was black with grime. Their hair hadn't been washed or combed for years. The Colombian government reckoned there were ten thousand street kids in this city alone, living in parks, under bridges and in sewers, stealing and begging to stay alive. They were called *los desechables* – the disposables. In some areas these small hungry thieves drove customers away from local businesses. The traders' solution was to hire local death squads to clean up the streets. Thousands had been murdered.

We headed for a steak and fish place with a Scottish theme and an indoor driving range in the basement. You could take a swing between courses. We'd been there many times, and we always steered clear of the fish. Bogotá was high up on a mountain plain. The sea was miles away.

Instead of street-lighting, this part of town had huge flaming gas torches. If you could see one, you knew you were in the right place – unless you were a *desechable*, in which case you knew to keep well away. The area teemed with Departamento

Administrativo de Seguridad (DAS), the national security police. Their remit seemed to be to look after civil servants, politicians and drug-dealers – people with money, basically.

They were always in civilian clothes, but they didn't exactly keep a low profile. During the day DAS cars would scream between the lanes of traffic on the decaying boulevards, bristling with Mini Uzis. The traffic parted like the Red Sea did for Moses.

At night, you'd see them lurking in doorways, usually in white armbands so they could identify each other if things kicked off. Everybody was wary of the DAS, and that included us. This was the drug capital of the world, and if you were in the secret police that didn't mean you'd turn down the odd line or two. Some of those lads were totally out of control, but they had the badge of authority – and a 9mm machine-gun at the ready.

84

A Merc pulled in at the kerb as we arrived, and bodyguards swarmed from the other vehicles in the cavalcade. The door opened and a pair of gold-tipped cowboy boots hit the pavement, followed by the principal, with slicked-back hair, an Armani suit, lots of gold, and a fur-coated beauty on each arm. It was like a scene from *Miami Vice*.

Gaz and I embarrassed ourselves for a moment, gawping at the women – the air-con was always on low in those limos: what was the point of trousering all that drug money if you couldn't drape your women in mink? Then we sliced a few balls down the driving range and tucked into T-bone steaks the size of cartwheels before wandering off in search of a bar that had the fight on.

We'd just turned down an alleyway towards a neon club sign when we heard gunfire about twenty metres ahead of us. Three or four short, sharp bursts. We hugged the walls for cover and drew down our weapons. We weren't looking for a fight, but we'd shoot and scoot if it came to it.

Five or six guys with Mini Uzis were silhouetted against the neon. I caught a glimpse of white armbands and heard laughter as they slung something onto the back of a pick-up.

'Fucking hell,' Gaz said. 'They're dropping the kids again.'

A tarpaulin covered the load. All that would be left were some bloodstains on the paving, and that was nothing unusual. We knew what was going on, but nobody talked about it. They called it social cleansing, as if it was some kind of rodent-eradication programme. Fuck knows where they dumped the bodies. They probably became pig feed.

Gaz looked like he wanted to take them on.

I shook my head. 'Soon as they see weapons they'll hose us down. Time to go.'

The DAS boys would be sparked up after their little spree, and they wouldn't worry too much about taking out a couple of extras.

I shoved my pistol back down my jeans. 'Come on, mate, let's bin it.'

The moment we moved, half a dozen kids who'd been hiding near the pick-up jumped up and ran straight towards us. They couldn't have been more than six or seven, but it was difficult to tell. Cartwheel-sized T-bones weren't on the menu for those guys.

The DAS lifted their 9mms but spotted us at the end of the alley in their arc of fire. They set off after the kids, shouting for them to stop.

Gaz tucked away his weapon just in time. The kids surged around us and we slid them between two wheelie-bins to get them out of the way. There was nowhere else to run.

The DAS drew level with us, sweating like pigs. They'd obviously been doing a lot of killing tonight. Each had a Mini Uzi on a sling over one shoulder, pointing straight at us. We kept our hands in view.

Our Spanish was good, but I pretended it wasn't. 'Inglaterra! Embassy! *Inglés! Británico!*'

Neither of us looked remotely like Our Man in Colombia. Drug-dealers, maybe; diplomats, unlikely.

The kids cowered at our feet. The stench coming off them was unbelievable. But the DAS couldn't give a fuck about them now. This was a different kind of challenge. The smallest and skinniest one hollered and jabbed his Uzi at us like it was his index finger. Every time he did so, the sling dropped further down his arm until it was taut.

His finger was on the trigger.

If he had the safety off, he could be zapping us any second.

'*Inglaterra!*'

The kids were whimpering.

Then one of the lads by the pick-up yelled up the alleyway. My Spanish was good enough to know he was saying they'd be severely in the shit if they dropped a couple of unarmed civilians from the embassy.

They stared at us, well pissed off, then turned and stalked away.

The kids stayed huddled between the bins.

I told them to scarper but they didn't budge.

Gaz pulled some US dollars from his pocket. As soon as they spotted them they saw the light. They grabbed the money and legged it back up the alley. They turned right, away from the embassy district. We watched them scatter in a blur of scabby feet and ripped T-shirts. Then, thinking about it, we ran a couple of hundred metres too, in case the DAS lads had second thoughts, decided to drive round the block and pick up the arseholes who'd fronted them. I didn't fancy ending the evening in the back of their pick-up.

We dived into the busiest bar we could find. Hundreds of locals were bunched around three different TVs. Gaz had already spent ten dollars so the Heinekens were on me.

We toasted each other with a clink of the bottlenecks on a job well done, but the celebrations were short-lived. Tyson beat Williams by a technical knock-out in the first, and remained undisputed heavyweight champion of the world.

We'd been cut off from the rest of that world, fighting our own little war. By the time we got back from Colombia, there was a big new one going on that we'd heard nothing about.

Saddam Hussein had invaded Kuwait, and the whole Regiment was gearing up to return to its desert roots.

Not Seven Troop, sadly: B Squadron were scheduled to take over the counter-terrorist (CT) team. Gaz was in charge, and I was his second-in-command.

85

November 1990

As the drums kept beating across the Gulf, every TV screen was filled with footage of Coalition forces preparing to put Saddam back in his box. American generals gave daily press calls to CNN in the Saudi desert about the urgent need to stop the rape and murder of Kuwaitis and kick out the Iraqi invader, while Saddam was telling another CNN crew he didn't know what the fuck they were on about.

Saddam promised the Americans the Mother of All Battles. The media loved it. Cameras in both corners of the ring! They hadn't had that in the Falklands.

Back in the UK, B Squadron were in a dark mood. It looked as if our stint on the CT team would take us into the spring of 1991 and beyond, and by then it might all be over. The Regiment was planning to be in the Gulf for the long haul. Not only were we going to miss the start of the war – for Special Forces the most important part, because we'd be involved before it was even declared – but we might also be stuck on the CT team for yet another tour: the three squadrons in Iraq might not be able to disengage.

There was stuff going on in Hereford that had never

317

happened before. Regimental HQ was preparing to move to Saudi, lock, stock and barrel. The communications centre was huge, and its equipment was dug in below its quarters. Scaleys lived like moles down there, receiving and transmitting signals twenty-four/seven. It was a huge undertaking, but with three squadrons committed to one operation, it had to be done.

The Regiment wasn't geared up for the scaling of weapons and kit. We were strategic troops, 'set to task'. There were green ops, very much like the impending Gulf War, with lots of weapons, vehicles and all that aggressive, kinetic stuff. There were black ops, which the CT team were part of. Finally there were grey jobs, the team jobs with long hair and trainers. We suddenly needed three squadrons' worth of green stuff, which was proving hard to get hold of.

We in B Squadron got on with our job, which was preparing for Islamic extremists to attack the UK mainland in retaliation for the invasion.

I was responsible for IA (immediate action). If the thirty-minute team got called out, I would grab an Agusta and a couple of signallers and fly straight to any incident – be it a hostage situation or helping the police blow in a few doors to get into a house and make arrests.

As the Coalition armies massed on the Saudi border, A and D Squadrons were already behind enemy lines. The CO called us into the Regimental HQ briefing room and announced that G Squadron would take over the team earlier than expected and B Squadron would deploy to the Gulf. We would deploy half a squadron at a time. The first to go would be the Red Team, which was us. Thank fuck for that: I was going to get involved in this war after all. It was why I'd joined the Regiment in the first place, having missed out on the Falklands.

But, first, four of us had to head off to Tucson, Arizona, to visit the world's biggest aircraft graveyard. We were meeting

SEVEN TROOP

up with some Delta patrols to practice methods of entry.

The place was like a mechanical sunset community. Thousands of aircraft had been mothballed and shrink-wrapped. The air was clean and dry, ideal conditions for military equipment and human beings in their twilight years.

Rows of ground-attack helicopters, fixed-wing fighters, bombers, you name it, stretched to the horizon. There were a few square miles of civilian aircraft, too, and those were the ones we were interested in. They'd been seized during drug operations or from African countries that had defaulted on their payments. We were allowed to blow up the ones that were beginning to show their age. I hoped the pensioners in their retirement homes wouldn't get wind of it or they'd be flapping good style.

We spent a very happy two weeks climbing like monkeys over 747s with the Delta lads until we'd got it just right. These guys were on the CT team Stateside, and were also bracing themselves for terrorist attacks.

We flew home via Washington DC. The UN Security Council had just passed Resolution 678, authorizing military intervention in Iraq if that nation did not withdraw its forces from Kuwait and free all foreign hostages by 15 January 1991. The TV screens at the embassy on Massachusetts Avenue were stuffed with US generals and plucky young soldiers telling the world how keen they were to implement it.

A technology expert talked about the first page that been written for something called the 'World Wide Web'. The Conservative Party had chosen John Major to succeed Margaret Thatcher as prime minister. In Germany, which had reunified a month ago, the very last section of the Berlin Wall had been demolished.

The military attaché mentioned that Des Doom was still in town, running a BG contract. Some of us thought it would be a good idea to hang around for a couple more days to see him, and familiarize ourselves with the Washington landscape, just in case. The embassy bought it. We didn't tell them we just needed time to shop for Cannondale mountain bikes, which were half the price there.

A gang of us piled into an embassy vehicle and headed out onto the Beltway. Des really was living the dream: his house was a plush executive mansion with a long gravelled driveway and lawns carved out of the Virginia woodland; there was a huge Lincoln Towncar out front, and the obligatory basketball hoop – not an improvised punch-bag in sight.

He ushered us into a lounge the size of a football stadium. The fireplace was wider than my whole front room.

'Great to see you all.' He handed round the Jack Daniel's with a big grin. 'You know I've got Nish working with me?'

86

Nish was going flying the next day – did I want to come along?

'Flying? Where did you learn?'

'Africa. Come on, it'll be a laugh.'

We met up the next morning. He lived at the bottom end of Massachusetts Avenue, the street all the embassies were on, in a very smart apartment. There was half a Mars bar and a can of Coke in the fridge, and that was about it, apart from a big pile of dirty cups in the sink and, of course, an overflowing ashtray. Otherwise it was completely bare.

We leapt into his company Saab. He drove like he was going for pole position in the Indy 500. I was amazed he hadn't been caught. Anything over sixty here and the police were usually all over you.

'I thought you were too busy in the bush, doing your David Attenborough bit with Harry . . .'

'There was downtime. Never took the test, though. I wanted a commercial licence and my instrument rating, so I came over here.'

The explanation was wrapped in a cloud of cigarette smoke.

The airstrip was forty-five minutes away. The morning frost had melted by the time we pulled up outside a small club-house. Several private aircraft sat in front of a couple of hangars. The two guys who ran the place knew Nish well. As he paid his ninety dollars for the hour's rental, one of them treated me to a huge grin and some prime Dick Van Dyke Cockney. 'You'll need your motor over there in the hangar, mate.' He didn't tell me why.

We drove to what I was hoping would be a state-of-the-art Jet Ranger with leather upholstery and a bar, but which turned out to be a tiny Robinson two-seater.

'Do us a favour, will you, mate, while I do the pre-flight checks?' Nish threw his fag end out of the window. 'Grab the leads out of the boot.'

'What the fuck you on about? We going to jump-start this thing?'

'Yeah.' He threw the map at me. 'You can navigate as well.'

He opened the bonnet and made the connections, then hopped into the cockpit. His pre-flight checks seemed to consist of adjusting his arse in the seat and getting another cigarette on the go. The heli coughed and belched black exhaust, then the rotors kicked off. I retrieved the jump leads and moved the car out of the way.

Nish gobbed pilot stuff into the radio and we lifted off.

'Where we going?'

'Back into the city. You're going to love this.'

Nish said he did this a lot to keep his hours up. He had his eye on a plane he was going to buy with the cash he'd made from this job and fly back to the UK.

'Across the Atlantic? Fuck me, what is it? An executive jet?'

'Nah, I'll bung a couple of jerry-cans in the back.'

Nish was in his element now we were airborne. We followed the Potomac river into the city. We were coming in low – very low – but that was the law here. Ronald Reagan airport was within spitting distance of the White House and aircraft were landing and taking off all over the place, so we almost had to roof-hop to keep out of the way.

'Any other city you have to be miles high. And in Europe,

certainly London, you need two engines so you can clear habitation if one fails.'

We were coming in to the city limits. I could see nothing but freeways feeding it with cars. There'd be no clearing habitation if this thing failed.

I talked a bit about the Regiment, told him things must be going downhill because I'd been promoted to sergeant. The Gulf came up, but I changed the subject when I saw Nish getting pissed off because he wouldn't be there. 'You still going for that record?'

It was like I'd opened a floodgate. 'Yeah.' His face lit up. 'Gonna beat Joe Kittinger's jump.'

'How high was it?'

'I've told you a million times. Twenty miles. Come on, keep up.'

'And he survived?'

'Of course he did, you dickhead. It's not a record for dead people.'

I knew very little about the attempt, apart from stories told in freefall circles. Nish knew everything, down to the inside-leg measurement of the guy's space suit. Joseph Kittinger was a US Air Force captain who'd jumped from a helium balloon with an open gondola 102,800 feet above New Mexico on 16 August 1960. He'd looked like the Michelin Man, but without his space suit his blood would have boiled and his organs exploded.

Towing a small drogue chute for stabilization, he fell for four minutes and thirty-six seconds, reaching a maximum speed of 614 m.p.h. – close on the speed of sound – before opening his parachute fourteen minutes later at 18,000 feet. Pressurization for his right glove malfunctioned during the ascent, causing his hand to swell. He set records for highest balloon ascent, highest parachute jump, longest drogue-fall, and fastest speed by an un-powered human through the atmosphere.

The jump was made in a rocking-chair position, descending

on his back, rather than in an arch, because he was wearing sixty pounds of kit on his arse and his pressure suit naturally formed that shape – it was designed for sitting in an aircraft cockpit – when it inflated.

And Nish was going to beat it. He was used to falling in the sitting position with a Bergen hanging off his arse.

'Who's going to finance it? You can't just hitch a ride in a hot-air balloon, can you?'

'Harry's got it all sorted. He knows one of the Guinness banking family.' Loel Guinness ran a company called High Adventure, set up to support sportsmen and -women involved in big performance and endurance events like climbing Everest. That must have been how Harry had got to know him.

He turned to me and grinned. Ash fell from the cigarette he still had clamped in his mouth. 'Joe was also the first guy to fly a gas balloon solo across the Atlantic, so I'm really following in his footsteps. Fucking great, eh?'

The cost was going to be massive and he'd need a shit-load of training, but he was up for it. As soon as Saad finished at Georgetown, it was going to become a full-on job. As long as he survived crossing thousands of miles of ocean in a single-engine aircraft first.

He pointed up at the clouds. 'Space ain't that far away, mate. If a car could drive straight up, it'd take less than an hour.'

'Driving the way you do, or legally?'

I got another big grin. 'Wonder if I'll see Frank's boss while I'm up there? He's a vicar now, you know.'

'You heard from him?'

'The odd postcard. Whenever he finds one of a nice busty nun.'

The Robinson shuddered into a hover. We were so low over a clapboard house we were making the shingles flap. A guy in the yard looked up and shook his fist at us.

Nish gave him a cheery wave. 'Shouldn't live there if he can't take a joke.' He gave another wave. We were about to blow the roof off. 'That's where they filmed *The Exorcist*. Great film. Have you seen it? Directed by William Friedkin.'

He pumped off left and back towards the river. Next stop was the White House, but we didn't stay long. We got a fearsome bollocking on the radio. Seconds later we were back over the river.

'What're all those crosses for, mate?' I pointed at the mass of felt-tip marks on the map. 'Landing sites?'

'There's loads of places to land in the city. But those are where I've scored.'

He'd land by a bar or a restaurant and go in for a Coke. Nine times out of ten, a woman would come up and start chatting because she wanted to go up in his helicopter. He would play the polite but stupid Brit, and they loved it.

I smiled to myself as he waffled away. He really was looking and sounding like he had in the old days. No talk of Hillbilly or Al, just flying, freefalling and women.

Almost the moment we were back in the Saab, it all changed again. He turned to me, his face serious. 'Listen, mate, you be careful in the Gulf. We do things in life that we're never able to forget.'

I nodded, not sure what he was on about. But, just as quickly, he broke into a smile, either to cover up his anxiety or to turn what he'd said into a joke.

87

January 1991

We'd been in Saudi a while, but now the Gulf War was really kicking off. A Chinook helicopter flew us into enemy territory north-west of Baghdad. On board was an eight-man foot patrol under my command. Our radio call sign was Bravo Two Zero.

Our mission was simple: to destroy a fibre-optic cable that ran from Baghdad into the western and north-western deserts, from where Saddam was deploying his Scud missile teams against Israel. His reasoning was simple. If Scuds continued to rain on Tel Aviv and Haifa, the Israelis would be provoked into fighting alongside the anti-Saddam coalition, and the alliance would crumble. There was no way Saudi or the others would countenance being brothers in arms with the Israelis, even if they just did their own thing.

Half-squadron groups from A and D Squadron were already combing the deserts, but they were up against it. The Scud launchers were small and mobile. Unless they were lucky enough to bump into one, all they could do was wait for a launch, then try to track and destroy it.

At one stage the whole Israeli Air Force was circling Israeli air space, poised to retaliate. George Bush cut a deal with

Yitzhak Shamir: the Israelis gave the Coalition a two-week window in which to take out the Scud threat. If we failed, Israel would attack.

All our planning and preparation changed overnight. We'd focused on traditional SAS tasks like the disruption of supply lines and communications, prime-target assassination and industrial sabotage.

We suffered from kit shortages just like everybody else. We had to make our own Claymore anti-personnel mines from nuts and bolts, plastic explosive and ice cream cartons. Everything else we begged, stole and borrowed, even down to ammunition and 40mm grenades for our M23 assault rifles.

And, of course, we were going out there in such a rush that we hardly had any information. Nobody knew exactly where the cable was, let alone how best to destroy it. The mapping consisted of air charts, which only showed major man-made and topographical features. But our attitude was: Fuck it, that's what Special Forces are all about – getting on with what you've got and improvising the rest.

It was nothing new. When the patrols from B Squadron had gone into mainland Argentina to do recces for the attack on the Marines' barracks and the airstrips, all they'd had to get them onto target were the maps in Michelin restaurant guides. There was plenty of detail on the ambience of various Tierra del Fuego eateries and the quality of their steaks but, strangely, absolutely fuck all on the location of the nearest Marines' barracks, its approach roads and defences. But that was all they could get their hands on at the time, so that was what they used.

Anyway, the primary task of Special Forces was to gain information. That was why, nine times out of ten, we went in without any.

Bravo Two Zero deployed, but we never found the cable. We only discovered later that it ran alongside the northern main supply route (MSR) from Baghdad and headed north-west towards the Syrian border. What we did find, at first light the next morning, was a pair of S60 anti-aircraft guns just four hundred metres from our lie-up position (LUP).

This was no big problem. Our most important weapon on this sort of job wasn't an assault rifle, a 60mm rocket or a light machine-gun, it was concealment. We would just lie up in daylight, move out at night and get on with the job. The problem was that our radios didn't work.

Steve 'Legs' Lane and Dinger had been trying everything they could think of to send our sitrep. I liked Legs. He had the longest and skinniest pair I'd ever seen, which made him a bit of a racing snake over the ground, even with a Bergen on his back. He'd started his army life in the Royal Engineers before transferring to the Paras and was still establishing himself after having passed Selection about six months before. Like all newcomers he was a bit on the quiet side, but had become firm friends with Dinger.

It wasn't difficult. Dinger was tall, with wiry blond hair, and he was wild. He was also ex-Para Reg and new to Seven Troop, and had taken up Nish's mantle as our resident smoker and wit. I think they even came from the same part of the world. It probably had something to do with the water. He was a great man to bounce off, just like Nish, and I took to him instantly.

No matter what Regimental HQ tried, we hadn't been able to let them know we were alive and getting on with the mission. But having no comms didn't mean everything stopped: we still had to get on with the job. The most important thing was the mission. Nothing else mattered.

There was a contingency plan in the event of radio failure: an RV with a helicopter the following night. But first I had to take out a four-man recce patrol at last light to try yet again to locate the fibre-optic.

Vince Phillips, my second-in-command, would man the LUP. He'd come from the Ordnance Corps. Aged thirty-seven, he had just under three years' service left with the Regiment.

He was a big old boy, and immensely strong – not only in body but also in mind. I valued his honesty, and his realism. His wild, coarse, curly hair, moustache and sideboards made him look like a mad mountain man, which was pretty much what he was. An expert mountaineer, diver and skier, he walked as if he had a barrel of beer under each arm. Most things were either 'shit' or 'fucking shit', but his main complaint in life was that his time in the Regiment was nearly up.

We were hiding up in a small wadi, waiting for last light. At about 1630, we heard movement about fifty metres away. A kid was taking his goats for a bit of a spin, and the lead animal had a bell. We stood to.

The goat came up and peered over the lip. He gazed at us and chewed away on a bit of old tumbleweed, then his mates came up and they checked us out too. We could hear the kid shouting, and it wasn't long before he was staring down at us, and we were staring up at him. He didn't have a clue what he was looking at, but eight weapon barrels told him it was a drama. He turned and legged it.

Vince scrambled up the wadi, but it was too late. The boy was making a beeline for the S60s. We were compromised.

Even if we'd caught him, we wouldn't have killed him. Special Forces don't roam the countryside with daggers drawn. We wouldn't kill a civilian unless it was absolutely imperative, and that had more to do with self-preservation than morality. If enemy troops rocked up to the outskirts of Birmingham or Manchester and slotted the first kid they bumped into, they wouldn't last five minutes when they were captured.

There were also tactical considerations. We'd have had a dead weight to carry, because everything we took in on the ground, we took out with us when we left. It was called hard routine. We pissed into containers and shat into plastic bags. We didn't cook, smoke – which Dinger hated – or leave anything to show the enemy we'd been there.

If Vince had caught the boy, he'd have found himself tied up out of sight of the S60s, with a stomach full of ration-pack chocolate to keep him happy. He might have OD'd on Yorkie bars, but he'd have been alive.

We had no option but to head for Syria, about 180 kilometres away. The CIA had organized a rat run for downed pilots and people like us, and we'd been told our contact would have a white sheet hanging out of his window in the first village we came to across the border.

After we'd all stopped laughing, we decided we'd give that one a miss and just find a friendly embassy in Damascus.

88

Over the next three days, three of my men died.

Vince went down on the second night. We'd gone out there expecting European spring weather. Instead we got a near-Arctic winter, the worst the area had seen for thirty years. Because we were on hard routine, we didn't have sleeping-bags. We slept in our Gore-Tex, always ready to move. After a contact that ended in hand-to-hand combat, Vince took the fight to the Iraqis, even though he'd badly injured his leg at our LUP. As the temperature plummeted past the freezing point of diesel, he perished from hypothermia.

Those men displayed skills and courage of the highest order when they were in the deepest shit – which wasn't easy when you were just over five feet tall. Bob Consiglio was of Swiss-Italian extraction and known as the Mumbling Midget. Despite his size he was immensely strong, and immensely stubborn. He insisted on carrying the same load as everyone else. All you could see of him from behind was a bloody great Bergen with two little legs going like pistons.

He'd been in the Royal Marines and lived life at full throttle. When he was out on the town, his favourite hobbies were dancing with and chatting up women a foot taller than he was. Hillbilly would have been proud of him. I certainly was.

The Mumbling Midget was the next to die. The night was a frenzy of death and chaos on both sides. Bob was up front with the Minimi light machine-gun. Everyone else was out of ammo. He ran into yet more Iraqis. As the contact kicked off, he stood his ground to give the rest of us time to escape, screaming at the incoming fire. Then his ammo, too, ran out, and he took incoming. He dropped like liquid. Without him we would all have gone the same way.

The patrol had got scattered, and Legs and Dinger had to swim the Euphrates to dodge their pursuers. Dinger didn't want to, but Legs showed the way and kept them both alive. They were captured the following day. Legs died some time later, almost certainly of hypothermia.

Only one of us made it across the border. Chris, the one with curly brown hair, was originally from the Territorial Army and had joined Mountain Troop about four years before the war while I was away in the Det. This was his first time on operations. He had spent a couple of years in Germany doing mountain stuff, and whatever they'd taught him certainly seemed to work: he continued on his own and finally made it to Damascus.

The other four of us were captured at different points along the Iraqi border on that third day, and spent the next seven weeks in interrogation centres in Baghdad. One of them was the infamous Abu Ghraib. Our hands were cuffed behind our backs and we were blindfolded, stripped naked and repeatedly beaten by the guards on our way into and out of interrogation.

There were two types of interrogator. Some of the military boys had been trained at Sandhurst during their war against Iran. And then there were the secret police; those lads really enjoyed their work.

We were whipped, and burnt with red hot spoons heated over paraffin stoves. We were hit with planks and steel balls swinging from sticks. My teeth had been smashed by toecaps and rifle butts when I was caught within spitting distance of the border, so a dentist was called in. He said he'd worked in Guy's Hospital for nine years, gave a chuckle and yanked out one of my back molars with a pair of pliers.

All of those lads wanted real-time information they could act on there and then. What had we been doing? Where was everybody else, and what would they be up to?

They knew the Regiment was out and about, because the Scuds were getting hit. They wanted information to help them counter those attacks. Our job was to keep that information from them.

The phrase 'prisoner of war' was a load of bollocks. We weren't prisoners *of* war, we were prisoners *at* war. We still had a job to do. The simple reason we weren't going to tell them what they wanted to know was that the guys on the ground were our friends. We knew their wives, their kids, even their dogs and cats.

The weeks that followed were all about trying to be the grey man, trying to minimize the number of beatings and make ourselves appear so insignificant we simply didn't matter.

It didn't really work. Baghdad was getting the shit blown out of it from an hour after last light to about two hours before first light. We were even taking incoming at the compound. There was no running water, no electricity, and the families and friends of our guards were getting killed and maimed. Meanwhile, their enemies were right under their noses, handcuffed, naked and in solitary confinement. Not unnaturally, they came in and took it out on us. Those kickings and beatings scared me more than the interrogations. My mind began to go wild.

Things got so bad I even tried talking to God, but He didn't answer. He was probably too busy having his ear bent by Frank.

And then I remembered a lecture by someone who'd had far more experience of this than I hoped I was ever going to get.

He was a United States Marines pilot who had flown Phantoms in Vietnam. He was shot down over Hanoi and spent six years in solitary confinement under continuous torture. Every major bone in his body was broken. He never got any medical care. He ended up with no teeth, no hair, no muscle mass. He was a mess, but he was alive. The Regiment invited him to visit. If prone-to-capture troops like us listened to the experiences of others, there might be one sentence that would help if we were ever in the same situation.

My mind was going haywire in my Baghdad cell, but I discovered his words did help me.

Hold on to the memory of those you love and want to see again.

I thought about the lads on the patrol, and particularly the ones I knew were dead. I swelled with pride. I hoped I was their equal. I had no worries about dying. We all knew you started from nothing and you were going to end with nothing. That was part of the deal. I almost felt jealous of Bob Consiglio, who'd gone down fighting; I might just be starved or beaten to death.

I even thought about Frank's tiger and his sheep, and decided the silly fucker had been right all along.

I didn't feel bitter and twisted. Nobody had forced me to be a soldier. I had no fear of being killed – fuck it, when it happened, I just wanted it to be quick, like Bob, while doing my job.

I could hardly take the kudos of being in the Regiment and then moan about it when things went wrong. People got killed. That was what happened. If you didn't like it, there were plenty of guys who wanted to take your place.

I managed the odd smile sometimes. I imagined Bob watching me. He'd be taking the piss out of the crap hat huddled in the corner in a pile of his own shit.

To begin with, I'd taken capture personally. It was the first time I'd really failed at anything since joining up. But then the optimist in me said, 'It'll be all right. I'm not dead yet. Maybe

334

I'll get to the next stage. I just need to get through the next interrogation, the next beating, the next day, the next hour . . .'

Again, the pilot was an inspiration. I remembered how he'd started off his talk. He'd held out his hands with his elbows tight against his sides, and he'd walked three and a half paces, turned, walked three and a half paces, turned again. I'd stared at him and wondered what the fuck he was on.

'This was my cell . . . this was my space . . . for six years . . .'

He went in there playing the big Marine, but all that shit was taken out of him. Get aggressive with two of them, and next time they brought in four.

'They have control of your life. There's nothing you have control of physically, they can do what they want. The only thing you can control is your mind. Let them have that, and you've lost.'

I sat in my cell and thought about his pain and fear. His family didn't even know he was still alive. I didn't know if anyone knew I was. There was nothing I had control over but my mind. I resolved to keep it mine.

I used the same thought process I had when I was a kid. However bad I thought I'd got it, there was somebody who had it worse. I was only on week three, week four . . . The American lad had had six years of it, and he'd survived. I'd been an infantry soldier and a Special Forces soldier for more than sixteen years. I was used to being wet, cold and hungry. I was used to fighting. I was even used to getting beaten up. I was in an infantry battalion, for fuck's sake. This guy was a pilot, flying from the cocoon of an aircraft-carrier, dropping a bomb from an air-conditioned office in the sky, then flying back for doughnuts, coffee and a spot of volleyball on deck.

Then, on his seventy-seventh mission, with just three to go before he got binned, he was shot down. The journey from cocoon to bamboo cage was short and sharp. At least I had a roof and a concrete floor.

I kept on and on, grasping at straws, trying to dredge the positive from the negative.

I was eventually released three days after the other three from the patrol, along with the remaining five or six American pilots who'd also been held in Abu Ghraib. There was some famous footage of General Norman Schwarzkopf, the Coalition's supreme commander, shaking hands with them as they came down the steps in Riyadh. The SAS prisoners were round the back of the aircraft, about to be whisked off to the British military hospital in Cyprus.

89

Hereford
May 1991

Back at the Lines, we had a couple of sessions with Dr Gordon
Turnbull, the RAF psychiatrist. He'd treated the mountain-
rescue teams at Lockerbie in 1988. The patrol's survivors sat in
a comfortable room in the officers' mess as Gordon explained
what post traumatic stress disorder (PTSD) was all about.

For starters, it wasn't a disease but it was a clinical condition,
a natural physical and emotional reaction to a deeply shocking
or life-threatening event. It could and did affect anyone, and
there was nothing unmanly about experiencing it.

One of the main symptoms of PTSD was an unwillingness to
talk about the events that had brought it about – so one of the
main challenges in helping sufferers was to engage with them
and get them to accept treatment. Some still felt misunderstood
by the medical establishment and society at large, and ended
up suffering in silence. Others carried so much guilt with them
– yet another symptom – that they felt unworthy of help.

PTSD could affect every aspect of a sufferer's life – not
surprising when the symptoms included insomnia, recurring
nightmares, persistent high anxiety levels, severe mood

swings, hyper-alertness, violent and aggressive outbursts, lack of concentration, sexual dysfunction and depression, self-loathing for surviving when others had not, self-isolation, inability to readjust to normal life, inability to communicate with loved ones, or to reciprocate love, and the desire to remain solely with others in the same position, who therefore 'understood'.

PTSD sufferers might also experience alcohol- or drug-related problems, often caused by an attempt to self-medicate their symptoms away. Some just lost it completely and resorted to violence – ranging from spousal abuse to murder when the stakes were cranked up.

I knew quite a few lads who fitted the bill one way or another.

Flashbacks brought on by reminders of the trauma could be the most debilitating feature of PTSD. They occurred when the brain was unable to process the imagery it had received during a severe traumatic incident; our brains needed to make sense of it before they could store it, so they played it over and over again, like an old record, until they did.

I took a long, hard look at myself. Nothing to worry about so far. I didn't have nightmares. I didn't feel depressed. In fact, I felt lucky. I was alive. But Gordon left me very aware that I shouldn't take anything for granted. I'd have to watch myself, maybe keep a mental checklist of the symptoms. Just in case.

Until quite recently PTSD had been perceived in the military as a sign of weakness, and stigma was still attached to therapy of any sort. Guys often wouldn't admit they were suffering; apart from anything else, they didn't want those close to them to think they were mad. This was certainly the Regiment's first foray into this landscape, and only happened because we'd been taken prisoner and tortured.

I already knew of a place in Wales that many from the green army had gone to after the Falklands. These were rough, tough Paras and Marines, but they'd needed help. I'd also heard that a couple of guys from the Regiment had gone there secretly.

Delta Force actively embraced therapy. They even had their own doctor. Why pay so many millions to train someone, then watch them fall apart at the seams? Why not try to stop it before it happened, or try to help them through it if it did? For the time being, jumping in a car and heading secretly for Wales was the only real option for the rest of us.

We spent about six months mincing around doing debriefs to a range of intelligence and military organizations, and receiving continuous medical treatment. My teeth took a lot of sorting, and I had some nerve damage in my left hand. The doctors seemed to like sticking little steel probes into my skin and passing a current through them to see if it jumped up and down like a frog's legs in a scientific experiment.

I learnt a lot more about the Iraqi side of things. Information came back from the CIA and our own spooks that the Iraqis had thought we were an Israeli raiding party, and that they had taken more than two hundred casualties, dead and wounded, as we legged it towards Syria.

We discovered why the radios didn't work. We were given the wrong frequencies, which was down to Regimental HQ's move from Hereford to Saudi. If you had to communicate with Hereford from anywhere in the world, you didn't just press a button on your radio.

With our Regimental HQ held together with gaffer tape in the middle of the desert, we had been given the frequency ranges for the southern footprint, covering southern Iraq and part of Kuwait, instead of the northern footprint nearer Syria and Israel. We'd been carefully laying out our antenna wires so we could transmit coded and encrypted signals in very short bursts to prevent interception by radio scanners, but the signals that reached Riyadh had been corrupted.

It was nothing new. There had always been fuck-ups, and there always would be. You couldn't hold it against people who were doing their best in difficult circumstances. At Arnhem, in 1944, they were given radios with a range of less than three miles even though the attack force was spread up to eight miles. With communication between units almost impossible, the battle had spiralled into isolated pockets of desperate action.

War isn't a science. Machines can go wrong. So can people.

90

Frank and I fixed to meet up at the Merton, a small hotel with a bar near the railway station. Frank was a curate now, whatever that meant. I'd heard he was wearing all the black and white kit and frocks and collars and all sorts, and I was looking forward to seeing him decked out.

I was disappointed. He was in the same old green checked shirt, blue Rohan trousers and red Gore-Tex jacket. The only thing different was an orange woolly tie. He looked like a deranged train-spotter.

'Frank! Where's the collar?'

'Working hours only.'

He saw me glance again at the tie.

'People really do treat me differently. I was called "sir" when I bought a train ticket yesterday.'

'That's because you look like a lunatic and he was scared you were going to smash the window and throttle him.'

He already had a pint of bitter in front of him and a pint of Stella for me. The bar was quiet; just a couple of old fellers in the corner. I pulled up a chair.

'What's it like, then, this curate business?'

'Great. My whole life has changed from physical to cerebral – what I believe in, what I do for a living, my friends—'

'Hey, I'm still your mate, aren't I?'

'It's different. I don't see you lot every day. Even my house is—'

'Fit for an ayatollah?'

He shook his head. 'Lodgings. Everything's changed. Even vocabulary.'

'Your accent has, for sure. You're not so Geordie.'

He chuckled into his beer. I obviously hadn't been the first to tell him that. 'They say every cell in the body renews itself, so the voice box probably does as well. I don't think there's a cell left in my body from my Regiment days.'

Yeah, I thought, and that's why you're dressed exactly the same as you were when you were in the troop – apart from the tie, of course. 'You're talking shit.'

He opened his mouth to answer but I pushed on: 'How long does it take to become an ayatollah?'

'Three years. I was just going to do the two-year diploma course, but I went for the degree in theology. It feels good having those letters after my name. I was ordained by the bishop in the cathedral. It was fantastic. Shame you missed it.'

'Now what?'

He paused. 'You know, at my ordination, I was helping administer wine at the service. There was this woman who kept looking at me. I thought, Do I know you? She wasn't smiling; she was looking daggers. I felt quite unhappy in her presence. And I thought, I wonder if she's a witch.'

I put my glass down. 'You administering the wine or drinking it, mate?'

'No, really, a witch. I felt unhappy in her presence. There is evil in the world, Andy. That's what I wanted to talk to you about. Are you OK?' He looked at me intently.

'You trying to do your spiritual healing bit here?'

He leaned across conspiratorially. 'It would help. Don't be embarrassed. I've had quite a few ex-Regiment guys come to me since I've been back. Whether you were the victim or the torturer, it's never going to go away.' He sat back.

'Maybe I can help. That's what I do now, remember?'

I shook my head. 'Listen, mate, when I start barking at the moon I'll give you a call.'

He smiled sadly. 'Remember over the water when we dropped all the wood off at the target sheds? Remember what I said? The door is always open. It still is, Andy.' He reached for his beer.

'I'd get yourself a wedge, mate. It might be like that for quite a while . . .'

Frank was connected to two churches. I knew St Peter's. It was slap-bang in the middle of town, with a huge spire you could see from miles around. I didn't get to find out where St James's was until one of the squadron lads got married there. I turned up at the wedding, and there was Frank in all the black and white gear. I felt proud of him. I was hoping to see him at the reception but he didn't turn up. I thought I knew why. Sinking the odd pint with me was one thing. Surrounding himself with the Regiment was quite another.

Frank did a lot more weddings and baptized a pile of babies for Regiment guys. He had also got himself involved in a lot of kids' support groups. He would take them canoeing or walking in the hills, anything to show them there was more to life than nicking cars or frightening old ladies. I admired him for that and wished there had been a Frank about when, as a kid, I'd needed one.

Towards the end of the year, the patrol was decorated with three Military Medals, for Vince, Steve and Chris, and a Distinguished Conduct Medal (DCM) for me. This made Bravo Two Zero the most highly decorated patrol since the Boer War, and me the most highly decorated soldier in the British Army. I'd have preferred it if everyone had stayed alive.

As the camp tailor was measuring me up and kitting me out in No. 2s, best dress uniform, I thought about Nish. He'd taken the piss out of me big-time the night before. 'Going to see her again, eh? Garden party this time?'

I couldn't even find my medals, and there was a bit of a flap on because none of us knew if you had to wear them. I couldn't remember what I'd done last time. We eventually discovered I didn't need them, which was just as well.

This investiture was totally different from the one I'd gone to when I was twenty. It included another group of people who wouldn't be given their awards in public – the Det.

We all arrived in a covered coach, curtains drawn, accompanied by wives, girlfriends, kids and all sorts. We went into Buckingham Palace and about twenty of us, plus companions, were led to a private room overlooking the garden. We hung around for quite a while. The Queen was having private meetings with the families of the lads who had died, and she wasn't rationing her time. I watched the kids run amok and jump all over the fancy furniture.

The Queen came in and asked us to sit down. We were called up one at a time to get our medals. There was an eccentric mixture of uniforms on display. The Jocks were in tartan trousers or skirts, and the CO had holes in his lapels from his previous rank. There was nobody there to tell us the correct protocol, so we each followed the guy ahead. The first one up had clicked his heels as he did a little bow, so we all followed suit. She must have thought she was decorating an SS brigade.

When my turn came, she smiled. 'Congratulations. We hear you were the commander of Bravo Two Zero patrol?'

'Yes, ma'am.'

'Well, you must feel very proud.'

'Of the men in my patrol, yes, I am, very much so.'

And that was that. Ceremony over, the Queen left for a cup of tea and a sticky bun. The big french windows were opened and we were invited into the garden. The kids ran riot and nobody complained.

One of my mates had a five-year-old, dressed up like a page-boy. He pointed up. 'Look!'

We all turned to see the Queen leaning on the banister halfway up the staircase, watching us fucking about in her garden. She was smiling.

The D Squadron lad picked up his boy, and he waved at her. 'That's the lady who gave you your new badge.'

The Queen waved back.

91

Snapper had written a book in November 1989 called *Soldier I*, after the letter designation he was given during the inquest on the embassy siege. He'd said he was going to write it when he was bouncing around just before he went on the Circuit, but none of us really took any notice. It was Snapper talking, after all.

The head shed had asked to read the manuscript, and so did the MoD, to make sure it didn't compromise national security. Everything was fine, until the book became a bestseller. All of a sudden gums were being bumped and it seemed Snapper had done a bad thing. The head shed waffled endlessly about how outrageous it was to profit financially from your Regimental experiences, but our reply was: 'Hang about, you're the ones who said it was all right and, anyway, he went through the process.'

Of course, the same didn't apply to senior officers writing about Special Forces activity. Those were 'memoirs', not revelations.

Snapper didn't care either way. He was out on the Circuit with his 'I'm totally sane' chit in his pocket, oblivious to the lot of it. For some of us, however, the sudden shift in attitude in high places was going to have far-reaching consequences.

There was a message from Andrew on my answer-phone when I got back. 'Give me a call. There's still a job for you if you want it.'

I went to a meeting at his new set-up. It wasn't the plushest I'd seen, but practical and fit for purpose. I soon discovered, over a brew in a chipped mug, that the offer wasn't for a specific job: he was asking if I wanted to be part of the company. He knew I was on the Wing, and he knew I was conscious. All the lads working for him had the same CV. Andrew had a new business model in mind: everybody working for the company would have a stake. I got out a calculator and did the maths.

There was no getting away from the fact that I could only stay in the Regiment until I was forty, whether I liked it or not. Seven years to go at a push, and that would be the end of my service. I was a senior sergeant, looking to becoming a staff-sergeant after I finished the Wing. I would probably leave as a warrant officer, but then what?

'Get out and be a part of something,' Andrew urged, from beneath his sandy moustache. 'Be a part of something you can help control.'

It wouldn't take me long to decide. I just wanted to run the idea past someone to make sure I was doing the right thing.

Next time I met Frank, I shoved a brown-paper bag across the table. 'Here, change that fucking thing, will you?'

Frank's orange woolly tie had to go. The replacement was from what the market stallholder called his autumn collection. It wasn't exactly designer gear, but the red polyester almost matched his Gore-Tex jacket. He told me that a few of the guys had approached him now he was all frocked up and they could tell him their problems in confidence. 'Same still goes for you, Andy. And if you don't want to talk to me, I know a secret place in Wales where you can go and get help if you need it.'

This was over a burger at what had become our regular

meeting place, the Micky Ds behind St Peter's. We called these lunches our McSummits – with fries.

He'd just bought a bag of coat hooks. The morning prayer meetings were popular.

'You get nightmares?'

'Yeah! I see you coming at me with a great big Bible, and I wake up screaming! Listen, I know about the place. Eat your chips and keep the sauce off that smart new tie.'

He hadn't been listening. 'Seriously, Andy.' It wasn't just his accent that was different, these days: the tone had become very clear, precise and measured. 'If you want, I can introduce you. It's OK, you don't have to be embarrassed about it.'

I stabbed my last chip into his tub of ketchup. 'Not for me, mate. I'm probably just too thick to realize I've got a problem. Tell you what, if you really want to help, why don't you pay for the burgers?'

That shut him up. But only for a moment.

'I'm thinking of being a stab. Joining them as a padre.'

We always gave the TA a hard time – Stinking Territorial Army Bastards. I didn't know why, because they were good lads. Frank said he'd been approached to be the chaplain of 23 SAS, one of the two territorial units up north.

'The money will come in handy. Plus I get to do some soldiering and I can be a padre.'

'Bollocks – you want back in. That's what it's all about. You want to play soldiers again.'

He shook his head. 'It might look that way, but I've just been over with Delta. They asked me to go back and conduct their annual prayer breakfast. I've got to tell you, Andy, it was a good experience. Every man attended. They wanted to be there – it wasn't a Scale A parade. I want to do more of it.'

I wasn't surprised. That kind of thing was standard operating procedure within the US Army. Religion was still an acceptable part of military life.

'Nice try. You're talking bollocks.'

He wouldn't have it. 'No, I just want to help the lads, that's all. Just as well I didn't give you my stable belt, eh?'

'If you can't find it, you can have mine.'

He did a double-take. 'You PVRing? It's a big step – and a horrible feeling walking out of that gate. You sure you won't regret it?'

'What? Like you?'

'Maybe. You going on the Circuit? Don't jump at the first job. Think hard, because once you're out, that's it, the end.'

'That's why I'm using you as a sounding board.'

I told him about Andrew's job offer. I was thinking of getting out after Christmas. The job didn't start until July, so I was just going to bum about until then. I'd never dossed. Joining up at the age of sixteen meant I'd never done anything but soldier, and now it seemed like time to move on. 'Why not, eh? Pony-tail, shorts and flip-flops, working on a beach somewhere.'

He slipped his hand into his Gore-Tex jacket and produced his wallet. I sat back, enjoying the moment.

'Here.' He ripped the Velcro open and handed me a folded sheet of paper. 'I got this from Delta, and I thought of Nish. You have it, I'll get another.'

I shoved it in my pocket. No way was I going to open it in front of him. It might have been a song. Frank might have wanted to start hallelujahing round the Ronald McDonald statue with me in tow.

'You seen him lately?' he asked.

'I've been away. He's still doing this skydiving from space thing, isn't he? Still in Russia?'

'Back soon.' He nodded thoughtfully. 'Listen, I'm worried. He's not looking good again.'

He picked up his coat hooks and what was left of my fries in their little greaseproof-paper bag, and we headed for the door. He smiled as he opened it and let me through with a flourish. 'Remember, Andy, it's always open. I know I can't talk you out of PVRing. I know you just wanted me to validate it. Just remember, it's possible that you want to avoid what you feel, escape from something you can't quite explain.'

That was experience talking.

We went our separate ways. When I got back to my car I unfolded the bit of paper. It was a poem about soldiers and God.

Psalm 35

A Prayer for Rescue from Enemies

1 Oppose, LORD, those who oppose me; war upon those who make war upon me.
2 Take up the shield and buckler; rise up in my defence.
3 Brandish lance and battleaxe against my pursuers. Say to my heart, 'I am your salvation.'
4 Let those who seek my life be put to shame and disgrace. Let those who plot evil against me be turned back and confounded.
5 Make them like chaff before the wind, with the angel of the LORD driving them on.
6 Make their way slippery and dark, with the angel of the LORD pursuing them.
7 Without cause they set their snare for me; without cause they dug a pit for me.
8 Let ruin overtake them unawares; let the snare they have set catch them; let them fall into the pit they have dug.
9 Then I will rejoice in the LORD, exult in God's salvation.
10 My very bones shall say, 'O LORD, who is like you, who rescues the afflicted from the powerful, the afflicted and needy from the despoiler?'
11 Malicious witnesses come forward, accuse me of things I do not know.
12 They repay me evil for good and I am all alone.
13 Yet I, when they were ill, put on sackcloth, afflicted myself with fasting, sobbed my prayers upon my bosom.

14 I went about in grief as for my brother, bent in mourning as for my mother.

15 Yet when I stumbled they gathered with glee, gathered against me like strangers. They slandered me without ceasing;

16 Without respect they mocked me, gnashed their teeth against me.

17 Lord, how long will you look on? Save me from roaring beasts, my precious life from lions!

18 Then I will thank you in the great assembly; I will praise you before the mighty throng.

19 Do not let lying foes smirk at me, my undeserved enemies wink knowingly.

20 They speak no words of peace, but against the quiet in the land they fashion deceitful speech.

21 They open wide their mouths against me. They say, 'Aha! Good! Our eyes relish the sight!'

22 You see this, LORD; do not be silent; Lord, do not withdraw from me.

23 Awake, be vigilant in my defence, in my cause, my God and my Lord.

24 Defend me because you are just, LORD; my God, do not let them gloat over me.

25 Do not let them say in their hearts, 'Aha! Just what we wanted!' Do not let them say, 'We have devoured that one!'

26 Put to shame and confound all who relish my misfortune. Clothe with shame and disgrace those who lord it over me.

27 But let those who favour my just cause shout for joy and be glad. May they ever say, 'Exalted be the LORD who delights in the peace of his loyal servant.'

28 Then my tongue shall recount your justice, declare your praise, all the day long.

I screwed it up and chucked it in a bin. That boy never gave up.

92

February 1993

The Robocops manning the main gate were MoD policemen, but they had enough weapons dangling off them to take on global crime. It was a really strange feeling driving past them out of the camp, seeing the Lines in the rear-view mirror for the final time.

I was even sorry to say goodbye to the red-brick campus buildings, crumbling though they were due to crap repair work or ground subsidence, depending whose lawyer you were. It had been home for the last ten years. I forgave myself the little lump in my throat.

The friends and relationships weren't going to disappear, but I was losing something that had been my life since I was sixteen. I knew now how Nish and Frank had felt. And, like them, all I really had to show for it was my stable belt and beret.

I'd had to go round the different departments to get my discharge papers signed and sort out my pay and taxes, get bombarded by questions about where I was going, what security company I'd signed up for. I also experienced that short, sharp, aggressive severance from the system that everyone talked about.

Being presented with my tankards was the final nail in my army coffin: one from B Squadron and one from the Wing, plus a statue of a military freefaller from Seven Troop; once you get that, there's no going back.

That's it, you're out, have a nice life. I comforted myself with the thought that this day would have come eventually whether I liked it or not, so I might as well get on with it.

Something that wasn't going to happen was my seven months of dossing around in pony-tail, shorts and flip-flops. Andrew needed me to start work for him straight away, and something else had come up.

Just before Christmas, I'd been approached by an officer and asked about Bravo Two Zero. The reason certain people were interested in my thoughts, he said, was because there was so much conjecture about the patrol in the press. We'd been attributed with everything from blowing up a power station in Baghdad to attempting to assassinate Saddam. Even the main MoD building in Whitehall was buzzing with theories. It was starting to take on a life of its own.

The suggestion was that, maybe, possibly, telling the true story would put an end to the rumours and get the whole thing over with. I wasn't averse to that, but then it was suggested that if I did agree to tell the story, maybe it could be part of a more wide-ranging Regimental history. I said I'd think about it. I did, and decided that if anyone was going to tell the story, I wanted it to be me.

I'd got to know John Nichol and John Peters, the Tornado crew shot down over Iraq in 1991 and paraded, battered and bruised, on TV for all the world to see. In fact, Nichol and I had stood next to each other in the line of prisoners waiting to be released at Baghdad airport. When they got back, and while they were still serving RAF aircrew, they wrote a book about their experiences called *Tornado Down*. I phoned them up and got some advice.

I decided to go for it. It wasn't going to be the cathartic

experience that Frank thought I needed but it would be a nice memento, and the few grand I hoped I might be paid would come in handy.

A few months later, the manuscript went to the MoD. They wanted a number of changes, which was fine by me. The fibre-optic cable had to be called a landline, for example, and they suggested different locations for the patrol's area of operations, and asked me not to talk about certain bits of kit that were still tactically sensitive. That was also fine by me. I wanted to tell the BTZ story, not compromise equipment and future operations.

The vetting process was deeply civilized, and I had a number of requests from the MoD for signed copies when the book was finally published.

While this was going on I continued to work for Andrew. I wasn't about to bin the day job.

93

Nish had finally bought himself a Cessna and flown it back to the UK. In typical Nish fashion, of course, he did it without any of the proper radios or safety kit the regulations said he required. Anything he did take was second-hand and stuck together with gaffer tape.

He'd nicknamed the four-seater *Zephyr*. Aircraft are much cheaper in the States, so his plan was to sell it once he got back and make some money to put towards the big skydive. By the time he landed, there wasn't much aircraft left to sell. He'd ripped out the two back seats to take an extra fuel tank. Then, because it only had one engine, which had already failed a couple of times during test flights, he removed most of the bolts from the door and decked himself out in an immersion suit. If he'd had to ditch, he planned to kick the door out and jump into his life-raft, a blow-up dinghy he'd bought at Toys Я Us. 'I might end up beating my dad's record,' he told me over the phone. 'He paddled for seventeen hours after parking his Spitfire in the Med. How long do you reckon it would take me from Newfoundland to Iceland?'

Nish didn't have the right radio or antenna, but he'd taken care of that. He tied one end of a roll of wire to a brick, which he dangled under the aircraft. To communicate with the various air-traffic controllers and jets zooming above him on the North Atlantic routes, he wound out or wound in a few more metres, depending on the prevailing frequencies. 'I knew all that antenna theory would come in useful in the end . . .'

Hare-brained as it was, he made it. He flew up into Canada, then across the Atlantic to Iceland, and eventually made it to Scotland, as you do. By the time he arrived, he'd changed his mind about selling. He'd got too attached to the single-engined heap of shit, I supposed.

As soon as he was back, the skydive from space took over his life. His house was turned into offices, and most of his time went into pestering the Russians for some of their Soyuz life-support suits. The Americans wouldn't cooperate in any shape or form. Maybe they were protecting Joe Kittinger's record.

There was something else on the bubble. Nish had a girl-friend – sort of. I'd never met her. I didn't even know if she was in the UK. They'd got together in DC, after I'd left. Her name was Anna, and depending on which week I spoke to him, she was either Russian or Russian/Filipina. One minute she played classical music, the next she was training to be a doctor. As long as she made Nish happy. If she was here, I wondered what she made of his company car: a battered old Ford Sierra with more rust than paint.

Frank always worried about everybody, all the time. Part of his job description, I supposed. All the same, I did call Nish to check up on him, but the phone kept ringing. The answer-machine was off, and that meant he was away – freefalling, or maybe flying *Zephyr* to Moscow. The boy had always been here, there and everywhere, and always at 100 m.p.h.

As for Frank, I wasn't sure if he knew that he had finally admitted he'd fucked up by getting out. I felt uncomfortable about him going off to play soldiers again. He'd got what he wanted, I thought: his church, his frock, his flock. I felt proud of him at weddings with all his gear on. He looked the business, especially now he had a decent tie.

You have to nail your colours to a mast at some stage, and it seemed Frank's hammer was still wavering in mid-air. Now he worried me almost as much as Nish did.

94

I'd met up with Nish a couple of times between his attempts to drum up support for the skydive from space and freefall gigs in Spain. While he and Harry, the Royal Marina Adonis, were busy sunning themselves, I was working on a BG job in the north-west of England, just outside Blackpool. Nish's shiny new brochure landed on my doormat and told me his jump was going to be from a ten-million-cubic-foot helium balloon. It said:

> *Fibre-optic cameras in [the parachutist's] helmet and a microwave transmission device on his body will allow viewers to see exactly what he sees as he reaches speeds of over 800 m.p.h. International best-selling authors Tom Clancy and Frederick Forsyth have agreed to provide commentary during the live TV coverage and subsequent documentary.*

I gave him a call to take the piss. He sounded happy. He said he'd done a deal that meant NASA were finally on board.

'What sort of deal?'

'I've got to help Harry get a scientist and his gear up a mountain.'

'Which mountain?'

'Everest.'

NASA had developed the Tissue-equivalent Proportional Counter to measure levels of solar radiation and their effect on the skin. It had already been used on several Shuttle missions, but the spacecraft moved too quickly to register any useful results. The scientist, Karl Henize, was going to measure the level of radiation reaching the Earth's surface at various altitudes during the climb. The data would be shared by NASA and High Adventure, Loel Guinness's company.

'Done any climbing yet?'

'It'll be on-the-job training. You sort of put one crampon in front of the other, don't you?'

Rather him than me, but he was looking forward to it and I was pleased for him.

Next time I saw him, a few weeks later, Nish just wasn't Nish. He'd lost a lot of weight, which I put down to training – combined with the fact he was trying to give up smoking. He sucked fruit gums non-stop, but it wasn't working. He'd get through a packet, then celebrate with a couple of cigarettes.

Frank was right: his condition was a cause for concern. He wasn't that happy-go-lucky any more. All his oomph had gone. He even seemed a little slow on the uptake, like he was thinking a bit too much before speaking. And he looked like shit.

I still hadn't met Anna. She was in her early twenties, about twelve years younger than him and, in Nish's words, 'exotic'.

Her father really was Russian, and her mother Filipina. And she really was studying to become a doctor. She could speak Italian, play classical music, all that gear.

She'd come over a couple of times after Nish had got back from DC, and must have liked what she saw. She had approached Bristol University, and was continuing her medical studies there. The strange thing was that there weren't any pictures of her in his house – but maybe that was because the place was so full of brochures and skydive from space shit.

'I don't have time.' He shoved another fruit gum in his mouth. 'Overworked. Know what I mean?'

'You'll be fucking overworked when you start humping up Everest.'

Nish wasn't the only one who had me worried. Frank was giving up St Peter's and thinking about joining the army full time as a padre. It wasn't very Christian of him. Who was I going to have my McSummits with from now on?

Nish went off with Harry, and *Bravo Two Zero* was published in November. It went straight into the bestseller charts, and ended up the biggest-selling war book of all time. I couldn't believe it. Not even the publishers had expected it be so successful.

It was during that first month of success that the problems started. Armchair generals were filmed muttering that I was giving away secrets and endangering national security. These so-called experts had no idea that the book had been cleared. I read articles that said the MoD were dismayed by the revelations. I couldn't make any sense of it.

'It's what sells newspapers, Andy.' The man next to me on the back seat of the staff car jabbed a finger at one of the offending broadsheets on my lap. 'Don't let them worry you.'

I wasn't about to argue with such a high-ranking member of the defence staff, especially as we were on the way to Sandhurst, where I was to deliver the Christmas lecture.

95

February 1994

Nish was still away; I hadn't seen him since he'd left for Everest last autumn. Frank had disappeared off the face of the Earth. This happened all the time; it wasn't as if we lived a nine-to-five existence and made a point of seeing each other at the end of the working day. Like bad pennies, they'd turn up. No news was good news.

Or so I thought.

I was overseas when I heard rumours that Nish had killed somebody. I couldn't get hold of Frank, Andrew, Harry, anyone reliable. In the end I had to phone the Lines. I got passed from pillar to post, and everybody had a different version. Nish had killed a man. Nish had stabbed a woman. He was in prison in France. He was in hospital in England.

'Any idea how I can get hold of Frank Collins? I think he's with the TA up north.'

'He's with 5 Airborne Brigade.'

I got him on the military extension at Aldershot. 'What the fuck's going on, Frank? He's killed a guy?'

'No, no, no. A guy died on the Everest trip. Nish was with him.'

'Thank fuck for that – I had visions of him locked away and—'

There was a brief silence at the other end of the line. Then: 'He has been. It was his girlfriend he tried to kill.'

'Anna? What the fuck's he playing at?'

'I don't know. He stabbed her. She's still alive. He hadn't slept for days. He had a complete breakdown. He thinks everyone's out to kill him. He thinks Anna's the devil. He's paranoid . . .'

'Where is he now? What can we do?'

'It's all been taken care of. He's been in an asylum in Chamonix.'

'France?'

'They were on holiday with Harry and his girlfriend.'

'He been charged?'

'I don't think so. They brought him back to the UK. I'm praying for him.'

'They?'

'Harry, Des and Schwepsy. They hired lawyers to get him out of there and into a London clinic. He's getting great support, but he's lost his mind.'

His nightmare had started on the Everest trip. There were twenty-four of them on the attempt to climb the North Face. The NASA guy, Karl Henize, was a keen amateur climber. Nish was the only inexperienced one.

Henize was an astronaut-scientist. He'd been on the support crew for Apollo 15 and Skylab missions, orbiting the Earth something like 120 times. During the Skylab-2 mission, he had been responsible for operating the Shuttle's robot arm, and conducting several scientific experiments. He was also a big-time astronomer with loads of technical papers to his name. He'd discovered more than two thousand stars, designated by the letters 'HE' in star catalogues. The boy was a bit of a star himself.

They were all humping up the North Face of Everest when, at about 17,000 feet, Nish began to suffer a severe headache. By

18,000 feet he was dropping behind. His head pounded. He vomited. His pulse rate shot up to 100 beats per minute. It was altitude sickness. His only chance was to go back down to base camp, reacclimatize, and start again.

He recovered after a couple of days and set off again to meet the rest of the lads, who by now were way above 20,000 feet. They'd stopped to acclimatize for a week before the next bound.

Nish was at 24,000 feet when he met Harry and a couple of other lads coming down. They were carrying Karl in a Gamow bag, a portable hyperbaric chamber. Through the small plastic window, Nish could see that his lips were blue and his eyelids were fluttering.

The bag had to be continuously pumped about once every five seconds – not to maintain pressure, but to flush fresh air through and prevent CO_2 build-up. At some point the next day, it was Nish's turn on the pump. He talked to Karl about his time in Africa with Harry, trying to keep his mind working even if his body wasn't. It was to no avail. They buried Karl on the mountainside under rocks and shale, as he had requested.

Nish was physically shattered and also devastated that yet again someone had died on his watch. And his problems were far from over. No sooner had he left one nightmare behind than he came home to another.

Nish and Anna travelled to France to spend New Year with Harry and his girlfriend, who lived just outside Chamonix. By the time they arrived, Nish was convinced she was the devil, and was out to kill him. He wasn't eating, in case her plan was to poison him. He was skinny as a rake now, a shadow of his former self. He also hadn't slept for seven days. He was a soldier; he was on stag, waiting to be attacked. He had to be really clever and manoeuvre around her, because he knew she could read his mind.

They picked up a car at the airport and headed for Harry's place. Anna drove. Again, Nish had to be hyper-vigilant. At any corner she might drive off the road and throw the car down the mountainside. They'd burst into a ball of flame, and because she was the devil, she would walk out of the blaze with not a scratch on her and he'd be burnt to a crisp.

As they came into Chamonix, Nish spotted a group of gendarmes on a street corner. He got her to stop the car. He jumped out and ran over to them, fucked, emaciated, face gaunt through lack of sleep. He couldn't speak French, and they couldn't speak English. He pushed and shoved to try to help them understand, but something seemed to be getting lost in translation. Why didn't they understand she was trying to kill him? She'd cast a spell over them; they were now on her side.

As the confrontation escalated into a gangfuck, Anna phoned Harry. He turned up just in time to save Nish from being arrested or beaten.

Harry got them to their hotel, but Nish just lay there on stag: his eighth night in a row without sleep. In the twilight hours it came to Nish that he was the chosen one, and must take up the sword against evil.

In the morning, Anna confronted him. 'Nish, you must eat something.' She tossed him a tangerine.

Not a fucking chance. He threw it back at her and she caught it.

She's sharp, he thought. As she would be: she's the devil.

Did he have to eat all of it? he wondered. If he ate all of it, it was going to kill him. If he only ate a bit, it might appease her. He might manage to stay on her good side, so she wouldn't turn him into a ball of flame. But once that was done, she'd have to die. He'd have to kill her. If not, she would also kill his son, Jason.

The four of them hit the slopes, and by now Nish was pleading with Harry not to leave his side, not even when he went to the toilet. Harry was the only person he could trust to protect him. He knew Harry was too smart to be taken over by Anna and drawn into her web.

On the drive back Nish started barking at the moon. He couldn't contain his thoughts any longer. He told the three of them that Anna had to die, and he explained his plan. As they came into Chamonix, Harry pulled up at a hospital where he knew one of the doctors.

Nish saw at once that Harry and his girlfriend had fallen under Anna's spell. They were now on her side. He couldn't hang about. He had to kill her before another moment was lost. As they walked into the hospital, he grabbed a pair of scissors from a tray and lunged at her. The blades glanced off her head and dug into her shoulder. He pulled them out as she went down screaming. He needed to get them into her eyes to kill her quickly.

Harry took Nish to the ground, just as the scissors sank into Anna's chest.

Nish was triumphant. 'Did I kill her? Did I kill her?'

Harry held him in a headlock until help arrived. Nish was sedated. The police handcuffed him and took him to a psychiatric clinic. He was locked in a white-painted room that reminded him of an ice cave. It had a ventilation hole high in one wall. The shining white guard who always stood outside was an iceman.

96

July 1994

I banged on the door of Nish's house in Hereford. I could hear the mid-morning talk-show waffle coming through the windows. He never actually watched the programmes. He just wanted them on so the noise and flickering screen stopped him thinking too deeply.

Even his smile of greeting was laboured. He was painfully thin. His whole body shape had changed. He would have been more at home on an Oxfam poster than an ad for Calvin Klein. His eyes were wet and dull, not sharp and feral. The wolf had fled.

As we headed past the brown sofa and the minging duvet he spent his life curled up beneath, a Daz commercial sparked up on the TV. 'You need to get hold of some of that, mate. Give that duvet a treat.'

He hardly ever left the front room. His world revolved around that brown velour sofa peppered with cigarette holes, and the duvet that looked like he'd found it on the towpath.

Overflowing ashtrays and plates of half-eaten toasted cheese sandwiches covered almost every horizontal surface in the kitchen. At least the drugs were making him hungry – after a fashion.

That wasn't the only side effect. He was like a zombie a lot of the time, yet he couldn't sleep. He had muscle spasms and shakes, a dry mouth and blurred vision. Chlorpromazine, one of the cocktail of anti-psychotic drugs he was taking, was a stupefier. It made him drowsy and lethargic. He still thought the whole world was against him, but he couldn't be arsed to do anything about it.

The kitchen looked like he'd furnished it from a car-boot sale, which he probably had. Cups and mugs were piled in the sink waiting for the washing-up fairy to visit. His white plastic garden chair still stood opposite the fridge. He would sit there and have a conversation with it if there wasn't anything on TV. He liked having a chat with the fridge now and again; it agreed with everything he said.

All the windows were shut, and the place stank of cigarettes and farts, but it wasn't funny any more.

Nish could only recall brief flashes of what had happened after the stabbing. He had a memory of lying on the floor with people holding his arms and somebody sitting on his back. He could hear Harry's voice, telling him everything was OK, not to fight it. The floor was cold against his cheek, and there was a strong smell of polish and disinfectant. For a while he thought he was back in the corridors of Para Depot as a young recruit.

Anna recovered and flew back to America, but things were touch and go for Nish. The French doctors wanted him sectioned; the police wanted to bring charges. His head was a car wreck. From the window of his ice cave, he had become preoccupied with fixing which way was north. He wanted to know if he had to cross the Alps to reach safety. He knew it was going to be difficult, dressed in just pyjamas and a dressing-gown, but these things had to be planned down to the last detail.

Harry had slipped into international-rescue mode. He called Des, Schwepsy, Loel Guinness and Saad Harari, Nish's old boss from Washington. The best Parisian lawyers were trying to sort something out.

Weak light penetrated the greasy net curtains behind the sink as he picked about in the landfill with nicotine-stained fingers. He scratched his stomach through his open denim shirt. 'Want a brew?'

'Yeah, why not, mate? But you going to give them a rinse this time?'

The milk would be off, as usual, and at least a dozen diseases clung to the bottom of each mug. Outside in the garden, the fence was still down after last year's storm. The grass was high enough to hide a hippo. The poor guy was fucked. It was all he could do to turn on the tap.

Harry had called Des in the States. He'd dropped everything and tried to get a flight, but it was easier said than done. Blizzards had brought America to a standstill and he'd spent two days snowed in at the airport before he could even get to New York. He immediately booked himself on more than twenty flights via the Far East and South America, anywhere as long as it meant getting to Geneva.

Des had breezed into Nish's ice cave, full of insults and banter. 'Hey, Big Nose – how's it going, madman? I always said you belonged in a padded cell.'

Schwepsy, ever Mr Formal, shook Nish's hand. They were working with the firm of lawyers that represented the French government, and getting the best medical advice. They had to find a British doctor to take responsibility for him, and a private jet, since no commercial airline would fly him, even in a straitjacket. Loel Guinness had offered his plane, and Saad was picking up all the other tabs. Des's contribution had been to organize champagne for the flight, and some very pretty nurses.

A few days later, they flew Nish home. An ambulance was

waiting to whisk him straight to the Charter Clinic in Chelsea. One of the psychiatrists there looked after the royal family. No expense had been spared.

As he minced around trying to put the kettle on, I pulled several bundles of fifty-pound notes from my jacket. I threw them on the kitchen worktop, trying to make it look casual.

He frowned. 'What's all this?'

'Your mortgage. If you don't pay it you'll be out, mate. The lads have had a whip-round.'

He hadn't been working. He hadn't even had the strength to fill in the DSS benefit forms. His mortgage payments were in arrears. I wasn't sure if he knew that – or if he did but didn't really care.

The drugs that were helping him were also fucking him up. Sometimes they didn't calm him, and he'd have another attack of paranoia. The last one had happened in the Stonebow Unit in Hereford General. After four weeks at the London clinic, he'd moved there as an inpatient, and then an outpatient when he gradually improved. One day, he punched a nurse because he thought she was out to get him. It was letters and cards and flowers straight afterwards, of course; he was horrified. She was OK about it – it was all part of the job, and she'd been there before. She'd even helped him fill out a couple of social-services forms that he'd filed on his kitchen table when he got home.

He pulled a bottle of milk from the fridge. I caught a glimpse of a Mars bar and a couple of lumps of cheese in there, and that was about it. He looked at the wad. 'I can't take it, mate. You know that.' His speech was slurred.

'It's not a question of can or can't,' I said. 'You have to. I can't give it back – I can't remember who gave what.' That was a lie. Everybody had put in five hundred quid, except Frank. He'd put in a grand. I'd said it had to be five hundred from him and five hundred from God, and no fucking about. I knew where both of them lived.

'Think of it as a loan.'

He looked at me blankly. 'That's all well and good, but I'll never be able to pay it back, will I?'

'Some loans are very long-term, all right?'

He dropped a mug on the worktop for me and studied the cash. After a while, he pulled a note from one of the bundles.

I shuddered as I tasted the tea. 'You might think of investing some of that in a carton of fresh milk . . .'

He pushed the money into the back pocket of his jeans. He didn't even try his tea. He obviously wasn't that mad.

'Fancy going to see Hillbilly?'

I nodded. 'Good thinking.'

Nish didn't go out that much because he didn't like people talking about him as he shuffled along the street. He liked getting a lift.

'Give us a minute.' He went into the front room and rummaged in a couple of shoeboxes.

I drove over the old bridge and through the town towards St Martin's.

We stopped outside a small Spar on the way and he jumped out.

'Get some soap while you're at it, mate,' I called after him. 'Take the Daz challenge.'

He didn't come back with milk and washing powder, or even the cigarettes I'd thought he'd gone in for. Instead, he was brandishing a bottle of Captain Morgan. 'You don't need that, mate. You got enough drama as it is. You don't need to throw that shit down your neck.'

'Shut up, you dickhead. It isn't for me.' He shut the car door. 'Well, what are we waiting for?'

97

I drove up the Ross Road in the direction of the Lines, and turned into the gravel car park by the church.

We walked along the hedgerows and into the Regimental plot. Traffic ran up and down the main drag, but trees, hedges and an old stone wall did a good job of blocking out the noise. I've never been sure if the noise actually stops at the wall, or if my mind just blocks it out while I'm there. Whatever, it was a peaceful spot.

We walked between the precise rows of headstones.

The low wall to our right was lined with the plaques of guys who'd gone home to their own people or been buried in-theatre.

I knew too many of them.

Some graves had flowers on them: some fresh, some getting on a bit. Some had nothing at all, but the whole plot was neat and crisp and well tended.

When I came to see the guys I usually stole a few flowers from the other graves and spread them about among my lot. Nish did the same. He bent over Hillbilly's grave and arranged a small bunch in a jam jar. These guys would always share a brew; it was madness not to.

He seemed more on the ball now. Maybe he'd just needed to get out.

I left him to his thoughts and had a few of my own.

Nish got up. His jeans were soaked from the knees down.

His face changed as he took the rum from his jacket. He unscrewed the cap. 'Time for the gunfire ration.'

He poured a tot over Hillbilly's grave. 'There you go, mate. Cheers.'

He took a sip himself. 'If only I'd done something about that cunt who jumped the gate.'

I wasn't too sure if he was talking to Hillbilly or me.

'If I hadn't been such an arsehole over the water, maybe I would have been with you.'

It was Hillbilly.

'Maybe I could have saved you.'

He fished in his back pocket and passed me a folded sheet of paper. It was a letter from the OC, dated 6 March 1986 – just a few weeks before he got binned. It was the one he'd told me about the night we went downtown.

Dear Nish,

As you know we have recently within the space of a week conducted two successful operations . . . My purpose in writing now is to acknowledge formally your contribution to these successes and to the currently encouraging situation . . . You have every right to be fully satisfied and indeed proud of the work you have done. Please accept my personal thanks and, on its behalf, the gratitude of the Regiment. Well done.

'If I'd just wound my neck in, I could have stayed in B Squadron with Hillbilly. I might have been with him on the Wing. I might have been there with him. Maybe, maybe . . .'

I handed it back. 'You can't beat yourself up. He'd want you to get on with your life.'

He handed over the rum and I took a sip as I followed him over to Al's. He did the same little ceremony there, had a drink with him, then looked down and shook his head. 'I know I keep telling you, but I'm sorry, mate. Not a day goes by . . .'

After a few moments in his own world he turned to me. 'Might as well do your lot while we're here, eh?'

98

We started with Bob Consiglio, whom Nish had never met. I told him he was a good man, and should have got the VC for what he did.

'He was like an Action Man-sized Rambo.'

I struck the pose, my imaginary machine-gun on my hip, my arms juddering back and forth like a schoolboy playing war. We laughed, but we both knew what the Mumbling Midget had done for the rest of us that night.

'Fucking brilliant.'

We toasted him and I poured a large one over his headstone as it started to spit with rain.

Nish had a sudden thought. 'Hey, did Bob like rum?'

I didn't know. 'Tough shit, he's got some now.'

He took the bottle and poured a little more over Bob. 'Just in case he does.' He laughed for the second time in as many minutes. He was the happiest I'd seen him in many months.

We went over to Vince. Nish kept the bottle. 'I'll do him – I know he likes a drop.'

He poured a generous measure. 'Here you go, big boy.'

He took another swig and passed it back to me, then rested his hand on Vince's headstone. 'I wouldn't have passed

Selection without him.' He slapped the marble. 'This boy saved my bacon.'

Nish told me what had happened on the Fan Dance. It came quite early in Selection, and involved running all over the Brecon Beacons with a Bergen hanging off your shoulders. It was the middle of winter. Nish was in shit state. His head was spinning and he was sitting in the mud. It was so cold he could no longer feel his hands or feet. His sweat was starting to freeze. He knew people died up there on Selection. He propped himself against a rock, and as he struggled to sort himself out, he heard, 'You all right, mate?'

'I looked up and saw a big fuck-off moustache looking down at me, and it was this fucker.' He slapped the stone some more. His eyes were welling up and he made no attempt to hide the fact. 'Didn't know him from Adam, but he made me take some sips of water, unwrapped his own Mars bars and forced two or three of them down me. "Come on, mate, you'll be all right." He got me up, and started me off again.'

He wiped the tears from his cheeks. 'If Vince hadn't been there, that would have been me fucked on the first week.' He looked at me. 'He didn't have to stop and help me. He didn't even know who I was. Fucking good lad.'

Nish spent the next fifteen minutes standing next to Vince, moaning and honking about how he had been portrayed in a book somebody else had written about Bravo Two Zero.

He was angry. The rum got passed backwards and forwards. I wasn't too sure how Captain Morgan got on with Mr Chlorpromazine.

'Don't worry, mate. The important thing is, we know him; everybody who matters knows him.'

We followed the low wall, pausing now and then to have a look at lads we knew and share a thought. We reached Steve Lane's plaque and I gave him a splash. I realized we were getting a little bit pissed here, because I missed it on the first attempt.

We sat on one of the old wooden benches like a couple of winos as the rain started to fall more heavily, and set about finishing the bottle.

There'd be five minutes of silence, and then he'd spark up. Then he'd go quiet again. I didn't mind. I normally came here on my own. It was good to spend time here with someone who talked back.

'What made you mad, mate – do you know yet?'

'They seem to think it's a chemical imbalance in my brain. And, by the way, I'm not mad.' His eyes sparkled. 'I've had a psychotic breakdown. The problem is, they can't say when this imbalance happened.'

'It had to be at birth – I've never known you any different.'

Either he didn't hear or he didn't get it. 'I just don't know, mate, I just don't know. Think of all those HALO jumps, on and off oxygen every five minutes. Right on the edge of hypoxia we were – I know that now. Maybe the whole of Seven Troop is affected. Maybe I'm just the first to fall. Maybe the trigger was Everest. I was in shit state up there. It was like I had a jackhammer in my head.' He took another swig and passed the bottle. There weren't many left. 'I don't know what caused it, but fuck it, I've got it.'

He went quiet again. 'You know, you're right – I'm officially mad, aren't I? No Snapper chit for me.'

Then, out of the blue, he made an announcement. 'I've got a sort of a girlfriend.'

'That's good, mate.'

'Yeah, early days.'

He lit a cigarette, suddenly worried that his fingers weren't yellow enough. I wasn't going to ask. If he wanted me to know, he'd soon tell me. It might have been somebody out of the Stonebow Unit who was just as mad, or it might have been his next-door neighbour. Who cared, as long as there was somebody with him? He was being looked after by friends: Harry, Des, Schwepsy, they'd all been in and out. Cameron

Spence, an A Squadron guy, had looked in whenever he'd got leave from protecting the Algerian oil fields. Everybody did as much as they could, but the guys were bouncing around all over the world; they had stuff to do.

We sat there for an hour before our bollocks started to freeze. Nish was shaking. I didn't know if it was the drugs, the temperature, or the fact that we were both soaked to the skin.

'Time for a cab?'

He nodded and rose unsteadily to his feet, sucking on yet another cigarette. 'Did it work for you?'

I straightened up as best I could. 'Did what work?'

'The book. You know – was it a cathartic experience?' He scrutinized me carefully through a cloud of smoke.

'No.'

We both swayed unsteadily. I knew he was trying to get serious.

'Maybe it would for me – you know, like a way of picking off the demons, then kicking 'em out.' He mimed pasting up a poster. 'Just published in hardcover today, ladies and gentlemen, Nish Bruce's epic, *How To Be A Fruit*.'

'Sounds good to me,' I said. 'It might help. You never know.'

99

I pitched up at 5 Airborne Brigade in Aldershot to talk to the Parachute Regiment. The NCOs were particularly interested in the command and control, planning and preparation aspects of the Bravo Two Zero patrol.

I bumped into their new chaplain. Round the barracks, his nickname had become Padre Two Zero once word got round that we'd been in Seven Troop together.

Frank loved being back in the army. He reminded me of a bright-eyed recruit, striding around in his frock with a spring in his step and his medals dangling.

We walked down Queen's Avenue, the main thoroughfare. He wore a maroon beret with a padre's cap badge, and a dog collar under his Para Reg smock. His SAS wings were emblazoned on his shoulder.

'Happy now, Frank?'

'Very. I've even taken up mountain climbing.'

I raised an eyebrow. I still couldn't understand why people wanted to climb up something and then climb right down again, just to be able to say they'd done it.

'And you're bringing God's word into poor, ignorant squaddies' lives?'

'Some of them.' He tapped the wings on his shoulder. 'This

lets them feel they can talk to me. I tell them even Stephen Hawking thinks there must be a God.'

Every now and then he was greeted by a beep from a car horn or a shout and a thumbs-up.

'Yes, I'm happy. I'm back. The money's good as well. I'm freefalling again, and I want to climb K2.'

'You should never have got out in the first place, should you, you dickhead?'

He smiled. 'You seen Nish lately?'

'Back in H. He's still dribbling, still on the meds.'

'I've been praying for him.'

'That's good, because I've been getting drunk with him in the Regiment plot.'

I was expecting a disapproving frown, but none came.

I left Frank to carry on God's good work, but before I jumped in the car back to Hereford he grabbed hold of my arm again. 'I want to write a book, you know.'

'About what, mate?'

'I want to talk about God – how it all happened, how I found Him. I know why He put me here, Andy, and that's to help people. I think it would help them to know my story.'

100

9 May 1998

I wandered back into the marquee with Nish. The Eurovision Song Contest was certainly giving everyone an appetite. Mountains of food and drink were being consumed as Terry Wogan reminded us briskly of the competing acts before the big vote. A chorus of cheers and boos rang round the tables.

Nish put an arm round my shoulder. 'Great party, mate. Now, where's Jackie Collins disappeared to?' Frank's *Baptism of Fire* had come out the previous October and turned him into a bit of a celebrity: Nish had instantly dropped the Father Frank handle and rebranded him.

The tabloids loved him too. He was an irresistible combination of Rambo and Mother Teresa. He still carried his Claymore bag over his shoulder, but he just had his Bible in it these days – and a bundle of photographs because people kept stopping him in the street and asking for his autograph. Not a day went by without a flood of fan mail and more requests to speak about his experiences than he knew how to handle.

Frank was out of the army again, still trying to find I don't know what. He'd finished the padre bit, and was being courted by every overseas charity and children's welfare group on the planet. He was still freefalling, and spent his weekends running up mountains to get closer to God Squad HQ.

Nish seemed to have banished his demons and got himself together enough to write a book. *Freefall* was coming out in three months. He gave me a sheepish grin. 'Then you'll see how mad I am.'

He spotted Livvy – who was living with him now – and went off to join her. She was in her thirties, very pretty, and juggling a job with being a single mum of two small girls. Nish was besotted. I was happy for him. Somebody was gripping him, and it looked like it was working. She must have seen something in him, too, if she was willing to stick around after taking one look at his sink and that terrible brown sofa.

He was still on the meds because he still had paranoid episodes. One time, he thought the IRA were out to get him, disguised as road workers. He'd been aggressive with people, angry, sad, morbid. He'd been in and out of the Stonebow Unit, drugged up to the eyeballs for days at a time, but Livvy had been at his side throughout. She'd cleaned up the house and seemed to have sorted out his life.

One of the upsides of his new medication was an obsession with personal cleanliness, although he still seemed intent on smoking himself to death.

Frank sat down beside me as the final votes came in. The Israeli transvestite won, and I was eighty quid to the good on the sweepstake. It didn't get better than this.

101

By mid-afternoon everybody who'd stayed overnight – in tents or sleeping-bags on the floor – had rattled off home. I minced around picking up empties and getting the marquee ready for collection.

At six o'clock, I heard the chug of a big old diesel engine coming up the drive. We weren't expecting more visitors. I went outside and stood on the bridge as Frank parked his Mercedes box van, the size of a small truck, in the mud. When he was away doing God's work, it was his travelling church and mobile home, all in one. He prayed, cooked and slept in it.

He'd put the family business to good use, kitting it out with a bed, bench seating, and cooker surround. Nish had nick-named it Pikey Two Zero when he'd first bought the thing and dossed on an old mattress on the bare metal floor at freefall meets, but now it was carpeted and had all mod cons he called it the Popemobile.

Frank rubbed his hands together as he walked up the path. 'Finished early, so I thought I'd see if there was any food left.'

There was, tons of it. But he was lying. When he'd left, it had been to go sky surfing at Peterborough, three hours away, en route to London. It was Frank's latest craze, jumping with a snowboard strapped to his feet and trying to slalom across the sky.

We sat in the kitchen and finished off the last of the chicken in creamy something or other with rice, and he told me about the latest offer he'd had to front a scheme for a children's charity in Africa. Initially, he'd been excited about it. Now it didn't look so good. 'I want to go out there and get my hands dirty, but all they're really after is another patron.' He'd had the same problem with inner-city charities. He was desperate to take the kids canoeing and climbing, but they just wanted him as a fund-raiser. He said it made him sad and frustrated.

'So what are you going to do? You fucked up, getting out a second time. You've got to get a plan together, mate.'

'I'm not sure things ever go according to plan. They didn't for Tommy Shanks, did they?' He played with his food like a child, pushing it around his plate. Not pissed off, but sad. Miserable, even. I'd never seen him like it. 'You know people for years, and they change and do things you'd never expect . . .'

'You all right, mate?'

'No, not really.' He fixed me with his cornflower blues. 'I've been thinking about Al. The waste and stupidity of it all. Why couldn't we have been there to save him? What are we doing with our lives?'

He was getting a bit too deep for me. He was the one who was supposed to know the answers, but he just kept coming out with more questions. 'I always try and do the right thing – be a good person. Why am I so lost?'

'I thought God sorted all that shit for you. Hasn't He got a plan?'

Frank stared into the middle distance. The pulpit voice was back, very clear and precise. The miserable face lit up. I was suddenly in the presence of the fervour of the convert. 'I do have a plan. God has given it to me.'

'Can He give me one?'

383

'No, not this plan. This plan is to stop the feeling of being lost. You don't need it. If you did, He would have given it to you as well.'

'So what's he got up his sleeve this time? Starting up an orphanage in Angola? Building a church on top of Everest?'

This evening Frank wasn't biting.

He got to his feet, helped himself to four or five cans of Coke and packed away some fruit and hunks of cheese. 'Free food and drink, that's what I came for. So that's it, I'm off.'

I walked him back to the van. He jumped in and I walked alongside as he reversed down the drive.

The window powered down.

'Call me as soon as you can tell me this plan of yours, OK? I'm doing book stuff in New York for a couple of weeks, but then we can get together. Have a McSummit, eh?' I suggested.

He stopped the van and stretched out his hand. 'Yeah, I'll see you, Andy.'

We shook.

'In London, when I get back.'

'Let's do that.' He locked his eyes on mine and didn't let go of my hand. I thought he was going to kiss me for a minute, but then he changed his mind.

102

17 June 1998

I threw open the door of my hotel room, which overlooked Central Park. The message light on the bedside phone was blinking. I hit the playback button, and heard a familiar voice. It was Mark Lucas, my literary agent in London, and the guy was almost crying. 'I've got some bad news.'

It had to be Nish, I just knew it. He'd done something stupid again.

'It's Frank . . .'

Oh, fuck. Parachuting accident, it had to be.

'He's committed suicide . . .'

No. I'd misheard. There had to be some mistake.

I sat down – collapsed – on the bed and hit the repeat button.

'He committed suicide . . . yesterday . . . give me a call.'

It was the early hours of the morning in London, but I picked up the receiver and dialled.

I hadn't misheard. There hadn't been a mistake.

Frank had plugged the gap under the door of a friend's garage, run a hosepipe from the exhaust into the cab, then locked himself in and turned on the engine.

I sat there on the bed in a Manhattan skyscraper with its

panoramic, 70mm movie view of the city that never sleeps, and all I could think was: *Frank, you cunt.*

103

24 June 1998

The line of mourners snaked along the pedestrian walkway of Hereford town centre and into St Peter's Church. I recognized former and still serving members of the Regiment, wives, friends and a whole lot of other people Frank had collected over the years. I stayed outside with my fellow pallbearers, waiting for the hearse to arrive.

A bell tolled. Shoppers stopped and watched. They all knew whose funeral it was. The local media had made it a big deal.

There were plenty of theories bouncing around as to why he'd killed himself. Some said he was angry with God. Some said he was angry with everyone. Others thought he was just angry, full stop. Look at the way he killed himself, they said. That was angry, no question. I wasn't convinced. I thought he was making sure people didn't forget him. He wanted to be a tiger for a day. The soft lad had certainly done that.

Frank was a searcher, who couldn't find what he was looking for. Did he even know what it was? He found God and got out of the army. But he missed his old life and missed Al, and missed the opportunity to kill the man who'd killed his mate. He was up and down, all over the place. Post-career anticlimax was the latest syndrome that Rumour Control had him suffering from, but I thought it was just another word for post traumatic stress disorder, and I had a feeling Gordon Turnbull would have agreed. But that was too easy an excuse.

Frank bounced around trying to work out what he wanted, and he couldn't because he'd fucked up when he left the army – he'd finally admitted as much that day in McDonald's, just around the corner from where I stood. The Church had never filled the vacuum. Even when he'd got back in as a padre, the gap was still there. He'd wanted to help people, but he'd still wanted to be a soldier. He'd wanted to come back to the Regiment.

He left a letter saying he wanted to be buried next to Al and the others in the plot, but that could never happen. They got him as close as they could in the civilian area, but even in death he couldn't find his way back into the fold.

The suicide was well planned and prepared. He'd known what he was going to do at the party, and that was just one of the things that pissed me off. He'd known exactly where he was going, and didn't even pull the safety cord. It made me fucking angry. We were his mates. He kept telling me he was there to listen and help others with their problems, so I made the mistake of assuming he didn't have any of his own. God was on his side – wasn't that supposed to solve everything?

He'd spent the rest of his days trying to replace what he'd walked away from. And he'd never managed it. Regret had consumed him. Maybe that was why he didn't feel he could tell anybody. But we were his mates, for fuck's sake.

My anger was probably a way of salving my own guilt; I knew I'd never quite forgive myself for not realizing what the fuck he was up to. It seemed so obvious now. Why hadn't I spotted it?

The hearse arrived, and we carried the coffin inside. I took my seat in the big old imposing stone edifice, but I took none of it in. I thought back to the time over the water when we'd talked about funerals in the van. I didn't listen to the waffle; I just thought about Frank and how he'd died. Like I'd said to him, the prayers meant nothing to me. Only the man did.

I looked around me. He'd certainly picked up a weird collection of people on his journey. There were friends from his evangelical, happy-clappy days, from the theology college, prayer groups, the cathedral lads down the road, the kids and youth groups he'd helped. You could tell the guys from the Regiment. Most had sun-tans and ill-fitting suits, and crammed the walkways and galleries rather than sitting down. It was the biggest crowd he'd ever pulled in this church.

I sat there listening to speaker after speaker say great things about him, but all I could think was: What a waste. He could have done so much to help people, if only he'd realized it was OK to ask for help himself. After all, he'd kept telling me it was OK to do that. We would have taken the piss out of him, of course. But we would have helped.

The Bishop of Hereford had opened one of the great halls of the cathedral down by the river, and most people headed down there after the service. The family had arranged a private burial at St Martin's, in a plot just ten metres or so from Al and the rest of them. We lowered his coffin into the ground, and then I stood back. I felt I was imposing. This was family shit.

I stayed a while after they'd gone. I was going to walk down to the corner shop and buy some gunfire ration.

One of the gravediggers approached me. We recognized each other from previous visits I'd made. He held up a carnation that had been left behind after the service. 'We're going to fill him in now, Andy. You want to say goodbye?'

I took the flower and stood there, telling the dickhead he'd chosen a fucking stupid way to die. Then I threw the flower into the grave and the lads got busy with their shovels.

I wandered down to the Spar and bought a half-bottle, then dropped by Al, Hillbilly, Vince, Bob, Legs, all the rest of the dickheads lying there. Then I went off to the cathedral for sandwiches, sticky buns and wine.

The hall was packed. It wasn't the first time any of us had been to a friend's funeral, and it certainly wouldn't be the last. We toasted Frank, and when the free drink ran out we melted away to clog up the pubs and wine bars. There were a few more smiles about the place now, and some laughter. Now we'd escaped the austere surroundings of the cathedral, we could take the piss out of Frank and remember him as friends should.

Nish actually bought me a drink, and we propped up the bar, ties loosened.

'You know, Frank came back on the Sunday, and he said goodbye. I didn't realize.'

'Why?' Nish looked bemused. 'I tell you what, Andy. There's many a time I've thought about being Frank's lead scout on this particular mission.'

'Not you as well, mate. What the fuck's going on here? You two been licking the same kill-me spoon?'

He took a big gulp of Stella and his hands started to shake. 'The nights are the worst. That's when I think about topping myself. I've worked it all out – how to do it, when to do it, what songs I want at the service, the whole fucking thing. And remember, I want burning. I don't want to rot in the ground like Frank.'

'That's the drugs talking, mate. Everything's all right. You've got a bit of control now. You've got Livvy, it's all right. Stop being a dickhead.'

'No, mate. I've got my Para Reg head on for this. I know what I'm talking about. It's all good. I've got it planned out. But don't worry – it's only when you decide you *will* commit suicide that you can. When that happens, you don't think about the service or where you want to be buried, you just go and do it.' He talked quite happily about it as the Stella made its way down the glass. He drained it with one final gulp. 'But he knows where's he going, doesn't he? He's going up to see his boss. Fuck knows where I'll be going.'

I wanted to tell Nish that I thought Frank's problem was that he kept looking for certainties in a world where they were a bit thin on the ground. But I thought there was time enough for that. 'Another pint? You're buying.'

Cameron Spence came and saved the day by offering to buy. I liked Cammy, even if he was from the Queen's Regiment. He still bit like a hungry fish when he got a hard time for it. He was a wiry, Road Runner type of guy, and the world's most intense and honest man – to the point at which he made men angry and women cry.

He raised his glass. 'Here's to Frank. I would've had him in my patrol any time.'

It was the highest accolade Frank could have received from any of us.

The next day, the *Sun* ran a story that said I'd been standing at Frank's grave with a carnation in my hand, crying. And I don't think they were wrong.

104

8 January 2002

The early-morning traffic snaked along the Oxford road. I was on my way from London to Hereford for a meeting with Andrew, then hoping to hook up with Nish the following day. I'd see him every month or so, unless he was away jumping.

He had married Livvy, but things didn't pan out. Last I'd heard she was in the Caribbean with her children, working as a property developer. I'd never asked him about it; I wasn't sure what the reaction would be. I didn't want to turn him even loopier than he already was. And just because we were mates didn't mean we had to do the big emotional thing every time we stopped off for a brew.

The meds kept him under control, and he was spending a lot of time freefalling in Spain. He still dreamt about the jump from the edge of space. Things were all right – as far as any of us could tell.

He'd called me the week before, sounding happy and upbeat.

'All right, mate? Listen, I'll be in H on the ninth – you there?' I'd asked.

He'd laughed. 'Yeah, I'll be there all right. Hey, I've got a new mobile number.'

'Wait.' I grabbed a pencil and pad. 'Go on.'

'I'll see you later on, mate.' He carried on laughing.

'Your number, dickhead – what's your number? Where are you, anyway?'

The phone went dead. I'd tried to call him back, but the number was withheld. That wasn't a problem. He knew I'd be in Hereford, and he knew I'd be with Andrew.

Since Frank's death I'd just been getting on with my life, much like anybody else. I was still writing, working on the odd movie and building the security company with Andrew. My big interest outside work was promoting army education. Al and Nish were my inspiration.

All infantry recruits, from the Guards to the Paras, received their basic training at the Infantry Training Centre at Catterick in North Yorkshire. At any one time, about eighteen thousand squaddies were based in the garrison town, making it Europe's largest military base. I did a regular turn. I stood in front of a roomful of recruits, all aged between seventeen and twenty-one, and began with an apology. Andy McNab wasn't six foot six and four feet wide, and he didn't wear a Superman costume. Then I talked about the first book I ever read as a boy soldier: *Janet and John* Book 10. It had been written for eleven-year-olds, which was just as well because that had been my reading age.

I showed them clips of film and bits and pieces of SAS derring-do, the gist of my message being: 'Look, lads, if I can do it, so can you. Use the Education Corps. Suck them dry, because that's what they're there for.' Then I finished by quoting the Education Corps captain who'd changed my life the day he told me and the rest of the zit-covered sixteen-year-olds at Infantry Junior Leaders Battalion: 'Everybody thinks you're thick as shit, but you're not. The only reason you cannot read or write is because you do not read or write.'

Not much had changed since then. These lads were still predominantly from the inner cities, and came with all the baggage: broken families, social deprivation, little or no education, exposure to drugs. Nearly half the new recruits still joined the army with the reading ability of an eleven-year-old. Nine per cent of them joined with the skill levels of five- to seven-year-olds. That didn't mean they were thick. It meant the state-school system hadn't gripped them.

Literacy skills were now as much part of basic training as weapons, fitness and battlefield tactics. You could be educated *and* a soldier. Go that route, and you had the world at your feet. I'd got quite passionate about it. Any minute now I'd turn into an ayatollah.

I smiled to myself and tuned in for the traffic news.

What I heard instead was the story of a man who'd jumped out of a Cessna yesterday, on the way back from Spain. It wasn't a freefall accident. He'd jumped out on purpose, without a parachute, while a female friend flew the aircraft. The man had been identified as Charles Bruce, forty-six, one of the world's best freefallers, with nearly four thousand skydives to his credit.

He had a friend and business partner called Judith, who was also a big-time pilot and freefaller. They owned a plane together. I guessed she must have been flying it. But I didn't have her number.

I called Andrew. 'You heard?'

'You didn't get my message?'

I hadn't bothered to listen to my voicemail. I'd been in too much of a hurry to get on the road.

I stayed in Hereford for three days, and the story became clearer by the hour. I phoned Jim Davidson. Minky had already called him, and he was in pieces.

Nish and Judith had been in Spain for a couple of weeks. That must have been where he'd phoned me from. They were doing a series of freefall displays. As they were making their way back to Hinton airfield in Northamptonshire, Judith radioed Brize Norton and requested permission to make an emergency landing. The wings were icing up.

Bad weather had forced them to land at La Rochelle. After the cloud had lifted they'd refuelled and set off again. The plane's wings started to ice up so Judith decided to take the aircraft up to 5,000 feet, above the cloud. Ten miles from Brize Norton, Nish had slid his seat right back and undone his belt. She'd tried to grab him, but he'd pushed open the door and gone out head first.

Judith descended over Fyfield and flew in low circles, trying to see where he'd impacted. She must have been absolutely traumatized. The locals watched the plane nearly roof-hopping before she finally had to bank away and head for Brize Norton. Soon afterwards, someone found Nish's body on a football pitch at the edge of the village.

We bounced around the pubs and wine bars, bumping into lads who'd known him, and a couple of his ex-girlfriends.

Nish had finally completed his skydive from the edge of space, and the general consensus was that he would have been smiling all the way down – a great big carefree wolfish grin that stretched from ear to ear. 'Nothing else comes close to those first few seconds after leaving the plane,' he had written in his book, 'because once you take that last step there is no going back. A racing driver or a skier or a climber can pull over and stop, have a rest, but with parachuting, once you cross that threshold, you have to see it through.'

That night, I had a dream.

Nish, Frank and Al flew towards me, pushing out their legs to catch more air. Their three heads were so close together they were almost touching. Frank opened his mouth and let go of the orange he'd been holding between his teeth. It bounced about between them for three or four seconds before being catapulted out of the vortex. I did a forward roll, then a backward roll and banged out of it to stable-on-heading. Al did a forward flip that took him into a rapid descent. Frank turned, drew his arms back into a delta wing, and tracked across the sky. Nish gave me a big thumbs-up, back-flipped out and disappeared.

105

Oxford Crematorium

It was standing room only in the crematorium chapel. Those who hadn't been able to make it that far were packed shoulder to shoulder in the corridor, and still others spilled into the courtyard and onto the lawns outside. Nish had touched so many lives.

The Red Freds were out in force, as well as mates from his Para Regiment days and, of course, the Seven Troop lads, which now included Dinger. I even caught a glimpse of Nish's next-door neighbour. It wouldn't have surprised me to see the guy from the corner shop on the Ross road, and the nurse he'd taken a swing at.

Harry looked around at them all and choked halfway through the eulogy. There was no singing. Nish just wanted to be burnt and have the whole thing over and done with.

Afterwards, we moved off to the airfield he used to jump from. The clubhouse was as jam-packed as the chapel, but a lot noisier. This was a celebration, not a doom-and-gloom affair.

A lot of us hadn't seen each other for a while. Ken was over in one corner. Rumour had it he was running around with a bunch of Russians. People didn't ask; if he wanted you to know, he'd say. He was waffling to Saddlebags, poking his chest. He looked as though he was about to drop him. He was probably just telling him a joke.

Ken had been right about the strategic war in Northern Ireland. Once peace negotiations were under way it had become very clear that our task had been to eliminate those who never intended to give up the gun. Martin McGuinness and Gerry Adams had wanted to get on with the politics, and we'd smoothed the path. Hard-liners who'd slipped through the net had resurfaced as the Real IRA.

Saddlebags now worked in the City as head of security for some financial institution, complete with Gucci car and even Guccier loft apartment.

Tiny was training to be a physics teacher. I wouldn't have wanted to be in his class. The kids would have nightmares.

Chris nursed a bottle of Pils. He was a pig farmer now. I thought that would suit him rather well. He didn't have to talk to them much; all he had to do was share a little grunt and a sniff with them from time to time.

Paul was on the Circuit, here, there and everywhere. Des Doom and Schwepsy were suited up and looked like moguls: they ran a security business and it was going strong. About a month ago I'd caught sight of Schwepsy from a taxi in the City. He was in a pin-stripe suit and carrying a briefcase, striding purposefully towards the entrance of an office block. Some poor fucker was about to be on the receiving end of an almighty bollocking. I leant out of the window and shouted, 'Oy, dickhead!' but he didn't look back. The insult couldn't possibly have been aimed at him.

Harry had stayed on in Chamonix, still soft in the head about climbing mountains. The hair had almost completely gone. It probably made him more streamlined at altitude.

As the shadows lengthened, the storytelling gathered pace and volume. We swapped memories of Nish's farts and bogeys and stitch-ups – just as he would have wanted – and also of his courage and skill, leadership and compassion, which we knew he would have hated.

I sat in the corner in the early hours and took a moment with my own thoughts. My dream replayed itself: the three of them freefalling like magicians just feet away from me. Their smiles widened in the slipstream as they watched the crap-hat new boy doing his best to keep stable.

I was the only one left alive.

Had Nish suffered from a chemical imbalance? Was it the cumulative effect of many episodes of hypoxia? Or was it PTSD? I knew he'd never really got over the deaths of Al and Hillbilly. Or, maybe, had he just thought, Fuck it, I've had enough, and jumped? There are some people who go for it full throttle, in life as well as death – and if things went on like this, the guy in the corner shop would be able to retire early.

I smiled. I knew Nish would have been laughing all the way down. He'd probably picked out the exact spot where he wanted to land and tracked towards it.

I now knew for sure he'd planned it all. It wasn't an impulse. He'd given the others the same mobile-number story. It had been his excuse to call us to say goodbye, like Frank had done on the day of the party without me realizing it. Maybe that was where he'd got the idea. I remembered him telling me at Frank's funeral, 'It's only when you decide you *will* commit suicide that you can . . .'

I raised my glass to him. I didn't know whether to feel sad or happy. I'd lost yet another mate, but he had died doing what he wanted to do – and how could you deny a friend that?

St Martin's Church, Hereford
January 2007

The guy behind the counter gave me a pitying glance when I bought a bottle of rum at ten in the morning. I was making a bit of a habit of this. I felt his eyes following me as I walked up the Ross road in the rain and nipped round to the back of the graveyard.

Frank got his first, not because he was the new boy but because his grave was on the way to the plot. I knew he'd never been that keen on the stuff, so I gave him a drop or two extra. He had some catching up to do.

I moved on, mouthing my thanks to Nish – this was a much better idea than flowers. I splashed Steve Lane's plaque, then walked through the lines of headstones. There had been a few new additions to the suicide club since Nish and Frank had set the thing up. One lad had left a complete order of service behind: which songs he wanted sung, where he wanted to be buried, even what flowers he preferred.

There were fresh flowers on Al's grave. I gave them a good sprinkle and moved on to Vince.

He got his ration next, and I spent a moment or two taking

the piss out of him for stopping to help Nish on the Fan Dance. Then I poured the last of the black stuff over Bob and headed for a brew and a waffle with a couple of the lads in town.

I'd visited the troops in Afghanistan and Iraq and come across a lot of the guys who were now out on the Circuit, and there was no doubt in my mind that a couple of them should have been queuing up outside Gordon Turnbull's door. I still give myself a mental MOT every now and then to make sure I'm not behind them.

I'd met up with Snapper in Kabul in 2006. It was great to see him, even if he did make me pay for the tea. He was still as mad as a box of frogs, and had enough weapons and radios dangling off him to take on the Taliban on his own. He was one guy who would never suffer from PTSD. There was far too much going on in his head to leave room for anything else.

Epilogue

After the 2003 invasion, I went back to the place where I was captured in Iraq. The Regiment had erected a cairn on the banks of the Euphrates to commemorate Vince Phillips, Steve Lane and Bob Consiglio. The locals were told it was booby-trapped; that if they tried to pull it down, it would pull them down too.

I couldn't stick around. If you stood still anywhere in Iraq for more than ten minutes the militants would be on their way. But I was there long enough to absorb it all. I still didn't feel bitter, resentful, guilty, anxious or violent. I just felt lucky to have come out pretty much unscathed, and privileged to be standing there next to something that the guys had built during the war to celebrate the memory of some brave friends who'd died.

I smiled to myself. Camaraderie hadn't gone out of fashion. I realized that was what I missed most. It was what Frank and Nish had missed, too.

Afterword

Anyone can get hit by PTSD, but the fact remains that soldiers experience a lot more trauma than most, and over much longer periods of time. It's a chilling fact that more guys have killed themselves since returning from the Falklands than the 255 that were lost in action there.

Soldiers adopt a fuck-it attitude. If they didn't, they wouldn't be able to do the job in the first place. If they went around thinking, Woe is me, I'm going to die, they'd have to get themselves straight down to the job centre. Fuck-it has always been the best policy, but it can prevent you asking for help. It can also backfire if you're thinking of taking your own life – or someone else's.

Special Forces are never going to have an easy time of it in the real world. They just have to try to get on with it, and some do that better than others. Maybe that's why I still feel my pulse race when I visit the recruits in Catterick and the infantry battalions in Afghanistan and Iraq. Mates I joined up with as zit-faced kids are fighting out there as senior officers. I enjoy going back, and I enjoy being part of it again, however temporarily. I guess I feel just a little of what Frank felt when he was Padre Two Zero.

From what I've seen of them in contact, the infantry has

never been in better shape. I joined a rifle company on a house assault in Basra last year, one of the most dangerous things a modern-day soldier can be asked to do. These lads were going in against armed insurgents who were ready and waiting. The first man through the door was a nineteen-year-old rifleman. Ten years ago, that would have been the job of Special Forces.

My first time in the Killing House with Hillbilly and Snapper, there were live bodies in the room. But they weren't firing back. When I did it for real in Colombia, they were. It doesn't come much worse than being number one through the door.

I've met an eighteen-year-old who only fired six rounds on his very first day in-country but killed three enemy insurgents. He hadn't yet had his first shave. I know a twenty-one-year-old sniper who killed three guys with four shots on his first job. When he got back, he had the piss taken out of him for wasting a round.

Those boys and their mates are going to see more shot and shell, and have more opportunity to kill the enemy, than their grandfathers did in the Second World War. Then, there was an army of more than a million, spread over several continents. Now a 'bayonet' (infantry soldier) has a contact every day and a half, often lasting for hours.

I try to keep some things tucked away in the dark part of my head, but I'll never forget Nicky Smith's blood splattering across my face, or the heavy 7.62mm rounds blasting into the chest of the first man I ever killed. I can still see the exit wounds that ripped his back open. And, twelve years later, I can still see the face of the last man I shot.

Soldiers hit by PTSD are casualties of war just as much as Vince, Bob and Legs were. A major mental-health crisis faces those who have served our country. We need to do something now, before we discover in another decade that more soldiers – regular and TA – have killed themselves since returning from Iraq and Afghanistan than were killed there in action.

We need to remove the institutional and cultural barriers discouraging soldiers from counselling, therapy – whatever you choose to call it. Seeking help should be seen as a sign of strength and professionalism, a desire to keep yourself at peak efficiency. The US Delta Force have been doing this for years, and I wouldn't have them down as a bunch of wimps.

We shouldn't be surprised by what happens to men who have seen conflict. The ancient Greeks recorded signs and symptoms in their soldiers after battle that we would recognize now as PTSD. We shouldn't need secret places in Wales for soldiers to slink away to. They're just like anyone else. They're human. They need support, not just from government but from all of us. There are hard-pressed organizations that can help them recover, but it's up to us to remove the stigma. They just need a little understanding and, dare I say it?, a whole lot of respect.

Photograph Acknowledgements

Author as a squaddy, Crossmaglen, 1977: courtesy Ken Hayward; Frank Collins in Malaysia, 1984: mirrorpix; Al Slater: BBC Motion Gallery; priest giving last rites, Belfast, 19 March 1988: mirrorpix; Vincent Phillips: Rex Features; Charles 'Nish' Bruce: mirrorpix; Frank Collins meeting the Queen: SWNS; Revd Frank Collins: mirrorpix.

Index

INDEX